D1117522

THE KING OF SWAT

THE KING OF SWAT

*An Analysis of Baseball's
Home Run Hitters from the
Major, Minor, Negro and
Japanese Leagues*

BY WILLIAM F. McNEIL

McFarland & Company, Inc., Publishers
Jefferson, North Carolina, and London

Front cover: Josh Gibson (right) accepting his most valuable player trophy for the 1941-42 season from Luis Rosario, Jr., sports director of *El Imparcial* newspaper (photo credit: Luis

British Library Cataloguing-in-Publication data are available

Library of Congress Cataloguing-in-Publication Data

McNeil, William.
    The king of swat : an analysis of baseball's home run hitters from
the major, minor, Negro and Japanese leagues / by William F.
McNeil
      p.   cm.
    Includes bibliographical references and index.
    ISBN 0-7864-0362-4 (library binding : 50# alkaline paper) ∞
    1. Home runs (Baseball)   2. Home runs (Baseball)—Statistics.
I. Title.
GV868.4.M36   1997
796.357'26—dc21   97-2179
                                               CIP

Manufactured in the United States of America

McFarland & Company, Inc., Publishers
  Box 611, Jefferson, North Carolina 28640

This book is gratefully dedicated to my family.
· To my wife Janet, who loves and understands me.
· To my children, Michael, Danny, Jeannie, and Eileen,
who make me proud to be a parent.
· To my grandchildren, Jessica, Jamie, Jeffrey, Jenna, Morgan,
Shannon, Shane, Connor, and Rachel, who make me young again.

ACKNOWLEDGMENT

Like most authors, I have imposed on many people during my research for *The King of Swat*. I realize that providing information to an unknown author is a thankless task at best but, strangely enough, in this business, most people respond in a pleasant and constructive manner. In fact, they usually go out of their way to be helpful.

I have requested and received assistance in locating photographs of the great sluggers, data on the various minor league parks (including field dimensions, prevailing winds, elevation, etc.), players' addresses and telephone numbers, and players' batting and slugging statistics. I have also interviewed several of the players featured in the book.

I would like to thank those people and those organizations who assisted me in my project. These included the Office of the Baseball Commissioner—Japan, Larry Lester, the Negro League Museum, John Thorn, Mark Rucker, John Holway, Masaru Madate, Jon Mark Beilue, *The Amarillo Globe-News*, Joe Hauser, Joe Bauman, Bob Rives, Morris Eckhouse, the Society for American Baseball Research, Bill Burdick, the National Baseball Library, Dick Clark, Dan Johnson, Bob Hoie, Stew Thornley, Ernest J. Green, Luis Alvelo, Larry Gerlach, Bob Bluthardt, Ted Lukacs and Gordon Brown.

CONTENTS

INTRODUCTION

Organized baseball has been played in the United States for over 140 years, and professional leagues have been in existence since 1871. Men of exceptional athletic ability have fascinated and seduced baseball fans since the inception of the game. The flashy, acrobatic shortstop going deep into the hole behind third base to make a dazzling stop, then turning and nipping the runner by a step at first; the speedy outfielder climbing the center field wall to rob a batter of a home run; the strong armed pitcher striking out batter after batter—these types of players have always stimulated the passion and adulation of the fans. But it is the home run hitter who commands the most reverence. He towers over his compatriots like the Colossus of Rhodes.

The clear, sharp impact as Appalachian hardwood meets Missouri cowhide—the small, white pellet whistling skyward into the night—50,000 fans leaving their seats in unison as the baseball settles into the far distant grandstand for a game-winning home run. This is the single most exciting and dramatic act in the game of baseball. Throughout the long history of the national sport, hitters who could propel baseballs long distances have been idolized by men and women everywhere.

SLUGGER! The name itself conjures up images of strapping, rawboned youths with muscles like Arnold Schwarzenegger and features like Robert Redford, young giants who can drive baseballs out of cavernous stadiums with relative ease and with monotonous regularity. The slugger is the ultimate hero.

Names of legendary home run kings, some fictional, some real, constantly fire the imagination. Ozark Ike McBatt, the comic book hero, always pulled the game out of the fire in the last inning with a mighty home run. The great Roy Hobbs, baseball's "Natural," nearly destroyed a baseball stadium with an electrifying ninth-inning round tripper to win the pennant. And Joe Hardy, of "Damn Yankees" fame, sold his soul to the devil to help his beloved Washington Senators defeat the New York Yankees in that famous Broadway musical of long, long ago.

In the real world, the heroes are made of flesh and blood, but still some of them are caricatures of their fictional counterparts. Rocky Nelson, a

1

throwback to the Gay Nineties, once claimed to have hit 84 home runs for the Brooklyn Dodgers. Unfortunately, according to Nelson, all but two were foul. Dick "Dr. Strangeglove" Stuart, the man who surrounded ground balls, slugged 66 round trippers for Lincoln, Nebraska, in the Western League in 1966, then banged out 42 for the Boston Red Sox seven years later.

The parade of authentic, larger-than-life heroes, is naturally led by Babe Ruth, the Sultan of Swat himself. He is joined by some of the great major league long ball hitters of yesteryear, men like Ned Williamson who hit 27 home runs in 1884, legendary nineteenth-century sluggers Big Dan Brouthers, Sam Thompson, and Roger Connor, and Babe's contemporaries, Gavvy Cravath and Tilly Walker, home run kings of the teens. Latter day heroes of the Big Show include Roger Maris, Hank Aaron, Ralph Kiner, and Harmon Killebrew.

Some sluggers never had the opportunity to play in the majors, for one reason or another; but they still thrilled the fans in other stadiums with their gargantuan blasts. Joe Bauman of the Roswell Rockets in the Class C Long-horn League hit 72 home runs in 1954, still the all-time professional record. Minor leaguer Joe Hauser of the AAA Minneapolis Millers sent 69 balls into distant stands in 1933, after having hit 63 home runs for Baltimore in the International League three years before. Bobby Crues matched Hauser's Min-neapolis output 15 years later, playing with the Amarillo Gold Sox in the West Texas–New Mexico League.

Many players who were denied the opportunity to display their skills in organized baseball because of the color of their skin demonstrated their prowess in other arenas—in the Negro leagues and in Cuba, Puerto Rico, and Venezuela. For more than 50 years, white baseball missed the chance to see some of the game's greatest players. The immortal Josh Gibson, catcher for the Homestead Grays, is credited with hitting the only fair ball completely out of Yankee Stadium since its construction in 1923, a feat that could not be accomplished by Babe Ruth, Lou Gehrig, Mickey Mantle, or Roger Maris. According to some baseball historians, the flamboyant catcher was the most prolific home run hitter in all of baseball. Other Negro leaguers, such as Nor-man "Turkey" Stearnes, Mule Suttles, and Chino Smith, also hit home runs with the ferocity and frequency of their white counterparts.

Across the water in Japan, Sadaharu Oh, first baseman of the Central League Yomiuri Giants, broke Hank Aaron's career home run record by pro-pelling 868 baseballs out of league parks over a period of 22 years.

Who, of all these men, is the greatest home run hitter of all time? Who deserves the title "King of Swat"? According to the simple statistics, Sada-haru Oh is the all-time career home run leader with his 868 recorded circuit clouts in league play, Roger Maris holds the major league season record of 61 homers, and Joe Bauman is the proud possessor of the overall professional record of 72 round trippers in a single season. But who is the man who hit home runs with the greatest frequency? Who had the best ratio of home runs per at bats, over his career, of all the celebrated sluggers? Was it the Babe? Kiner? Aaron? Maris? Perhaps Bauman? Or Gibson? Or Oh San?

Who is baseball's King of Swat? The answer lies within the pages of this book. Admittedly, it is not possible to arrive at a universally acceptable answer because of the many variables involved, because of incomplete playing records in some cases, and because of the subjective nature of some of the evaluations. This book presents one answer to the question. Perhaps, that answer will stimulate other researchers interested in the same subject matter to conduct their own studies and draw their own conclusions.

Many variables affect a batter's performance, and these variables have to be factored into the final equation to arrive at a fair assessment of each player's talents. Some of the most obvious variables are

Quality of the opposing pitching
Size of the baseball parks, particularly the home park
Liveliness of the balls
Major league expansion
Night baseball
Geographical location/altitude

These and other considerations come into play when evaluating the various candidates for the title of "King of Swat." How does one compare the achievements of Joe Bauman in the Class C Longhorn League with those of Sadaharu Oh in the Japanese Central League, half a world away? How can the slugging prowess of Dan Brouthers of the Detroit Wolverines in 1886 be weighed against the record-breaking season of Roger Maris with the '61 Yankees? And how can the legendary feats of Josh Gibson be compared with those of the mighty Babe Ruth?

Some comparisons are readily available. Others are less obvious. This book examines the feats of baseball's most proficient home run hitters, taking into account the variables noted above. It analyzes their achievements, puts them into proper perspective with respect to each other, and arrives at a subjective rating of their skills. In the end, when all evaluations have been completed, only one mighty slugger will stand front and center. The competition will have fallen by the wayside.

That man will be the world's greatest home run hitter.

THE KING OF SWAT.

CHAPTER 1

THE MINOR LEAGUES

The search for baseball's King of Swat must necessarily begin in America's minor leagues, where some of the game's most enduring home run records were established. The minors were, and are, the training ground for the major leagues; nevertheless, some of the game's greatest sluggers spent their entire careers in the minors. For one reason or another, some players simply refused the opportunity to play in the majors. Others suffered injuries that restricted their overall performance. And some players had severe defensive liabilities or personality shortcomings that prevented them from achieving major league status. But all of them could drive a baseball great distances.

Minor league baseball began in 1877 with the founding of the International Association. The league was composed of seven teams; the league champion Tecumseh Stars of Ontario, Canada; Maple Leaf of Guelph, Canada; Manchester, N.H.; Lynn, Mass.; Buckeye of Columbus, Ohio; Rochester, N.Y.; and Allegheny of Pittsburgh, Pa. William "Candy" Cummings, the celebrated inventor of the curve ball, served as the league president. Other future major leaguers to play in the International Association included Ned Williamson, Pud Galvin, Fred Goldsmith, and Harry Stovey. This league, like subsequent minor leagues, was poorly organized and ineffectually run, however, resulting in its early demise.

One league that did survive the chaotic development of the minor league system was the Western League, founded in 1879. It managed to endure many painful growing pains over the next twenty years, continually improving the quality of its play despite player raids by National League teams and by other minor league clubs. It eventually became the most talented minor league in the country. League President Ban Johnson renamed it the American League in 1900, and it became a full-fledged major league the following year, competing successfully with the older, more established National League.

It was not until 1882, with the formation of the Northwestern League, that minor league baseball came into its own. The Interstate Association (IA) began operations the following year. In 1884, the IA was renamed the Eastern League, and, in 1913, it became the International League. It remains the oldest minor league still in operation.

By 1900, the minors had grown to 19 leagues. During this time, there were continuing disagreements between minor league teams and National League clubs over the rights to individual players. Finally, in 1901, seven minor leagues joined together to form the National Association of Professional Baseball Leagues, establishing rules that would protect them from incursions by major league teams.

In 1902, the minor leagues included 17 leagues in four classifications. Over the years, the number of minor leagues fluctuated considerably, but continued to grow as the popularity of the game captivated the American sporting public. The minors reached their peak just after World War II, in 1949, when there were 59 leagues operating, with a total of 433 individual teams. Once television became available to the general public, and expansion brought major league baseball to fans in the western sections of the country, attendance at minor league baseball games declined dramatically. By 1992, only 18 minor leagues were operating, including four short-season rookie leagues.

The minor leagues refused to die, however. They are now experiencing another resurgence, thanks to the greed of major league players and owners. The long and bitter baseball strike of 1994, which resulted in the cancellation of the last third of the '94 major league baseball season, the corresponding loss of the '94 World Series, and the cancellation of 18 regular season games in 1995, alienated millions of baseball fans around the country. The viewing public is once again visiting minor league parks, where young men play the game with the enthusiasm of old and money hasn't yet corrupted them.

The minor leagues have operated, in one form or another, for 120 years. During that time there have been in the neighborhood of 2,600 teams, representing 49 of the 50 states (Alaska excepted), the eight provinces in Canada, as well as Cuba, Mexico, the Dominican Republic, Puerto Rico, Panama, and Venezuela. In general, the leagues consisted of six teams each, with each team employing approximately 15 baseball players. Assuming the average career of each player was six years, a total of 45,000 different players have competed on a minor league level since 1877. As we review the foremost sluggers in minor league history, keep these figures in mind. The men we will study competed against 45,000 other players, and they were the best of the best.

Professional baseball has changed dramatically over the past 125 years. The game, as we know it today, hardly resembles the game our forefathers played on the Elysian Fields in Hoboken, New Jersey, on that warm summer day in 1846. In the beginning, these larger-than-life heroes enjoyed more of a gentleman's encounter, swinging gaily at balls lobbed underhand by a pitcher 45 feet away. Today's fast-paced game of 95 mile-per-hour fastballs, hook slides, home runs, and back-to-the-plate catches in deep center field, would be mind boggling to the athlete of the nineteenth century. It is obvious, therefore, that it will not be possible to compare each and every professional baseball player, side by side. In some cases, specifically those involving nineteenth-

Brainard Park in Artesia, N.M., where Joe Bauman hit home runs number 70, 71, 72. View from right field to plate (credit: Bob Rives).

century players, direct comparisons with twentieth-century players are beyond the scope of this study. For this reason, the nineteenth-century players will be evaluated entirely within their own era.

During the embryonic stages of the game, the playing fields were nothing more than wide-open pastures. Spectators stood along the baselines and around the extremities of the outfield. There were no fences until team owners began to charge admission to the games and took the necessary steps to enclose the fields, to prevent fans from viewing the games free of charge.

When the professional game first began, many baseball diamonds utilized grounds that were designed for other purposes. The original New York Polo Grounds, as the name indicates, was built as a polo field, by James Gordon Bennett, the publisher of the *New York Herald*. It was subsequently occupied in 1884 by the New York Metropolitans of the American Association. The early fields were often oblong in shape and had an oval track around the outside, to accommodate other athletic events. Bicycle racing was in vogue in the late 1800s, and many parks, like Hampden Park in Springfield, Massachusetts, home of the Springfield entry in the Eastern League, held bicycle races at the park when the baseball team was out of town or during the off season. Early fields also entertained racing and running events, as at the Downing Racetrack in Decatur, Illinois, which hosted harness racing when Three I League baseball was not being played there. Athletic Park in Milwaukee, Wisconsin, home of the Milwaukee Creams of the Western Association, sported a tiny oval-shaped park whose dimensions were restricted by the city-block grid layout. The outfield distances, left to right, were 266 feet, 395 feet, and 266 feet. At the other extreme, Athletics Park in Terre Haute, Indiana, another Three I League franchise, had monstrous outfield distances of 440 feet to left, 592 feet to straightaway center, and 440 feet to right. Needless to say, not many home runs were hit in Terre Haute—and none of those that were hit left the confines of the park. Future Hall-of-Famers Branch Rickey and Three-Finger Brown strutted their wares in Terre Haute. Brown, in fact, compiled a sparkling 23–8 record there in 1902. Brainard Field, in Artesia, New Mexico, where Joe Bauman set the single-season, professional baseball home run record, had a distant right field fence, 349 feet from home plate, but the center field fence was only 355 feet deep because a street ran across it, according to Bob Rives. Sulfur Dell, in Nashville, Tennessee, had a chummy 250-foot right field foul line and a 25-foot incline behind first base that made life interesting for the right fielders.

The game of baseball has gone through a continuous evolution over its first 125 years. The architectural design of parks has changed considerably, from the open fields of the 1860s, to the oblong monstrosities of the 1880s, to the first steel stadiums of the early twentieth century, to the symmetrical ballparks of the 1990s. The first steel structures, like Panther Park in Fort Worth, Texas, and Bennett Park (later Tiger Stadium) in Detroit, Michigan, were built to fit into the existing urban road network. Their counterparts in the majors, like Ebbets Field and Fenway Park, had a unique personality and charm all their own. Sadly, the individuality of the old parks, like Brooklyn's slanted right field wall, Boston's "Green Monster" left field wall, and similarly unique characteristics in dozens of minor league parks, are slowly giving way to the sterile stadiums of the twenty-first century.

The baseball itself has been improved from the soft, hand-constructed ball of 1880 to the scientifically manufactured, hard ball now in use. The specifications used to manufacture today's baseballs closely dictate the type and amount of yarn used, the number of stitches, and the type of leather used for the cover. There are also physical tests to measure the ball's resiliency and dimensions. Bats have also been standardized to prevent one man or one team from gaining an unfair advantage through the introduction of a new, innovative material or design.

Protective equipment kept pace with improvements in the balls and bats. Catcher's masks, shin guards, and chest protectors became standard equipment around the turn of the century. Fielder's gloves, too, were adopted during the same period. In the beginning, fielders caught the ball barehanded, without the benefit of protection. When gloves were first introduced, in the 1880s, most players refused to wear them, considering it unmanly to catch a ball with artificial hands. It was a full ten years before all players started to use fielder's gloves. Even then, the gloves were no more than a thin kidskin covering. As late as the 1940s, fielder's gloves were small, padded mitts that still required the player to catch the ball in the pocket and to use two hands when catching it. Today's gloves are large, pocketed coverings with mammoth webbing systems. A modern-day player has only to throw his glove in the right direction and the ball will disappear into the vast horsehide trap.

Over the years, the minor leagues have produced some of the most celebrated sluggers in baseball. Many of them, like their major league colleagues, were assisted by the small dimensions of their home ballparks. The first recorded "home park" advantage in the minor leagues went to Charlie Reilly of St. Paul in the Western Association, in 1889. Reilly led professional baseball with 27 home runs, most of them hit out of the tiny park at State and Eaton Streets. In addition to Reilly, two other St. Paul sluggers, Joe Werrick and John Carroll, finished second and third in the home run derby, with 25 and 24 home runs, respectively.

Another long ball hitter, whose reputation was built around a four-base bandbox, was Perry Werden of the Minneapolis Millers in the Western League. Werden was a giant of a man. In an era when the average ballplayer stood about five-foot-seven and weighed in the neighborhood of 150 pounds, Werden topped out at six-foot-two and 210 pounds. The St. Louis native began his major league career as a pitcher when he was just 18 years old, and his spectacular 12–1 record in 1884 with the St. Louis Maroons in the Union Association helped them capture the pennant by a whopping 21 games. After he hurt his arm, Werden moved over to first base, where he became a renowned slugger. He went on to lead two major leagues in triples, pounding out 20 three baggers for the Toledo Maumees of the American Association in 1890, then rapping out 29 triples for the National League St. Louis Cardinals in 1893.

Home runs were almost unheard of in Toledo and St. Louis during this period, due to the distant outfield fences. The same was true in most big league parks. Fences, in general, were at least 400 feet from home plate, with the center field fence 500 feet away, and they seldom came into play. The big sluggers of the day specialized in doubles and triples, not home runs. In 1890, the Maumees hit only 24 round trippers in 134 games, but they led the league in triples with 108. Robison Field in St. Louis was murder for righthanded hitters, with distances of 470 feet to left field and 500 feet to center field. The entire Cardinal team managed only ten round trippers in 1893.

When Werden asked owner Chris Von der Ahe for a salary increase after his outstanding season in 1893, he was quickly and unceremoniously traded to Minneapolis. Playing in Athletic Park, with its short fences (275 feet to left field and 250 feet to right), Werden suddenly blossomed into a home run threat. He blasted 43 home runs in 1894. The following year, the righthanded slugger hit 45 round trippers, establishing a professional record that lasted for 25 years. In fact, the rangy first baseman was the only player in professional baseball to hit 40 or more home runs during the dead ball era. Babe

Ruth broke the record in 1920, with the advent of the lively ball, when he hit 54 home runs for the New York Yankees. In 1896, the Millers moved into Nicollet Park, with its 334-foot left field fence and 432-foot center field fence, and Werden's home run totals plummeted. He still led the league in home runs, but his output was a more modest 18. He also led the league in triples, with 18, which was 11 more than his 1895 total.

Perry Werden was a consistent home run hitter, who won six home run crowns during his career; but only in his Minneapolis tenure was he able to hit more than 12 home runs in a single year. Minneapolis established a team home run record in 1895 by hitting a total of 219 four baggers. Their record lasted for over three decades.

In addition to Werden's lofty home run totals in Minneapolis in 1894 and 1895, four other Miller sluggers took advantage of the cozy dimensions of Athletic Park to slam their way into the record books. Henry Hines (34) and Frank Burrell (32) also broke the old mark of 28, in 1894. The following year, Bud Lally (36) and Joe Werrick (32) zeroed in on the short fences to join baseball's elite circle of home run hitters.

Putting Werden's statistics into perspective, he was the number one career home run hitter in the minor leagues during the dead ball era, totaling 169 home runs in 6,233 at bats. He averaged 15 homers a year, per 550 at bats. His major league average of five home runs paled by comparison— until you consider his output of three base hits. Werden averaged 17 triples a year in the majors, a number that put him in elite company. Wahoo Sam Crawford, the major league leader in career triples with 312, averaged 18 triples a year. Shoeless Joe Jackson led the way with an average of 19 triples a year. Harry Stovey and Dan Brouthers followed with 17.

Werden, however, was not the nineteenth-century minor league home run king, based on the average number of home runs per 550 at bats. That honor belonged to Edward L. "Home Run" Breckinridge. The big first baseman packed 190 pounds of muscle on his six-foot-two frame, and he used that bulk to great advantage, leading all minor leagues in home runs three times in twelve years. During the Gay Nineties, when home runs were the exception rather than the rule, the righthanded power hitter smashed 16 home runs for Grand Rapids in the Northwest League in 1891. He followed that with 20 homers for Columbus in the Western League and Troy in the Eastern League in 1892, and climaxed his assault on home run crowns by slamming an unheard-of 25 round trippers for Brockton in the old New England League in 1896. In all, Home Run Breckinridge piled up 120 home runs in 3,337 at bats during his minor league career, an average of 20 home runs for every 550 at bats. It was, by far, the highest home run average in nineteenth-century minor league baseball. In fact, it was the highest average in professional baseball, far exceeding the 12 home runs a year hit in the major leagues by Sam Thompson.

Breckinridge checked out of professional baseball early, retiring after the 1899 season, at the young age of 30. In his final season, he slugged 12 home runs for Brockton in only 274 at bats, while averaging .321. He left behind an excellent career batting average of .322.

Other early sluggers included 160 pound Buck Freeman, who slammed 23 home runs with Toronto in the Eastern League in 1898. The lefthanded slugger went on to lead the American League with 25 circuit blows in 1899. He also chipped in with 25 triples that year. Five years later, Home Run Joe Marshall smoked 25 home runs for Butte, Montana, of the Pacific National League. The major league leader that year, coincidentally, was Buck Freeman, of the Boston Red Sox, who hit 13. In 1907, Freeman, once more back in the minors, led all professional baseball in homers, with 18. Dave Brain of the Boston Beaneaters topped the major leagues that year, with ten round trippers.

Truck Eagan, an early minor league legend, led all professional baseball in home runs in 1904 and 1905, hitting 25 and 21 home runs, respectively, with Tacoma of the Pacific Coast League (PCL). The most home runs hit in the major leagues during those years was ten, by Jasper Davis of the Philadelphia Athletics in 1904. Eagan's numbers, impressive though they are, were assisted by the long Pacific Coast League playing schedule and by the small dimensions of his home park. The Tacoma Baseball Park, where Eagan played half his games, had a claustrophobic, 200-foot left field fence and a correspondingly short, 342-foot center field fence. The righthanded slugger also benefited from the 200+ game schedule in the PCL. His home run totals, if factored over a 550-at-bat season, would be more normal at 19 and 15 and still good enough to have led the league. It should be pointed out that while other players had the same advantages as Eagan, they couldn't come close to his numbers. In fact, in 1903, when Eagan hit a league-leading 13 home runs, the second-place hitter had only 7. Eagan's home run total that year represented 13 percent of the league's total of 103 homers. The burly shortstop, who twice more led his minor league in home runs, was, in fact, the leading minor league slugger during the first decade of the twentieth century. He had a short major league trial with Pittsburgh and Cleveland in 1901, going to bat 30 times with just four hits and no home runs. Eagan ended his professional career with Richmond of the Virginia League in 1911, finishing with a career total of 123 home runs, an average of nine a year.

Some long ball hitters arrived on the baseball scene around the time the lively ball was coming into play, and they took advantage of it in a big way. One of these big boomers was Clarence "Big Boy" Kraft, a burly first baseman, who helped usher in the modern game of baseball in the early 1920s. The 6-foot, 190-pound strong boy was on the downside of a mediocre minor league existence when the new lively ball was introduced in 1920. The "jackrabbit" immediately rejuvenated Kraft's sagging career. His home run output skyrocketed, and his batting average jumped from .286 to .340. Kraft hit more than ten home runs in a season, eight times in sixteen years, but his best seasons were with the Fort Worth Panthers of the Texas League, where he feasted on lively ball pitching most of the time. After totaling 20 home runs during his first three years in the league, Kraft suddenly exploded in 1921, sending 31 of the new balls out of Panther Park and other minor league enclosures. He led the league with 32 homers the following year, and slugged another 32 in 1923. In 1924, Big Boy had a career season. In addition to leading the league in at bats (581), runs scored (150), and runs batted in (196), the towering righthander sent 55 balls screaming into the Texas sky, setting a new minor league record. He was the first minor leaguer to break the 50–home runs barrier. Babe Ruth had established the professional record with 59 home runs in 1921. Kraft's scintillating season propelled the Panthers to the sixth of their seven consecutive Texas League championships. Their 109–41 record left second-place Houston a frustrating 30½ games behind.

Kraft's home run averages accurately reflect the differences in the construction of the baseballs from the dead ball era to the lively ball era. Prior to 1921, Big Boy averaged 12 home runs a year. After the introduction of the lively ball, he pounded out 36 round trippers a year.

After the 1924 season ended, Clarence "Big Boy" Kraft did what very few professional athletes do. While at the top of his game, he put away his bat and glove and retired to open an automobile dealership in Fort Worth. He was 37.

Another minor league legend whose career straddled the dead ball-lively ball transition, was Anthony "Bunny" Brief. This native of Remus, Michigan, is generally recognized as one of the top ten all-around players in minor league history. His 19-year-career was spent mostly in the top classifications, with four short coffee breaks up in the big time. The 6-foot, 185-pound first baseman won seven home run titles and four RBI crowns from 1910 through 1928. He hit more than 30 home runs a year four times, and twice exceeded 40. His high was 42 with Kansas City of the American Association in 1921. From 1911 through 1919, when the ball was heavy, Brief clouted an average of 13 home runs a year. From 1920 through the end of his career in 1928, hitting a juiced-up ball, he banged out 28 round trippers a year.

The righthanded slugger had four trials with major league teams, but never could solve the pitching in the Big Show. His career average in the majors was a minuscule .223, with only five home runs in 569 at bats. His minor league stats, however, were something else again. Over a nineteen-year period, Brief tattooed bush-league pitchers for a .331 batting average, while slugging 342 home runs in 8,945 at bats. He holds the American Association all-time career record for runs scored (1,342), hits (2,196), doubles (458), home runs (276), and runs batted in (1,451). Bunny Brief was one of the brightest stars to illuminate the AAA sky. He just couldn't take that last giant step to the top.

Isaac "Ike" Boone arrived on the minor league scene in 1920. When he retired, 17 years later, he left a legacy that has never been equaled. He was the greatest pure hitter in minor league history. Ike Boone got off the mark quickly, hitting a stratospheric .403 for Cedartown in the Georgia State League. The following year, he led the Southern League in hitting, with an average of .389 for New Orleans. He went on to win five batting titles in five different minor leagues, including the top three AAA leagues: the International League, the American Association and the Pacific Coast League. While playing with the Mission in the PCL in 1929, Boone had a sensational season. He established the professional record for total bases with 553, while leading the league in batting (.407), home runs (55), and runs batted in (218).

The big, lefthanded batter slugged his way to a career .370 batting average in the minors, the number one professional career batting average of all-time. Ty Cobb was second at .367. Boone amassed a total of 2,521 hits in 6,807 at bats, with 217 home runs, 1,334 runs batted in, and 1,362 runs scored. He was a solid hitter in the major leagues as well, piling up a creditable .319 average in 1,154 at bats over eight years. His lack of speed and his defensive liabilities prevented him from becoming a long-term major leaguer, however.

As can be seen from the above numbers, Ike Boone was a solid hitter with an occasional sock, but he was no world class slugger of the Babe Ruth caste. He had one glorious season, where everything came together for him, and he made the most of it. Except for 1929, Boone's home run totals were modest. He hit 32 home runs in 1926 and 22 home runs in 1930. Those were the only other seasons, out of 17, that Ike Boone hit more than 18 home runs.

The minor leagues had other famous sluggers over the years, names that are familiar to baseball enthusiasts; names like Bauman, Hauser, Crues, Dick Stuart, Bob Lennon, and Tony Lazzeri. There were also less well-known sluggers like Moose Clabaugh, Pud Miller, Ken Guettler, Frank Gravino, and Frosty Kennedy. As you might expect, the home park advantage contributed significantly to the records of many of these minor league hitters.

The Society for American Baseball Research (SABR) published a three-volume statistical work titled *Minor League Baseball Stars*. In volume one, they pointed out the benefits of playing baseball in a small park. The example they used was Sulphur Dell, the home park of the Nashville Vols of the Southern Association.

The right field fence at Sulphur Dell stood only 250 feet from home plate. Over the history of the Southern Association, according to SABR, "There were eight players who hit 40 or more four baggers, All were left-handed hitters who played for Nashville. Here are the hitters and their homer totals by year, all somewhat tainted by the smell of Sulphur":

(1954)	Bob Lennon	64
(1948)	Chuck Workman	52
(1930)	James Poole	50
(1951)	Jack Harshman	47
(1949)	Carl Sawatski	45
(1948)	Charlie Gilbert	42
(1949)	Babe Barna	42
(1930)	Jay Partridge	40

Ten minor league sluggers slammed 60 or more home runs in one season. It became evident, after analyzing their records, that some of them were probably aided by small parks and favorable atmospheric conditions. Many of the big boomers played in the so-called "homer havens" scattered around minor league America: Minneapolis, Salt Lake City, Roswell, Nashville, and Amarillo. Those players usually didn't fare as well when they played in larger parks. Other hitters just put together that "one big year," when everything went right for them, a year when the ball looked as big as a melon and everything they hit went out of the park. Athletes in all sports experience that type of year occasionally, when they are "in a zone." There were some long ball hitters, however, who hit home runs wherever they played. They were the true, world-class sluggers.

One of the best-known minor league home run leaders was Tony Lazzeri, the famed second baseman of the New York Yankees during the heyday of Babe Ruth. Lazzeri played with the Bronx Bombers from 1926 through 1937. Known as "Poosh-em-up" Tony, he was the first professional baseball player to hit 60 home runs in one season. The precocious young bomber blasted his record total for the Salt Lake City Bees of the Pacific Coast League in 1925, at the tender age of 20. The same year, he set records for runs batted in with 222 and runs scored with 202. Tony's achievements were greatly assisted by the long, 200-game schedule in the PCL, as well as by the 4,000-foot altitude and tailing wind at Bonneville Field in Utah. If his statistics were adjusted to a normal 550-at-bat season, even with the advantage of the atmospheric conditions in Salt Lake City, his home run total would shrink from 60 to a more normal 44.

In the majors, the hard-hitting Lazzeri chalked up a .292 career batting average over 14 years. Seven times in his career, he knocked in more than 100 runs in a season; and on four occasions, he hit 18 home runs, two more than his career average. Poosh-em-Up Tony could hit the ball, but he was no Babe Ruth—except for 1925 in Salt Lake City.

An interesting sidelight to Lazzeri's fantastic season in Salt Lake City is the effect it had on one of his teammates, Frank "Lefty" O'Doul. O'Doul was a pitcher when he arrived in Salt Lake City, having spent seven years bouncing around between the minors and the majors. But, when the crafty left-handed hitter saw how easily balls sailed out of Bonneville Field, he quickly discarded his toe plate and grabbed an outfielder's glove instead. The move was a great boost to O'Doul's career. He went on to punish major league pitching to the tune of .353 over the next seven years, capturing two National League batting championships along the way. He slugged the ball at a .398 clip for the Philadelphia Phillies in 1929 and hit a resounding .368 for the Brooklyn Dodgers in 1932, at the age of 35.

John William "Moose" Clabaugh of Albany, Missouri, played minor league ball for 18 years. During that time, he displayed his talents in sixteen different cities in thirteen leagues. His 346 career home runs were evidence that "Moose" could hit the long ball anywhere. Seven times he exceeded 20 home runs in a season, and three times he led his league in homers. Only once, however, did he hit more than 32 home runs in a year. In 1926, playing for Tyler in the Class D East Texas League, the 25-year-old slugger cracked 62 home runs into the thin Texas air. For his efforts, he was rewarded with a two week look-see by the Brooklyn Robins of the National League. Unfortunately, his .071 batting average during the trial did not impress the Robin front office, and he was quickly sent back to the minors, never to return. Clabaugh's second highest home run total came in the infamous Sulphur Dell bandbox. In 1932, the big lefthander parked 32 balls over the 250-foot right field fence in Nashville.

Moose Clabaugh, not only hit home runs, but he also hit for average. He captured five batting crowns in four different leagues, including the Class D East Texas League, the Class B Southeastern League, and twice in the Class A Southern Association, with averages ranging from .363 to .382. He also averaged .323 over five years in the Class AA Pacific Coast League. Clabaugh played in over 100 games in 12 different seasons, and he never batted less than .305 in any of them. When he retired at the age of 39, he left behind a lifetime batting average of .339.

Russell Louis "Buzz" Arlett is considered by many experts to be the greatest player in minor league history. The native of Oakland, California, starred both on the mound and at the plate over a memorable 20-year career. He began his career as a pitcher with Oakland in the Pacific Coast League in 1918. After a so-so 4–9 rookie season, the righthanded spitball artist blossomed into a bona fide star. Appearing in a league-high 57 games, Arlett won 22 games against 17 losses, while compiling a solid 3.00 earned run average. The following year, he led the PCL in victories, with 29, and hit five home runs along the way. In 1923, after two more winning seasons on the mound, the six-foot-three, 225-pound hurler went down with an arm injury, ending his pitching career. His final mound stats show 108 victories against 93 losses, with three 20-victory seasons.

Fortunately for Arlett, his all-around athletic skills allowed him to make a successful transition to the outfield, prolonging his baseball career. Almost overnight, the switch-hitting Arlett became one of the most feared hitters in the Pacific Coast League. He batted .330 in 1923, with 19 home runs and 101 runs batted in. Then he went on to knock in more than 100 runs for eight successive seasons, leading the league with 140 in 1927. The cellar-dwelling Philadelphia Phillies, seeking some badly needed offense, brought the 32-year-old slugger up to the Big Show in 1931. Arlett was an immediate offensive success, batting .313 with 18 homers and 72 runs batted in, in just 418 at bats. His lackadaisical outfield play, however, brought about his quick return to the minors.

Playing in Baltimore's Oriole Park in 1932, the big switch hitter took advantage of the 300-foot left field fence to deposit 54 baseballs out of the park. Twice within a period of five weeks, the six-foot-three, 225-pound outfielder slammed four home runs in one game, once on June 1 and again on July 4. He is still the only professional player ever to hit four home runs in one game, twice. Two years later, hitting in another comfortable park, this time in Minneapolis, the handsome Californian piled up 41 home runs. Arlett's career home run total of 432, is second to Espino in minor league annals. His average of 30 home runs per 550 at bats is impressive, and compares favorably with Roger Maris' average of 30 home runs per year, but it does not come close to the numbers generated by the likes of Ruth, Oh, Gibson, or Bauman.

Joe Hauser, a slugger whose numbers do compare favorably with the top boomers of baseball, is the only player in professional baseball history to hit more than 60 home runs in one season, twice. He accomplished that feat by smashing 63 round trippers for the Baltimore Orioles in 1930 and 69 home runs for the Minneapolis Millers in 1933. Hauser is also the only world-class minor league slugger discussed in this study whose offensive and defensive skills were both of major league caliber. He might well have had a long, successful career in the majors if the injury jinx hadn't cut him down in his prime.

"Unser Choe" ("Our Joe"), as he was called by the Milwaukee German community, was born in that Wisconsin city on January 12, 1899. A five-foot-ten, 175-pound lefthanded batter, Hauser began his professional career as an outfielder with Providence, Rhode Island, in the Eastern League in 1918. He eventually moved up to the Philadelphia Athletics as a hard-hitting first baseman in 1922. Unser Choe seemed to come of age in 1924, batting .288 with 27 home runs and 115 runs batted in. His home run total was second in the American League to Babe Ruth's 46. On August 12th of that year, the handsome, blond slugger smashed three home runs and a double, good for 14 total bases—an American League record at the time.

Hauser's major league potential was reflected in his performances against Walter Johnson, generally regarded as the greatest pitcher in baseball history. To Unser Choe, The "Big Train" was just another tiny choo-choo. In 1924, Johnson was touched for ten home runs—three off the bat of Joe Hauser. Over the course of a 21-year career, Johnson yielded a total of only 97 homers.

Joe Hauser's 27 home runs for the Philadelphia Athletics were second to Babe Ruth in the American League. Hauser later became a minor league legend, hitting 63 home runs for the Baltimore Orioles in 1930 and setting a professional record by hitting 69 home runs for the Minneapolis Millers in 1933 (credit: Joe Hauser).

Babe Ruth hit ten in 14 years. Joe Hauser was second with five in just 2½ years.

Tragically, Joe Hauser was never able to realize his potential. The 26-year-old's world came crashing down the next spring, when he suffered a broken right kneecap in a freak spring training accident. He missed the entire '25 season and was unable to perform at a major league level in three subsequent trials. He did hit 16 home runs for Philadelphia in 300 at bats in 1928, but then drifted back to the minors. Hauser finished out his career with seven years in AAA ball, followed by six years in the lower classification Wisconsin State League.

From 1930 through 1936, the Wisconsin native terrorized the pitchers in the International League and the American Association. Playing in Baltimore's Terrapin Park, in 1930, Hauser led all professional baseball with 63 home runs, breaking the old International League record by 19. The 335-foot right field foul line in Terrapin Park was similar to most modern stadiums, but it was considerably more distant than both Yankee Stadium (295 feet), where the Babe spent most of his career, and Korakuen Stadium (297 feet) where Sadaharu Oh set his home run records. The center field wall in Baltimore was a healthy 450 feet from home plate. Righthanded hitters had a slight advantage in the park, shooting for the inviting left field foul pole, only 300 feet from home plate. Lefties, like Joe Hauser, were kept honest, taking aim at the challenging right field targets.

Putting Hauser's performance in perspective, only three other players hit more than 50 home runs in a season for Baltimore in 41 years, and none of them exceeded 54.

Three years after his International League performance, the compact lefty set a professional baseball record, since broken, by hitting a staggering 69 home runs for Minneapolis in the American Association. He broke his old record of 63 homers in a morning-afternoon doubleheader against St. Paul on Tuesday, September 5. In the morning contest, he became the first player to hit two home runs in the same game over the 365-foot right field fence in St. Paul's Lexington Park. The second home run set a new season home run record of 64. Hauser continued his barrage with home run number 65 over the left field fence in Minneapolis's Nicollet Park in the afternoon game.

Four days later, on the next to last day of the season, he smashed numbers 68 and 69 in an 8–6 loss to Kansas City; however, he missed a chance to crack the magic 70 barrier when the season's finale was rained out. Fifty of Hauser's 69 home runs were hit in the Millers' home park, Nicollet Stadium, where the short, 279-foot right field grandstand provided an inviting target for the veteran pull hitter. The monumental significance of Hauser's feat is reflected in the fact that only Nick Cullop, with 54 round trippers in 1930, hit more than 50 homers in one season during the 54-year history of Nicollet Park. Over a 31-year period, from 1930 through 1960, only four International League players hit 49 or more home runs in a single season. Joe Hauser did it twice. The best Ted Williams could do was 43 with Minneapolis in 1938.

One trivia footnote relating to Hauser's historic season involves a local cereal manufacturer, the General Mills Company. General Mills, in honor of the Millers' 1932 International League championship, rented a large billboard on the outfield fence at Nicollet Stadium for the 1933 season, proudly proclaiming, "Wheaties—The Breakfast of Champions." It was the first time that famous slogan was ever used. And it all began with the Minneapolis Millers.

The year after his record-breaking achievement, Unser Choe was on track to break the 60 barrier a third time. He walloped 33 home runs in Minneapolis's first 82 games, a pace that would have given him 62 for the season. Unfortunately, the injury gremlin struck the powerful slugger a second time. Hauser went down with a broken left kneecap in mid season and was lost for the rest of the year.

Over the seven-year period, however, Unser Choe averaged 50 home runs for every 550 at bats, a figure exceeded only by Babe Ruth's 52 home runs per 550 at bats from 1926 through 1932. Hauser stands fifth on the all-time minor league career home run list, and is near the top frequency-wise with 34 home runs per year. His major league home run average was just 21, but it was on the rise when he was injured. Still years away from reaching his peak, and six years before he scaled the heights in Baltimore, the Milwaukee strongman's major league home run totals had increased from 9 in his rookie season, to 16 in his second year, and to 27 in his third year. If his luck hadn't suddenly deserted him, there is no telling what he might have accomplished.

Gabriel "Pete" Hughes, dominated the lower minor league classifications during the late '30s and the early '40s. Hughes was an offensive powerhouse, whose unique accomplishments have never been equaled in the annals of baseball. Over a productive 12-year career, the husky, 190-pound outfielder compiled a .350 career batting average and won two batting titles. He also captured four home run crowns in four different leagues over that period. The native of Hurley, New Mexico, averaged 35 home runs a year, but was more than a big, muscle-bound slugger. He was an all-around run producer, adding 39 doubles and 7 triples to his annual extra base hit barrage. He also had a keen batting eye, as evidenced by his extraordinary bases on balls record. He led the league in walks nine times in 12 years, averaging an amazing 205 walks a year. His 1,666 career bases on balls is a minor league record.

Pete Hughes is now recognized as the all-time professional leader in on-base percentage, beating out Ted Williams by a comfortable margin. The "Splendid Splinter" had an on-base percentage of .483 in the major leagues, followed by Babe Ruth at .474. These numbers pale by comparison to Hughes's numbers. The hero of the southwest had a career on-base percentage of .530, the only professional baseball player ever to exceed the magic .500 level. He had season OBPs of .577, .574, .569, and .566. This right-handed hitter is also one of the few players ever to score more than one run a game over a career, tallying 1,339 times in 1.333 contests. His RBI percentage of 0.98 is one of the highest ever recorded in professional baseball.

Gabriel "Pete" Hughes was a one-man army.

D. C. "Pud" Miller" was a beefy six footer who feasted on the pitching in the southwest. The lefthanded-hitting outfielder plied his trade with 15 teams over a checkered 14-year career. He pounded the ball wherever he went, but he couldn't seem to settle down with one team. In 1949, playing for Lamesa in the West Texas–New Mexico (WT-NM) League, the 215-pound slugger rapped out 52 home runs in 109 games. He added another 3 homers in 27 games with Gladewater in the East Texas League, giving him a total of 55 home runs for the year.

Pud Miller hit the ball for average, as well as for distance. He won two batting titles with Hickory of the North Carolina State League, hitting .369 in 1950 and a sizzling .425 the following year. When he retired, he had accumulated 268 home runs, an average of 37 home runs a year. His career batting average of .350 is one of the highest in minor league history.

Ken Guettler was another minor league slugger who had one magic year. The compact outfielder was a genuine home run hitter, averaging 33 home runs a year over a 15-year career. Unlike Miller, however, Guettler was not a high-average hitter. He did win one batting crown, hitting .334 with Portsmouth of the Piedmont League in 1952. He also had three other .300 seasons in his career, but intermixed them with several mediocre seasons, finishing with a career batting average of just .289.

The solidly built righthander won eight home run crowns in five different leagues. He won four of his crowns with Portsmouth in the Piedmont League, between 1951 and 1955, with home run totals of 30, 28, 30, and 41. The year after hitting 41 homers, Guettler moved on to Shreveport, Louisiana, in the Class AA Texas League. In 1956, at the age of 29, the 190-pound outfielder slammed 62 home runs and drove in 143 runs in 140 games. Many of his homers disappeared over the 320-foot left field fence at Spar Stadium. That was Guettler's last full season in organized ball. Three years later, he retired from the game after hitting .232 in the South Atlantic League.

Forrest Edward "Frosty" Kennedy, a five-foot-eleven, 180-pound outfielder-infielder from Los Angeles, California, capitalized on the unusual playing conditions in the southwest, to become a home run hero. Kennedy was a decent hitter during his first four years in the minors, averaging well over .300 with teams in California, Georgia, and Florida. He was a good RBI man with reasonable power, but he was not a big home run hitter, with just ten round trippers a year to show for his efforts. Once he hit the Class B and C leagues in Texas and New Mexico, however, he turned into a fearsome slugger. In five full seasons in the southwest leagues, Kennedy's batting averages ranged from a low of .301 to a high of .411. His home run production included 25 homers with Lamesa in the West Texas–New Mexico League, 38 with Plainview and 35 with Amarillo in the same league, and 30 with Yuma in the Arizona-Mexico League. His most successful year was 1956, when the 30-year-old slugger spanked 60 home runs and drove in 184 runs in 144 games for Class B Plainview in the Southwest League. His career home run average was 27 home runs a season, but his average in the southwest was a lofty 39 home runs a year—respectable but not remarkable, considering the caliber of the opposition in the lower classifications, the small ballparks, and the light air.

It was noted earlier that Bob Lennon, a big, six-foot, 200-pounder, had feasted on the short right field fence in Nashville. In 1954, the 26-year-old, lefthanded batter hit 64 balls into orbit over Tennessee. Lennon's second highest home run total was the 31 he hit out of cozy Nicollet Park in Minneapolis. In larger ballparks, the free swinger's home run production was less impressive. He hit 28 and 25 homers for Montreal in the International League, the only other times he exceeded 13. Over a 17-year career, the Brooklyn native hit 278 round trippers, an average of 25 per year.

One of the most notable home run hitters in all of organized baseball was Dick Stuart, who bashed 66 home runs for the Lincoln (Nebraska) Chiefs in the Class A Western League in 1956. One of Stuart's mammoth blasts was measured at 610 feet, the second-longest measured home run in history. The six-foot-four, 212-pound first baseman went on to accumulate a total of 228 round trippers in the major leagues, primarily with the Pittsburgh Pirates and Boston Red Sox.

Known as "Dr. Strangeglove" because of his defensive deficiencies, Stuart led one of the major leagues in errors for seven straight years. But how he could hit. Not a high-average hitter, the colorful slugger smashed 38 homers for the Pirates in 1961, 42 homers for the Red Sox in 1963, and 33 more homers for Boston the following year. Moving on to Japan after his major league career ended, the big righthander made 49 balls disappear in 208 games for the Taiyo Whales of the Central League, averaging 39 home runs for every 550 at bats. While this compared favorably with his major league average of 32 home runs per 550 at bats, his minor league average was a lofty 46!

It is often stated that Stuart's 66 home runs in Lincoln were aided by the playing conditions in his home park, but such assistance is difficult to rationalize. Sherman Field was not a tiny ballpark, by any means. Both foul lines stood 330 feet from home plate, with the center field fence 380 feet away. The elevation was 1,176 feet, according to Ernest J. Green in *The Baseball Research Journal*, about average for a minor league location. And there were no prevailing wind conditions that would benefit a home run hitter. Teams representing Lincoln participated in professional baseball over a period of 56 years and no other Lincoln player even hit as many as fifty home runs in a single season. In fact, during the twelve years that Lincoln was in the Class A Western League, from 1947 through 1958, no league leader, with the exception of Stuart, exceeded 44 home runs in a single season. Four times during that span, the league leader hit less than 30 home runs.

Larry Gerlach, who attended many of Stuart's games in Lincoln, claimed the big first baseman wasn't noted for hitting cheap home runs. According to Gerlach, Stuart's patented uppercut swing usually sent balls far over the left field fence, with many of them clearing the scoreboard in the left center field power alley.

Actually, the rangy righthander could have been discussed in the chapter on the major leagues' lively ball era. He had more at bats, more hits, and more home runs in the majors than he did in the minors, but his 66 home runs in Lincoln made him a minor league legend. In the majors, he averaged 34 home runs per year with Boston and 32 home runs per year with Pittsburgh. These numbers are comparable to those put up by Willie Mays (33), Reggie Jackson (31), and many other world-class sluggers.

Dick Stuart had the potential to reach the upper echelons of power hitting. The colorful first sacker hit them out of every park he played in. It made no difference if he was in Lincoln, Billings, Hollywood, Atlanta, Pittsburgh, or Boston. When he put good wood on the ball, it went out of sight. Over a storied 18 year career, spanning the globe, the big righthander hit a total of 487 home runs in 6,869 at bats—an average of 39 homers a year. It is sad that his defensive liabilities restricted him from reaching his full potential. If he could only have fielded his position at a major league level, he might well have challenged the great home run hitters of all time. Still, his impressive offensive achievements do qualify him for recognition with the game's top sluggers.

The minor leagues' all-time career home run king is Hector Espino, A five-foot-eleven, 185-pound slugger who played most of his career in the Mexican League. Espino hit 484 home runs over a 25-year career, an average of 29 homers per year (per 550 at bats). He shunned several offers to play major league ball, preferring instead to remain in his home country. Espino was not a power hitter of the Crues or Bauman type. He produced his high career totals through consistency over a protracted period of time. Only once did he hit more than 40 home runs in a season, smashing 46 round trippers in 1964. That was the same year he played 32 games for Jacksonville in the International League, his only experience in the United States. Espino hit three home runs and batted .300 in his short American career, but returned to Mexico after feeling the sting of American prejudice.

Frank Gravino terrorized Northern League opponents for three years during the early '50s. The compact outfielder packed 186 pounds on a five-foot-nine-inch frame, and he generated tremendous power with a go-for-broke, freewheeling swing. Gravino was no more than a journeyman minor leaguer until he found a home in the northwest. From 1940 through 1949, with three years out for World War II, the righthanded hitter bounced around the minors, playing erratic baseball and drawing little attention from major league scouts. His low batting average (.292) and limited defense prevented him from advancing into the higher minor league classifications. Once he hit the northwest, however, his fortunes changed. During his last four years in professional baseball, the righthanded slugger won four home run titles, hitting 42 homers for St. Jean in the Provincial League, and 32, 52, and 56 round trippers with Fargo-Moorehead in the Northern League. In 1953, when Gravino walloped 52 homers, the number two man in the league totaled only 18.

There are two interesting sidelights to the '53 season. Gravino's outfield sidekick that year, 18-year-old Roger Maris, was able to put only nine dingers on the board. The following year, with Keokuk in the Three I League, the future major league home run king poled 32 homers. Dave Roberts, a noted minor league slugger, hit 15 round trippers in '53 as a 20-year-old rookie for Grand Forks. The next year, he planted 33 of them for Aberdeen. Roberts went on to average 21 homers a year over 15 minor league seasons. The lefthanded-hitting first baseman also became a slugger of note in Japan, where he starred in the Japanese Central League for seven seasons. His home run average in the Land of the Rising Sun was an impressive 37 homers a year.

In 1954, Gravino's 56 homers put him 33 homers ahead of his nearest rival, according to *Minor League Baseball Stars*. The publication also notes that he outhomered four other teams. The native of Newark, New York, retired after the '54 season at the age of 31. His career stats showed a total of 271 home runs and a .292 batting average. His home run average was a sensational 38 homers per year, the fourth best average in minor league history.

The minor leagues in the southwest produced some of the mightiest offensive statistics in professional baseball history, beginning in the late '30s, and continuing into the mid-'50s. This was particularly true of the West Texas–New Mexico and Longhorn Leagues, both operating in the border towns along the Texas–New Mexico divide. These leagues produced two of the top three single-season home run hitters in professional baseball history, as well as the top three run producers. Gordon T. "Gordie" Nell was part of that offensive barrage. The righthanded hitting outfielder bounced around from league to league for several years in the early '30s, displaying a good batting eye, as well as above average power, but not showing the consistency required to move to the top classifications. He led the Western Association in home runs twice, hitting 27 round trippers for Muscogee in 1930 and 44 homers for the same team in 1931. Along the way he sat out all or parts of nine seasons. Four of these seasons were related to World War II, while the other five years were for personal reasons.

From 1939 through 1949, Nell played in the WT-NM League, where he proceeded to carve out a name for himself in Texas baseball lore. He won one batting title along the way, as well as three home run crowns and three RBI crowns. When he finally retired, after the '49 season, he left behind a career .337 batting average, a total of 365 home runs, and 1,416 runs batted in. His

Bobby Crues pounded out 69 home runs for Amarillo in the West Texas–New Mexico League in 1948, tying the professional record (credit: Amarillo Globe-News).

home run average was an imposing 37 homers per year, which puts him in the upper class of minor league sluggers, but doesn't seriously challenge Dick Stuart, Bobby Crues, or Joe Bauman for the minor league King of Swat crown.

In run production, however, Gordie Nell was the prince, if not the king. His 1,416 RBIs were achieved in only 1,351 games, giving him a sensational average of 1.05 RBIs per game. That performance gave him second place on the all-time run production list for professional baseball. Only Bobby Crues exceeded his numbers. No major league player has come close to the magic 1.00 number in 125 years.

Another legendary minor league home run king was the aforementioned Bobby Crues, the tall Texan. Crues was born in Frisco, Texas on December 31, 1918. Twenty years later, as a strapping six-foot-two, 185-pounder, he began his professional career as a pitcher for Lamesa in the West Texas–New Mexico League. The hard-throwing righthander logged a 20–5 record in 1940, but arm problems sidelined him periodically over the next two years. After spending three years in military service, Crues returned to baseball as an outfielder. By this time, he was 27 years old, too old to aspire to major league stardom. Instead, he spent six full seasons, and parts of two others, playing ball in the Class C and D leagues on the Texas–New Mexico border. Along the way, he made himself a legend in the southwest.

In 1947, playing for the Amarillo Gold Sox in the WT-NM League, the big, righthanded hitter took advantage of the unique playing conditions in the Texas city, to smash 52 home runs in 139 games. The following year, he tied Joe Hauser's professional baseball record of 69 home runs in one season. His 254 runs batted in that year, in a 140-game season, established a professional record that may never be broken.

Bobby Crues played two more full seasons, hitting 28 and 32 homers for San Angelo in the Longhorn League, before hanging up his spikes after the

'53 season. His career total of 232 home runs in 3,216 at bats, averages out to be 40 home runs for every 550 at bats, making him the number three home run hitter in minor league history. He has the sixth highest home run average in professional baseball, including the major leagues, the Japanese leagues, and the Negro leagues.

Crues's high frequency rating was significantly affected by his two year stint in Amarillo. He hit more than half his career home runs during that period, aided and abetted by a small park, the 3,676-foot altitude, and favorable wind conditions. The foul lines in Gold Coast Stadium were only 324 feet from home plate, with center field just 360 feet away.

The kid from Frisco established one other offensive production record during his abbreviated career in the West Texas–New Mexico and Longhorn Leagues. Bobby Crues knocked in 905 runs in just 843 games, an average of 1.07 runs batted in per game. That is the all-time professional baseball record.

Dozens of world-class sluggers have flexed their muscles on minor league fields across the United States over the past 100 years or so, but the king of these big bruisers has to be Joe Willis Bauman, the burly Oklahoman. Bauman was the property of the Boston Braves early in his career, but three years in the U.S. Navy during World War II took away his big opportunity to play major league baseball. Returning home from military service in 1946, the towering, six-foot-five-inch, lefthanded power hitter pulverized West Texas–New Mexico League pitching to the tune of 86 home runs in two years.

In 1952, following contractual disputes with Boston and a subsequent three-year hiatus from the sport, during which time he played semipro baseball, the 235-pound behemoth made his second comeback. Playing with the Artesia Drillers in the Class C Longhorn League, Bauman tore opposing pitchers apart, batting a lofty .375, while leading the league with 50 home runs and 157 runs batted in—in just 139 games. The following year, the 31-year-old Sooner ripped the ball at a .371 pace, again leading the league in home runs with 53 and driving in 141 teammates. Home runs were not cheap in Artesia either, in spite of the 3,200-foot elevation. The right field fence at Brainard Park stood 349 feet from home plate, and the dead-pull hitter had to power the ball through the teeth of a constant 10–20 mile per hour headwind.

In 1954, Joe Bauman experienced a career season, putting together the most overpowering offensive display ever seen in organized baseball. Playing for the Roswell Rockets of the Longhorn League, he captured the triple crown with numbers that may never be equaled. He coupled a dazzling .400 batting average with 72 home runs and 224 runs batted in. His home run total established a new professional record, breaking the old mark of 69 held jointly by Joe Hauser and Bobby Crues. Bauman hit his record-tying 69th home run at Park Field in Roswell, New Mexico, during the last week of the season; then he traveled 38 miles south to Artesia where he hit numbers 70, 71, and

72 in a twi-night doubleheader to close out the season. Home run number 70 went out of Brainard Park over the 352 foot marker in right center field. His 224 RBIs that year are second on the all-time professional list, behind Bobby Crues's 254.

Bauman set another record of note that year. His 456 total bases in 498 at bats gave him a new, organized ball, slugging percentage record of .916.

The big first baseman was a bona fide home run hitter. Although he was in organized ball for 16 seasons, he played only six full years. He lost three years to military service, was inactive during four years, and played less than 100 games in three other campaigns. In his six full seasons, however, he was awesome. His home run totals ranged from 38 to 72. On a frequency basis, his home runs per 550 at bats averaged 43, 48, 59, 63, 80, and 46.

Bauman played in the Longhorn League for four-and-a-half years, from 1952 to 1956. The league was in existence for only nine years, and Bauman led the league in homers in four of those years, averaging 55 home runs a year, adjusted to 64 for a 550 at-bat season. The home run leaders during the remaining five years of league play averaged only 37 home runs a year, which, when adjusted to 43, are a full 33 percent fewer than Big Joe.

As with most home run leaders—including major league sluggers like Ruth, Maris, and Aaron—Bauman's statistics were aided by his playing environment. Some people have tried to minimize Bauman's accomplishments by casting aspersions on the playing conditions in the southwest parks. These charges are not entirely accurate. The high elevation in the southwest, no doubt, did assist his smoldering wallops. Roswell and Artesia are located at an elevation of approximately 3,700 feet. By comparison, however, Coors Field in Denver, the home of the Colorado Rockies, sits 5,280 feet above sea level. The dimensions of the playing fields in the Texas–New Mexico area have also been denigrated without justification. The dimensions of most of the parks in the WT-NM League and the Longhorn League were of average size. Park Field in Roswell, where Bauman established his home run record, was 329 feet down both foul lines and 380 feet to center. Brainard Park, as was noted previously, had a relatively long 349-foot right field foul line, buffeted by a steady headwind. By comparison, Hank Aaron took aim at a 320-foot foul pole in Atlanta, with a following breeze, and a 1,057 foot elevation. Babe Ruth, Mickey Mantle, and Roger Maris had the friendly, 295-foot right field seats in Yankee Stadium to shoot at. And, in Tokyo's Korakuen Stadium, where Sadaharu Oh enjoyed his greatest success, the stands were only 297 feet from home plate.

The effect of park dimensions and atmospheric conditions on home run totals can be best understood in the career statistics of Hank Aaron. "Hammerin' Hank" averaged 31 home runs a year in Milwaukee's County Stadium. In Atlanta, where he played his last eight years, Aaron averaged 41 homers a year. The foul lines in both stadiums were similar (320 feet in Milwaukee and 325 feet in Atlanta), but the friendly atmospheric conditions in Atlanta's Fulton County Stadium earned the park the nickname, "The Launching Pad." It routinely led all National League parks in home runs.

Joe Bauman retired from the game in 1956, after the recurrence of an old ankle injury, leaving behind some of the most impressive statistics ever generated. In 1,019 games, he put together a .337 career batting average, with 337 home runs and 1,057 runs batted in. His average of 1.04 RBIs per game is one of the top marks ever achieved in professional baseball. Sam Thompson of the old Philadelphia Phillies holds the major league mark with 0.92 runs batted in per game.

Perhaps Bauman's most impressive record, however, is his home run frequency. His average of 10.3 at bats per home run translates into 54 home runs per 550 at bats, easily beating Dick Stuart (46) as the all-time minor league home run king. Here is the complete list of world-class minor league sluggers, along with their home run averages:

> Joe Bauman . . . 54 home runs per year
> Dick Stuart. . . . 46 home runs per year
> Bobby Crues. . . 40 home runs per year
> Frank Gravino . 38 home runs per year
> Gordie Nell . . . 37 home runs per year
> Pud Miller . . . . 37 home runs per year
> Pete Hughes. . . 35 home runs per year

As the above list reveals, there have been many great long ball hitters throughout the glorious history of minor league baseball, but none of them have come close to putting up the numbers generated by the big bomber from Oklahoma. Joe Willis Bauman's 54 home run average is the best career frequency of any baseball player in the world, exceeding that of such renowned sluggers as Sadaharu Oh, Josh Gibson, and Babe Ruth.

In the arena of famed home run hitters, Joe Willis Bauman resides with exalted company.

CHAPTER 2

MAJOR LEAGUES, THE DEAD BALL ERA

Professional baseball has been played in the United States since 1869, when the Cincinnati Red Stockings, a group of full-time professionals under the direction of manager Harry Wright, terrorized baseball opponents from San Francisco to Long Island. The mighty Redlegs compiled an unmatched record of 79 victories and one tie before being derailed by the Brooklyn Atlantics 8–7, in eleven innings, on June 14, 1870.

Over that span, Cincinnati outscored their overmatched opponents by an average score of 43–10. Their leading batsman, shortstop George Wright, slugged the ball at a torrid .518 clip in 52 games, with 59 home runs and 339 runs scored. The five-foot-nine, 150-pound bundle of dynamite was America's first King of Swat. Since there were no fences surrounding the early parks, home runs were all inside-the-park affairs, favorable to line-drive hitters and speedy baserunners. Wright fit the bill perfectly.

Shortly after the demise of the Redlegs, the first professional baseball league was formed. The National Association of Professional Baseball Players operated from 1871 through 1875. It was succeeded by the current National League of Professional Baseball Clubs, formed in 1876.

The first quarter century of professional baseball was an evolutionary period, during which the rules of the game were constantly being adjusted to optimize the competition and to put the pitcher, batter, and fielder all on an equal plane. The biggest change in field dimensions concerned the distance from home plate to the pitcher's mound. Initially, the mound was only 45 feet from the plate. It was extended to 50 feet in 1881 and, finally, to sixty feet-six inches in 1893.

Initially, pitchers had to throw the ball with an underhand motion, and they could not twist their wrist to curve the ball. In 1881, they were permitted to throw sidearm; in 1884, the present overhand delivery was legalized.

The number of balls and strikes was also in a state of flux during the 1880s. In 1881, nine balls were required before the batter was awarded first base. The four-ball rule was finally put into effect in 1889. The number of strikes required to record an out was set at three in 1889. Prior to that time, it took four strikes to retire the batter.

Other important changes came into force in the late 1880s and early 1890s. The flat bat was outlawed, and only round bats could be used from 1893 on. In 1887, the strike zone was defined as being from the top of the shoulders to the bottom of the knees. Beginning the same year, batters could no longer request where they would like the ball pitched. Until then, the batter could call for a high pitch or a low pitch.

By 1893, the modern game of baseball, as we know it, became a reality. The dimensions of the field were firmly established, the balls and strikes were set at their present levels, the construction of the balls and bats were standardized, and fielders' gloves were in general use. Most players began using gloves on their catching hand by 1886. Bid McPhee, however, was an exception. The Cincinnati second baseman, generally regarded as the best second baseman of the nineteenth century, considered gloves to be unmanly, and he refused to wear them. In spite of that, the barehanded McPhee led the National League in fielding percentage nine times. In 1896, when he finally did relent and started to wear a glove to protect an injury, he established a fielding record that endured for 29 years. Sparky Adams of the Chicago Cubs finally topped his .978 fielding percentage in 1925. The biggest changes in professional baseball between 1893 and 1920 had a significant effect on home run production. They involved the introduction of the cork centered ball in 1911 and the use of the so-called "lively ball" beginning in 1920.

Home runs were a rare commodity in the early days of baseball (the Redlegs' George Wright excepted), primarily because of the poor quality of the balls and the outlandish dimensions of the ballparks. The balls were soft and poorly constructed compared to today's balls, and they did not travel nearly as far when hit. Additionally, only one ball was used in a game, and it became badly misshapened as the game progressed. The baseball fields themselves were often not enclosed, so long hits were always in play. It was a game of speed, with doubles and triples the fashion of the day. Those parks that were enclosed tended to be so large that the outfield fences seldom came into play. Often, the center field fence stood 500 feet or more from home plate.

In 1876, the National League's premier season, the entire eight team membership hit a total of only 40 home runs over a 65-game season. No one team had more than nine homers. Only George Hall of Philadelphia with five and Charlie Jones of Cincinnati with four hit more than two home runs during the entire season. Hall, a slightly built five-foot-seven, 142-pound lefthanded hitter, accounted for the Ruthian total of 12.2 percent of the home runs hit in the entire league. He outhomered four teams in the league, and accounted for all but two of his team's home runs. He retired after the 1877 season, leaving behind a seven year batting average (including National Association games) of .345. No home run data is available on his five years in the Association.

Charlie Jones, on the other hand, was the first true slugger in the National League. His four home runs in 1876 represented 10 percent of the league's home run totals. Jones, a native of Brooklyn, New York, was the first big man to star in the National League. Standing five-feet-eleven-inches tall and weighing a robust 202 pounds, the righthanded-hitting outfielder towered over the average player, who stood only five-foot-seven and weighed 150 pounds. In 1879, Jones slugged a league-leading nine home runs for the Boston Red Stockings, a whomping 15.5 percent of the league's total. His home run percentage may be the highest major league percentage of all time. Babe Ruth accounted for 13.7 percent of the league's home runs in 1927 when he hit his record setting 60.

Nicknamed "Baby" because of his enormous size, Jones, a noted carouser like Babe Ruth, was in constant trouble with his team and with the league. He was blacklisted for two years over a salary dispute after the 1880 season, returning to action with the Cincinnati Reds of the American Association in 1883, where he immediately left his mark by slamming 11 home runs, 10 percent of the Association's total.

Charlie Jones left other marks on the major leagues, as well. In 1880, he pounded two home runs in one inning: a major league record that has never been broken. Four years later, he hit three triples in one game, tying an American Association record. The big slugger retired from the game in 1888, closing out a successful though often controversial eleven-year career. His lifetime batting average of .299 included 55 home runs. His National League home run average of eight homers per 550 at bats puts him in the top echelon of nineteenth-century home run hitters. It should be noted, however, that when Jones began playing, the pitching rubber was only 45 feet from home plate, and pitchers were restricted to underhand or sidearm deliveries. During his last five years in the league, the pitching distance was 50 feet, and pitchers were allowed to throw overhand. Those changes apparently affected Jones's power statistics, as his home run average fell from 11 to 6 home runs per year after 1883.

During the formative years of the league, small ballparks popped up now and then, jeopardizing the credibility of the game. The Cleveland Blues, playing in tiny National League Park, had special ground rules whereby balls hit over their short left field fence were scored as doubles. Their western rivals, the Chicago White Stockings, carried the "small park" syndrome to the extreme in 1883 and 1884. Their home park, Lake Front Park, on the shores of Lake Michigan, was the smallest baseball park in major league history. The left field fence stood only 180 feet from home plate, making left field in the Los Angeles Coliseum seem like the Grand Canyon. The right field fence was not much further away, hovering only 106 feet behind the first baseman. Center field was a cozy 300 feet from the batter.

In 1883, players hitting balls over the left field fence in Lake Front Park, were credited with doubles. The White Stockings, of course, led the National League with 277 two-base hits, 68 more than their closest rivals, the Boston Red Stockings. Third baseman Ned Williamson was the pacesetter with a record total of 49 doubles. With those ground rules in effect, Chicago batters hit only 13 home runs for the year. The following year, with balls hit over the left field fence counting as home runs, the White Stockings' two-base hit output dropped sharply to 162, but their home run production exploded. Cap Anson's sluggers pounded out 142 round trippers, almost as many as the rest of the league combined. Four Chicago batters exceeded the 20 home run mark, led by Williamson's unprecedented total of 27. Second baseman Fred Pfeffer (25), left fielder Abner Dalrymple (22), and first baseman/manager Cap Anson (21) all broke the old mark of 10 set by New York's Buck Ewing the year before. Right fielder King Kelly, with 13 homers, also exceeded Ewing's mark.

Ned Williamson's record stood for 35 years, until 1919, when Babe Ruth unloaded 29 four baggers, ushering in the era of the lively ball. The Chicago third baseman carried the reputation of being baseball's first bona fide slugger for more than sixty years, but it was a reputation built on "design" rather than on ability. Research eventually uncovered the secret of his success. Of Williamson's record breaking 27 home runs, all but two of them were hit in chummy Lake Front Park.

The following year, the White Stockings moved to the new West Side Park, an oval-shaped field with 216-foot foul lines and a 500+ foot center field, much like the Polo Grounds. Williamson's home run production almost disappeared completely in the new surroundings. He hit only three home runs: two at home and one on the road. Dalrymple led the league with 11 round trippers, while Cap Anson hit seven and Fred Pfeffer hit six—a far cry from '84.

The five-foot-eleven, righthanded-hitting Williamson toiled in the major leagues for 13 years, amassing 4,553 at bats over that period. His 1884 home run total amounted to 43 percent of his career home runs. The most he ever hit in any other year was nine, in 1887. Of his 63 career homers, only seven were hit on the road. His 49 doubles were also a career mark for the 170-pound slugger. His next highest totals were 27 in 1882 and 20 in 1887.

Ned Williamson was one of the top third basemen of his day, an outstanding defensive player who led his position in double plays six times and in assists seven times. He was not a dangerous hitter, however. His lifetime batting average was only .255. Never once did he hit above .294, and never did he drive in more than 84 runs in a season.

There were, however, some giants among the hundreds of young men who toiled on America's baseball diamonds during the last twenty years of the nineteenth century. There were some authentic sluggers, who were worthy of comparison with Babe Ruth, Hank Aaron, Sadaharu Oh, and Josh Gibson. The most notable of the group were Roger Connor, Sam Thompson, Dan Brouthers, and Harry Stovey.

Roger Connor, the New York Giant first baseman, was the career home run champion of the nineteenth century, piling up 137 circuit blows over an 18-year career. Connor was a big man, standing six feet and three inches tall and carrying 220 pounds on his muscular frame. He was one of several big men on the New York team, causing manager Jim Mutrie to exult repeatedly about "My boys, my giants." The name was eventually picked up by newspapermen, and has been the team nickname ever since.

Connor was a consistent long ball hitter who counted 441 doubles, 233 triples, and the aforementioned 137 home runs among his 2,467 career hits. He led the league in home runs once, and seven times exceeded ten home runs in a single season. Triples were his forte, however. The speedy Connor led the league with 18 three-base hits in 1882 and with 20 triples in 1886. Overall, he legged out 15 or more triples ten times in his career, four times exceeding the 20 mark. He ranks fifth, career-wise, in that category, trailing only Sam Crawford's record total of 312 triples, Ty Cobb's 294, Honus Wagner's 252, and Jake Beckley's 243. He led the National League in batting in 1885 with a sizzling .371 average. The big, lefthanded batter hit .300 or better eleven times in 18 years. His lifetime batting average of .317 is fiftieth all-time. He was voted into baseball's Hall of Fame in 1976.

Roger Connor's home run frequency of nine home runs per 550 at bats is among the top five home run averages of nineteenth-century sluggers.

Big Sam Thompson was another behemoth of the diamond. In an era when the average player was shorter and slighter than today, Big Sam topped out in his prime at six-feet-two-inches tall and 207 pounds. Like Connor, he hit from the left side of the plate, and he drove baseballs to all fields with awesome power. Although he batted 1,810 fewer times in his career than the Giant first baseman, Big Sam only trailed him by ten career home runs.

Thompson's 15-year career was spent primarily with the Detroit Wolverines and the Philadelphia Phillies. It was in the City of Brotherly Love that Thompson became a member of the only .400 hitting outfield in major league history. His .404 batting average was matched by his outfield partners, Ed Delahanty (.407) and Billy Hamilton (.404).

Big Sam led the league in home runs on two occasions, with 20 round trippers in 1889 and with 18 circuit blows in 1895. He led the league twice in doubles, once in triples, twice in runs batted in, and once in batting average. His 1,299 RBIs in 1,407 games translates into 0.923 runs batted in per game, making him the all-time major league run producer. Lou Gehrig was a close second, with 0.920 RBIs per game, while Hank Greenberg was right on

Gehrig's heels, with 0.915 RBIs per game. Thompson's 166 RBIs with Detroit in 1887 is a nineteenth-century record and was the major league record for 34 years. The Bambino finally broke it in 1921, driving in 170 runs. Ruth's record stood for only six years, before being smashed by Lou Gehrig's 174. In 1930, Hack Wilson of the Chicago Cubs knocked in 190 teammates, which is still the major league record. Gehrig's 184 RBIs in 1931 stands as the American League record.

On a frequency basis, Sam Thompson led all nineteenth-century batters in home runs, hitting an average of 12 home runs for every 550 at bats. After 1893, when the pitching distance was increased from 50 feet to its present sixty feet-six inches, Big Sam's bat exploded. He capitalized on the new pitching distance more than any other batter in baseball. Prior to 1893, Thompson showed a .312 career batting average to go along with ten home runs. From 1893 through the end of his career, the husky slugger batted .362 and averaged 14 home runs per year. His extra base totals, in 5,984 career at bats, show 340 doubles, 160 triples, and 127 home runs. When he retired, the big outfielder had a .336 career batting average. He was admitted into the Hall of Fame in 1974.

Dan Brouthers, yet another big, lefthanded slugger, played with a variety of teams over a 19-year career, but he is primarily associated with the Buffalo Bisons and the Detroit Wolverines. The six-foot-two, 207-pound first baseman showed the way in doubles three times, in triples once, in home runs twice, in RBIs twice, and in batting average five times. His stratospheric batting performances included averages of .370, .368, .374, .373 and twice .350.

Big Dan Brouthers was a true baseball superstar, creating havoc in the National League for almost two decades. His .342 lifetime batting average was the highest batting average of any nineteenth-century batter and remains ninth on the all-time list. As a home run hitter, he ranks sixth on the nineteenth-century list, hitting a round tripper on 1.58 percent of his at bats, an average of nine home runs per season.

Considering the playing conditions in the nineteenth century, such as parks with no fences or with fences outside the playing area, total extra base hits may be a better measurement of a batter's slugging prowess than just his home run totals. In that regard, Big Dan Brouthers is number one. Combining doubles and triples with home runs gives Brouthers an 11.5 percent extra base hit percentage, one percentage point or more above his nearest competitors. In pure slugging percentage, Big Dan again came out on top of the pack. His .519 slugging percentage, nineteenth all-time, ranks first against his peers. Sam Thompson was second at .505.

Harry Stovey was the black sheep of nineteenth-century sluggers. Whereas Connor, Thompson, and Brouthers were all big, ponderous, lefthanded-hitting sluggers, Stovey was a sleekly built six-foot, 180-pound greyhound. The righthanded batter had tremendous power, as evidenced by the

*Harry Stovey was the Willie Mays of the 1880s. He combined awesome power with blaz-
ing speed. He was the first major league slugger to hit 100 career home runs. He led the league
in home runs six times and in stolen bases three times. He stole 156 bases in 1888 and hit
19 home runs in 1889 (credit: National Baseball Library, Cooperstown, N.Y.).*

fact that he led the league in home runs six times—more than any of his contemporaries. Stovey was the National League's premier slugger during the 1880s. He was the first professional baseball player to amass 100 career home runs. His career total of 121 home runs is the third highest in the nineteenth century, trailing only Roger Connor and Sam Thompson. His home run frequency is second to Thompson, at 2.00 percent of his at bats, an average of 11 home runs per year. Admittedly, Stovey took advantage of the field dimensions at Philadelphia's Jefferson Street Grounds (the same park that George Hall played in). The park was shaped like an oval, similar to the Polo Grounds, with short foul lines and a 500-foot center field fence. Stovey probably parked a few over the cozy left field fence, but he also had the disadvantage of a 400 foot power alley in left center. The fact is, though, that it didn't matter where Harry Stovey played. He smoked the ball everywhere. His titanic blasts were just as much in evidence when he played for the Worcester Ruby Legs and the Boston Beaneaters, as they were when he played for the Athletics of Philadelphia.

From 1883–85, when the Philadelphia flash won three home run titles, with a total of 38 circuit blows, the rest of the Philadelphia team could muster only 37. In 1883, when Stovey sent 14 balls into the Pennsylvania sky, no one else on the team hit more than one! In fact, Stovey outhomered five of his seven remaining teams. In 1884, when Stovey hit 11 round trippers, third baseman Fred Corey was next with five. In 1885, when he accounted for 13 home runs, center fielder Henry Larkin chipped in with eight. And in 1889, when Stovey slugged 19 homers, third baseman Denny Lyons was second with nine.

Harry Stovey was a better all-around player than his long ball hitting contemporaries. In addition to his slugging prowess, the fleet-footed Stovey was an outstanding fielder with a strong throwing arm. He was also a weapon to be reckoned with on the bases, as evidenced by his 744 stolen bases in 931 games, a frequency of 0.80 stolen bases per game. By comparison, Ricky Henderson, the current all-time stolen base leader has a frequency of 0.56.

Stovey led the league in stolen bases three times. Four times he stole more than 100 bases in a season, with highs of 143 in 1887 and 156 in 1888. Unfortunately, no stolen base records were kept during Stovey's first six years in the majors. His recorded stolen base totals began after he reached the age of 29. Based on his other offensive statistics, it is possible that Stovey had another 478 stolen bases that went unrecorded. If that were the case, Ricky Henderson's 1,117 career stolen bases would still leave him 105 behind Stovey's total.

The Philadelphia flyer was credited with using the first sliding pads in the major leagues. He is also recognized as one of the first baserunners to slide feet first into bases.

Harry Stovey was a versatile performer, both offensively and defensively.

He possessed all the qualifications of a bona fide superstar: he could hit (.321 lifetime batting average), hit with power (121 home runs), run (744+ stolen bases), field, and throw. Sadly, the Baseball Hall of Fame in Cooperstown, New York, still has not admitted Stovey into its inner sanctum. Hopefully, the veterans committee will correct that oversight in the near future.

This study, however, is concerned only with Stovey's ability to hit baseballs out of the park. Suffice it to say, he was one of the foremost sluggers of his time. His .484 slugging percentage trails only Brouthers, Thompson, Delahanty, Orr, and Connor for nineteenth-century honors.

A humorous sidelight concerning Stovey involved his family name. It was really "Stowe," but Harry used the name "Stovey" during his baseball career so as not to embarrass his mother, who considered the sport to be less than honorable. After his retirement from baseball in 1893, the 36-year-old outfielder returned to his hometown of New Bedford, Massachusetts, where he resumed his given name. He served the citizens of the coastal community for many years as a police officer. When he died in 1937 at the age of 80, there were not many residents left who knew that their friend and neighbor had been one of the greatest home run hitters in baseball history.

One last nineteenth-century slugger needs to be recognized. Big Dave Orr was a superstar for the New York Metropolitans of the American Association (AA) during the 1880s. The five-foot-eleven, 250-pound first baseman hit the ball with authority, leading the AA in triples twice, home runs once, batting average once, and slugging average twice. He was also an above-average fielder. Tragically, Orr was cut down in his prime, suffering a career ending stroke during the 1890 season. He was 30 years old.

The righthanded power hitter bowed out with a .342 lifetime batting average (tied for ninth all-time), a .502 slugging average (fourth in the nineteenth century), and 108 triples in 3289 at bats. Unfortunately, Dave Orr did not play enough years or accumulate enough at bats to qualify for an official recognition of his accomplishments.

As professional baseball moved into the twentieth century, new names began to dot the sports pages, and new heroes carried the appellation, "slugger." The most outstanding long ball hitters of the last two decades of the dead ball era were Buck Freeman, Frank "Home Run" Baker, Tilly Walker, and Gavvy Cravath.

Buck Freeman, a native of Catasauqua, Pennsylvania, came to the attention of the baseball world in 1898 when, playing for Toronto in the Eastern League, he led the entire minor leagues in home runs with 23. Moving up to the Washington Senators the following season, the slightly built lefthander proved it was no fluke by leading the National League in home runs with 25. The five-foot-nine, 169-pounder also hammered out 19 doubles and 25 triples that year.

Freeman moved over to the American League in 1900, spending the rest of his 11-year major league career with Boston. The hard-hitting outfielder continued to hit the long ball for the Red Sox, finishing second in the league in home runs in both 1901 and 1902, then capturing the home run title in 1903 with 13 circuit blows.

Buck Freeman finished his major league career in 1907. He left a career batting average of .293, with 82 home runs in just 4,208 at bats. His home run average of 11 per 550 at bats places him in third place against his peers, and in fifth place all-time, from 1876 through 1919. Even as a 36-year-old retread, the southpaw swinger could still drill the ball. After leaving Boston early in 1907, Freeman caught on with Minneapolis of the Class A American Association, where he captured his second minor league home run crown, smashing 18 dingers for the Millers.

One of the most famous sluggers of the early twentieth century was John Franklin "Home Run" Baker, celebrated third baseman of the Philadelphia Athletics. The 170 pound southpaw swinger earned his nickname in the 1911 World Series when he hit home runs off Rube Marquard and Christy Mathewson of the New York Giants on successive days. Baker's two run shot off Marquard in the sixth inning of game two proved to be the game winner, as the A's prevailed, 3–1. The following day, he clipped the great Matty for a game tying home run in the top of the ninth. The A's went on to win in eleven, and eventually captured the Series, four games to two.

Home Run Baker's Series feats were no flukes. The 25-year-old slugger had captured the American League home run title that year by slamming 11 balls out of various league parks. He repeated as home run king in 1912 (10), 1913 (12), and 1914 (9). Over a 13-year major league career, Frank Baker earned a well-deserved reputation as one of the greatest third baseman of all time. He was a valuable cog in Connie Mack's famed $100,000 infield, teaming with Stuffy McInnis, Eddie Collins, and Jack Barry, to carry the Athletics to four American League pennants and three World Championships in five years.

Baker's career batting average was .307, which included 96 home runs and 1,012 runs batted in. His World Series statistics are even more impressive. The handsome infielder slugged the ball at a .363 clip in 25 Series games, with 18 RBIs. His hits included seven doubles and three home runs.

Frank "Home Run" Baker stands out as one of the top home run hitters of the dead ball era. His home run average of 9.0 ranks fourth against his peers and seventh overall from 1876. The slugging third baseman did not have the advantage of a small ballpark to hit in, either. When he played in Shibe Park, it took a solid poke to clear the fences. The left field fence was 378 feet from home plate, center field was 502 feet distant, and Baker's power alley in right center field was a 393 feet away. Even the right field foul pole was 340 feet away.

Clarence William "Tilly" Walker's bat exploded after the introduction of the lively ball in 1920. The 33-year-old Walker slugged 17 home runs in 1920. He followed that with 23 homers in 1921 and 37 the following year (credit: National Baseball Library, Cooperstown, N.Y.).

Clarence William Walker, commonly known as "Tilly," was another of the dead ball era's top home run hitters. The native of Telford, Tennessee, spent 13 years in the majors, playing for Washington, St. Louis, and the Boston Red Sox before settling down with the Philadelphia Athletics for six years.

Tilly Walker was small as sluggers go, packing only 165 pounds on a five-foot-eleven-inch frame; but he could hit the ball with the best of them, including the great Babe Ruth. In 1918, the righthanded hitter tied the Babe for the league home run championship with 11. As the lively ball era dawned, home run totals exploded, with Ruth's 29 circuit clouts in 1919 and 54 circuit clouts in 1920 leading the way. Walker was second to Ruth in 1919 with 10 home runs, and third in 1920 with 17.

In 1921, when Ruth put 59 balls into orbit, Tilly Walker was fourth in the league with 23. The following year, the 35-year-old outfielder outhomered the Sultan of Swat, 37 to 35. He trailed only Ken Williams of the St. Louis Browns, who led the league with 39.

The 1922 season was Tilly Walker's swan song. Connie Mack, the owner of the A's, concentrating on pitching and defense, had moved the outfield fences back 30 to 40 feet over the winter. The 36-year-old Walker played in only 52 games in 1923, hit but two home runs, and drifted back to the minors for a six-year finale.

Tilly Walker's career stats credited him with a .281 batting average and 118 home runs in 5,067 at bats. His 2.3 percent home run average, or 13 homers per year, is number two all-time for the dead ball era. With the advent of the lively ball, Tilly's home run average shot up to 26 for a three year period. It was still increasing when he retired!

Another big home run hitter around the turn of the century was Gavvy Cravath, also known as "Cactus" because of his sharp wit. Cravath was a late bloomer as far as major league players go, arriving in the Big Show to stay when he was 31 years old. The five-foot-ten, righthanded hitter tore the minor leagues apart for many years, but failed to impress major league brass in three early trials with the Red Sox, White Sox, and Senators.

As early as 1903, Cravath displayed his powerful home run stroke on the west coast. Playing for the Los Angeles Angels in the Pacific Coast League, the stocky outfielder rapped out seven home runs, second in the league to Truck Eagan's 13. What made Cravath's numbers even more impressive was the disadvantage under which he hit them. While Eagan was popping chip shots over a short 200-foot left field fence in Tacoma, Cravath had to outmuscle a 345-foot left field fence and a 427-foot center field fence in Prager Park.

In 1911, the California native cracked 29 home runs with Minneapolis in the American Association to lead all minor leagues in that category. His performance brought him to the attention of the Philadelphia Phillies, who were striving for respect in the National League, having finished no higher than third over the previous nine years. The Phils purchased the not-so-youthful slugger's contract and immediately inserted him in right field. In his first season in the Senior Circuit, Cravath hit 11 home runs, three behind the league leader. The next year, he captured the home run crown by banging 19 dead balls out of the park. He led the league in home runs in six of the next seven seasons, with totals of 19, 19, 24, 11 (finishing second), 12, 8, and 12. He also led the league in RBIs twice and was a consistent .280–.300 hitter.

The tobacco-chewing Californian played in tiny Baker Bowl for nine years. Right field in the Bowl was only a short, 272-foot pop from home plate, while the right center field power alley measured an inviting 300 feet to the fence. Left field was a more distant 335 feet away. In spite of the fact that Cravath was a righthanded hitter, he learned to hit the ball to the opposite field to take advantage of the short porch. His success in Baker Bowl is reflected in his home run totals, with 93 of his career 119 home runs being hit at home. In 1914, all 19 of his home runs were hit at home. The following year, he hit 19 of 24 home runs in Baker Bowl.

The 39-year-old outfielder retired in 1920, after playing in only 45 games. Over an eleven-year career, he compiled a .287 batting average with 119 home runs in 3,951 at bats. His 3.0 percent home run rate averaged out to 17 home runs a year—by far the highest total in the first 45 years of major league play.

It is too bad that Cravath could not have competed against Babe Ruth on equal terms. It might have been quite a battle. Both players dominated their league's home run statistics. In Cravath's case, he accounted for 6.2 percent of the entire home run production of the National League from 1912 through 1919, far ahead of Tilly Walker's impressive 4.5 percent in the American League from 1914 through 1922. Both Cravath and Walker outdistanced their nineteenth-century rivals by a wide margin in that regard.

Cravath and Walker were fortunate in one respect. During the first decade of the twentieth century, the home run had fallen out of favor with the baseball establishment. The owners returned to a conservative style of play, stressing speed, pitching, and defense at the expense of the long ball. With the introduction of the cork-centered ball in 1910, however, the home run once again became a formidable offensive weapon. Soon, home run production returned to its pre–1900 level, putting Cravath and Walker on an equal competitive footing with Brouthers, Thompson, and Stovey.

Roger Connor was the official home run leader of the dead ball era with 137 career circuit clouts to his credit. On a frequency basis, however, it was Cravath who stood out from the pack.

Gavvy Cravath was the undisputed King of Swat of the dead ball era.

CHAPTER 3

MAJOR LEAGUES, THE LIVELY BALL ERA

As the year 1920 dawned, professional baseball was in the midst of a revolution. The arrival of Babe Ruth as a major league hitter, with his record breaking 29 home runs in 1919, had caused quite a stir around the majors. The excitement his long blasts generated in the ballparks did not go unnoticed by the team owners and, with thoughts of increased revenues dancing in their heads, they took immediate action to capitalize on the crowd-pleasing phenomenon.

A new, "lively" baseball was introduced in 1920, and the home run suddenly became the dominating factor in the game. Major league home run totals increased from 447 in 1919 to 631 in 1920. They continued to increase for several years as more and more players began gripping the bat down at the end instead of choking up on it, as had been the practice since the days of Cap Anson. Slap hitting became passé, and swinging from the heels was the in-thing to do. Home run totals reached 937 in 1921, and the following year they broke the 1,000 barrier, with 1,055 circuit clouts being recorded between the two leagues.

Not surprisingly, one George Herman "Babe" Ruth was the major beneficiary of the change. Blessed with a powerful upper torso and lightning-fast wrists, the Bambino cracked the unheard of total of 54 home runs in 1921, almost double the old record. He upped his record to 59 the next year and, in 1927, established a mark of 60 home runs. Babe Ruth stood alone as a slugger. All other hitters paled by comparison.

Ruth, a graduate of St. Mary's Industrial School for wayward boys, began his baseball career as a pitcher with the Baltimore Orioles of the International League in 1914. Within a year, he was an 18-game winner for the Boston Red Sox, and soon became the top southpaw pitcher in the American League. From 1915 through 1918, the Babe won 78 games against only 40 losses. In head-to-head pitching duels against the great Walter Johnson, Ruth came away a winner eight times in ten decisions. He had a 3–0 record in two World Series competitions, hurling a record 29 consecutive scoreless innings along the way.

43

As great a pitcher as Babe Ruth was, however, he was even more valuable as a hitter. During his four years on the mound, the smooth-swinging lefty ripped the ball at a .301 clip, with 20 home runs and 110 runs batted in, in 668 at bats. In 1919, Ruth alternated between the mound and right field, going 9–5 as a starting pitcher and shattering the major league home run record with 29 circuit blows.

Over the next 16 years, from 1919 through 1934, the legendary Sultan of Swat, now a full-time outfielder, hit 688 home runs, an unbelievable 8.4 percent of the home run output of the entire American League. Gavvy Cravath, the number two man in that regard, had accounted for 6.2 percent of the league total during the dead ball era.

In 1920 and 1927, Babe Ruth, by himself, outhomered every other team in the league. In his record-breaking year of 1927, his 60 home runs represented 13.7 percent of the home runs hit in the American League. By comparison, Roger Maris's 61 home runs in 1961, represented 4.0 percent of the American League home run total. To match the Babe's percentage, Maris would have had to hit the astonishing total of 225 home runs!!

Over the course of his career, Ruth hit 714 home runs in 8,399 at bats, an average of 47 home runs per 550 at bats. That represents a frequency of 8.5 percent: number one all-time. This average includes six years in Boston in the dead ball era, during which time the mighty Bambino averaged 24 homers a year, which was seven more than his chief competitor, Gavvy Cravath. Once the Babe was comfortably ensconced in his new home, New York's Yankee Stadium, and took aim at the new jackrabbit ball, his home run averages exploded.

George Herman "Babe" Ruth, the Sultan of Swat, the barometer by which all other home run hitters are measured, averaged 50 home runs a year, home and away, after the advent of the lively ball.

Babe Ruth was not the only slugger of note during the early years of the lively ball. His teammate Lou Gehrig, Jimmie Foxx, and Mel Ott also propelled balls out of major league parks with monotonous regularity.

Lou Gehrig arrived on the major league scene to stay in 1925. When he was finally inserted into the New York Yankee lineup on May 31, 1925, he played every game for the next fifteen years, finally taking himself out of the lineup on May 2, 1939. His record of playing in 2,130 consecutive games was the major league standard for 56 years. Baltimore's Cal Ripken Jr. finally broke the record on Wednesday, September 6, 1995.

"The Iron Horse," as he was called, was born in New York on June 19, 1903. The big, six-foot-one first sacker made eyes pop at Columbia University with his prodigious home run wallops, setting a one season school record with seven circuit blows and a .444 batting average. He began his professional career as an 18-year-old, with Hartford of the Eastern League. After hitting 61 home runs for Hartford in 731 at bats over a two year period, he

Jimmie Foxx, known as "The Beast" by admiring opponents, smashed 534 home runs in 20 seasons. When he retired in 1947, he trailed only Babe Ruth in career home runs (credit: Transcendental Graphics).

was called up to the Big Show by the New York Yankees. In his first full year in the majors, the 212-pound, lefthanded slugger pounded 20 balls out of the park, taking particular advantage of the cozy right field seats at Yankee Stadium.

Batting fourth behind Ruth for much of his career, Gehrig hit a total of 493 home runs. In 1927, when Ruth hit his record-breaking 60 homers, the big first baseman knocked out 47 homers of his own, a staggering 10.7 percent of the league total. His career average of hitting 5.6 percent of the league home run total is one of the highest in history, ranking third behind Ruth and Cravath. His home run frequency of 6.16 percent is eleventh all-time and represents 33 home runs for every 550 at bats.

When Lou Gehrig retired in 1939 at the age of 36, he left behind a .340 lifetime batting average and a total of 1,990 runs batted in, in 2,164 games. His average of 0.920 RBIs per game is second all-time, behind Sam Thompson.

Lou Gehrig was one of the greatest players ever to don a major league uniform, unquestionably the all-time, all-star first baseman.

James Emory Foxx, old Double-X, was the strongest man in baseball during the 1930s. Built like a weightlifter at five-foot-eleven and 190 pounds, Foxx had arms like anvils. The Maryland farm boy began his professional career with Easton in the Class D Eastern Shore League at the age of 16, in 1924. That same year, he played in ten games for the Philadelphia Athletics, batting .667 on a six-for-nine performance.

By 1927, the 19-year-old Double-X was in the majors to stay, and two years later, he became the regular first baseman of Connie Mack's American League powerhouse. The free-swinging, righthanded hitter smashed 33 home runs as a 21-year-old, driving in 117 runners, and batting a lofty .354. Foxx, like Ruth and Gehrig, was not only a home run hitter. He also hit for average. The Philadelphia strong boy won the triple crown in 1933, batting .356, with 48 home runs and 163 runs batted in. He won another batting crown with the Boston Red Sox in 1938 with an average of .349, en route to a career mark of .325.

Jimmie Foxx won a total of four home run titles and three runs-batted-in crowns during his 21-year career. He still holds the major league record for hitting 30 or more home runs in 12 consecutive seasons. He is tied with Gehrig for knocking in 100 or more runs in 12 straight years. When he retired in 1945, Foxx had accumulated a total of 534 home runs in 8,134 at bats, an average of 36 home runs per year. That level of productivity places him eighth all-time and second behind Ruth during the period of 1920 to 1940.

Old Double-X had a distinct home park advantage during his career. Whether taking aim at Shibe Park's 334-foot left field wall or Fenway Park's inviting "Green Monster" screen only 315 feet from the plate, Foxx feasted on home cooking. He averaged 43 home runs a year at home during his stay in Boston, compared to 32 homers on the road. In Philadelphia, his home average was 39; his road average 31. Jimmie Foxx was definitely a home body.

The National League had a few sluggers of its own in the early days, the most notable of whom was Melvin Thomas Ott. The lefthanded slugger with the unique leg kick, à la Sadaharu Oh, dominated the Senior Circuit's power stats for 17 years. The compact five-foot-nine, 170-pounder, went directly from the Louisiana sandlots to the major leagues at the age of 17. He moved into the New York Giants' starting lineup as a 19 year old, becoming one of the mainstays of Bill Terry's powerful teams of the 1930s.

Mel Ott won six home run titles during his 22 years in New York. Eight times he hit more than 30 homers in a season, with a high of 42 homers in 1929. When he left the game in 1947, he had accumulated a total of 511 home runs, the third man in history to break the 500 barrier. Ruth and Foxx were first and second.

The powerful right fielder led the New Yorkers to three pennants during his career. He sparked the Giants to their lone World Championship in 1933, stinging the ball at a .389 clip in five World Series games. His two-run homer in the first inning of game one proved to be the winning margin, 4–1, as Carl Hubbell stifled the Washington Senators on five hits. His second home run of the Series, in the tenth inning of game five, won the championship for New York.

Mel Ott averaged 30 home runs a season during his career, a solid figure, but not one that would challenge the Babe as the King of Swat. If "Master Mel" had been able to play all his games in the Polo Grounds, however, it might have been a different story. The little lefthander was born to play ball in the oblong stadium along Harlem River Speedway. His uppercut swing and his ability to pull the ball over the short, 258-foot right field fence paid him handsome dividends over the course of his career. His 39 home-run-per-year average in the Polo Grounds was almost double his average on the road, where he banged out 21 homers a year.

Hammerin' Hank Greenberg, the Jewish slugger from New York City, was another story completely. He terrorized major league pitchers for 13 years, during the '30s and '40s. The big, six-foot-three, righthanded hitter came up to the American League with Detroit in 1933 after three years in the Tiger farm system. He proceeded to lead the league in home runs on five occasions, losing another season to injuries and missing an additional 4½ years to military service during World War II.

In just his sophomore season, the 23-year-old phenom led the American League in doubles with 63, just four behind Earl Webb's major league mark of 67. In a sign of things to come, Greenberg laced out 201 hits, scored 118 runs, batted in another 139, and hit a sizzling .339. The following year, the muscular first baseman led the American League in both home runs (36, a tie) and runs batted in (170), complementing his .328 batting average. His extra base hit output also included 46 doubles and 16 triples, giving him a total of 98 extra base hits for the year. That figure has been exceeded only six times in major league history, three times by Babe Ruth, twice by Lou Gehrig, and once by Jimmie Foxx. Ruth holds the record with 119 extra base hits in 1921. Gehrig is close behind with 117.

After missing a year with injuries, Greenberg once again took the RBI title, this time with 183 ribbies, the third-highest total in major league history behind Hack Wilson's 190 and Lou Gehrig's 184. His other offensive statistics were almost as impressive; 200 hits, a .337 batting average, 137 runs scored, 49 doubles, 14 triples, and 40 home runs.

In 1938, Greenberg came close to breaking Babe Ruth's record of 60 home runs in one season. Thanks, in part, to a major league record of 11 multi-homer games, he pounded out 58 round trippers in Detroit's first 150 games. Unfortunately, the New York strongman drew the collar over the final five games. In addition to the home run title, he also led the league in runs scored with 144, while batting .315.

Hammerin' Hank had another banner season two years later when he led the league in three offensive categories; doubles (50), home runs (41), and runs batted in (150). He had a career high batting average of .340, although it gave him no better than a fifth place finish behind Joe DiMaggio's league leading .352.

Four years of military service during his prime severely hampered Greenberg's chase for baseball's brass (home run) ring. In the four years prior to his enlistment in the Air Corps, he had piled up 172 home runs, an average of 43 a year. By the time he returned to the baseball wars late in 1945, he was a well-worn, 34-year-old veteran. He did manage to hit 82 home runs over the next 2½ years, but the grind was too much, and the big man called it quits in 1947.

Hank Greenberg had one major obstacle to contend with during his career that differed from most of the other home run hitters. Unlike Ruth, Gehrig, and Aaron, who had cozy parks to hit in, the Tiger first baseman played most of his games in roomy Briggs Stadium. Left field, Greenberg's favorite target, was a distant 340 feet from home plate. The center field barrier stood 450 feet away. Only Josh Gibson and Harmon Killebrew were at a similar disadvantage.

As it is, his home run frequency is ninth on the all-time major league list. His RBI average of 0.915 RBIs per game is the third highest total ever, just slightly behind Sam Thompson and Lou Gehrig, both of whom had essentially the same average. His lifetime slugging percentage of .605 is fifth in the majors, and his extra base percentage of 15.0 percent is exceeded only by the Babe himself.

The towering, 215-pound slugger left behind a total of 331 home runs in 5,193 career at bats, an average of 35 home runs per season—one more than Hank Aaron. If he had been able to realize a full career, without war and without injuries, and if his home ballpark was better suited to his swing, his home run totals would have challenged the greatest home run hitters of all time. He would certainly have had a shot at Mays's 660 home runs and may well have exceeded Ruth's and Aaron's totals.

As the years passed, more and more players went for the fences, determined to be the next Sultan of Swat. Whereas only a few hitters had swung from the heels in the '20s and '30s, it seemed as if almost everybody became a free swinger after World War II. By 1950, the major league home run total exceeded 2,000 for the first time. Six years later, every team in the National League hit more than 100 home runs for the season. Brooklyn had six batters with ten or more home runs. The Milwaukee Braves had six. The Cincinnati Reds had eight, including five with 28 or more!

New sluggers arrived on the scene yearly, to challenge the Bambino's most famous records. The new breed, taking up the hunt between 1940 and 1960, included Ted Williams, Ralph Kiner, Mickey Mantle, and Willie Mays. Theodore Samuel Williams, the lanky, six-foot-four southpaw swinger from San Diego, may well have been the greatest natural hitter of all time. Blessed with a smooth, compact stroke and exceptional eye sight, the Boston Red Sox hitting star was unstoppable at the plate from day one. In his rookie season, he led the American League with 145 runs batted in, while hitting .327 with 31 home runs.

Just two years later, at the tender age of 23, the "Splendid Splinter," as Williams was called, became the last of the .400 hitters, rapping the ball at a torrid .406 pace in 1941. He also led the league with 135 runs scored and 37 homers that year. The character of the man was demonstrated on the last day of the season when, assured of an even .400 batting average for the season, Williams refused his manager's offer to sit out the final two games in order to protect his average. Instead, he proceeded to go six for eight, upping his average to the final .406.

Over a much-interrupted, 19-year career, the 190-pound left fielder led the league in hitting six times, runs batted in four times, home runs four times, doubles twice, and runs scored six times. A Navy pilot, Ted Williams missed a total of five years to military service; three years in World War II and another two years in the Korean Conflict. In spite of the interruptions, he still amassed 521 career home runs and 1,839 RBIs in 14 full seasons.

The "Splendid Splinter" was one of the few home run hitters who had a working knowledge of the strike zone. He struck out only 709 times in 7,706 at bats, a home-run-to-strikeout ratio of 0.73. Three times in his career he had fewer strikeouts than home runs. Of the great modern sluggers, only Sadaharu Oh (5 times) and Joe DiMaggio (7 times) surpassed that performance. Negro league slugger Josh Gibson had fewer strikeouts than home runs two years in Mexico, but the Negro league statistics are not complete enough to measure his performance there.

Ted Williams, Boston's own "Splendid Splinter" was indisputably baseball's greatest hitter over the last 65 years. He may have been the greatest hitter of all time—period. He was the last hitter to crash the magic .400 barrier, hitting .406 in 1941 (credit: Transcendental Graphics).

Williams hit a home run in 6.76 percent of his at bats, an average of 37 home runs a year. Williams's statistics over his last few years in the American League give an indication of how great a talent this man was. In 1957, at the ripe old age of 39, Williams led the league in batting with an average of .388. Not quite through, he led the league again the following year with an average of .328. In his final season, the aging veteran hit a healthy .316, with 29 home runs in just 310 at bats. His home run average that year, based on 550 at bats, was 51—not bad for a 42-year-old graybeard. Supposedly, Boston's favorite son had some choice pickings in Fenway Park. The right field foul pole was only 302 feet from home plate, but his favorite target, the right center field bullpen, was 380 feet deep, protected by a short 3½ foot fence. Ted Williams didn't get many cheapies down the line, however. His fluid swing usually propelled long, high fly balls that landed well back in the bleachers behind the bullpens.

Ted Williams's .344 lifetime batting average ranks fifth all-time. He ranks second in bases on balls, second in slugging average, and first in on-base percentage. His home run frequency of 37 home runs per year makes him the fourth most productive home run hitter of all time. Had Williams not lost five years to military duty, he most certainly would have hit over 700 home runs, and may have challenged Ruth's and Aaron's marks. He would definitely have established a new major league mark for runs batted in. From a strictly statistical standpoint, if the "Splendid Splinter" had played another five years (or only 4.82, to be exact) and if he had had the benefit of playing in an average, home run hitter's park, he would have been the all-time career home run leader with 781 circuit blows. He would also have taken over the career RBI crown, with an incredible total of 2,472 runs batted in, 175 more than Hank Aaron's existing major league mark.

Ralph McPherran Kiner arrived on the National League scene in 1946 and proceeded to set the Senior Circuit on its ear. He led the league in home runs during his first seven years in the majors, then quietly retired from the game three years later.

The quiet-spoken Kiner was born in Santa Rita, New Mexico, on October 27, 1922. He broke into organized ball with Albany, New York, in the Eastern League at the age of 18, batting a respectable .275 with 11 home runs. The next year, he led the Eastern League with 14 home runs, then was called to active military duty during World War II. When the war ended, Kiner reported to the Pittsburgh Pirates training camp as their new left fielder.

In 1946, as a rookie, the powerful, 23-year-old slugger topped the National League with 23 home runs. Over the winter, the Pirates acquired Hank Greenberg from Detroit and immediately redesigned their park to accommodate the two righthanded home run hitters. They installed a double bullpen in left field, reducing the left field home run distance from 365 to 335 feet and the power alley in left center from 406 to 355 feet. The bullpen area eventually became known as "Kiner's Korner," for obvious reasons. The six-foot-two, 195-pound Kiner responded with 51 circuit blows in 1947, then followed with totals of 40, 54, 47, 42, and 37, all league-leading numbers.

Back problems slowed Kiner to a crawl in 1953, and Pirate management, desirous of reducing the payroll on their last-place club, traded him to the Chicago Cubs in mid season. Two years later, still playing in pain, the 33-year-old warrior put away his bat for good. He left behind some impressive statistics.

Ralph Kiner hit 369 home runs in 5,205 at bats over a period of ten years, an average of 39 home runs per 550 at bats. That average is the second best in major league history, trailing only Babe Ruth's 47.

A blond bombshell from Oklahoma stormed the Big Apple in 1951 to give major league fans some of the most unforgettable thrills in baseball history. Mickey Charles Mantle, named after Hall-of-Fame catcher Mickey Cochrane, was born in Spavinaw, Oklahoma, on October 20, 1931. Raised in Commerce, 70 miles northeast of Tulsa, the 19-year-old switch hitter made the jump from farm to big city in just two years.

Arriving in Yankee Stadium in 1951 with all the typical New York hoopla, the easygoing Mantle, heir apparent to Joe Dimaggio, settled into center field to become the most powerful switch hitter in major league history. Standing

Ralph Kiner exploded on the major league scene in 1947, when he hammered out 51 home runs. He went on to lead the National League in home runs his first seven years in the league (credit: Transcendental Graphics).

only five-feet-eleven-inches tall and weighing 195 pounds, the "Commerce Comet" generated tremendous power from both sides of the plate. He hit some of the longest home runs ever seen in the major leagues, five times denting the facade on the Yankee Stadium roof. He hit tape-measure shots in most major league parks, including a 565-footer in Washington. Some of his legendary blows were estimated at more than 600 feet.

Mickey Mantle was a free swinger who hit, not only for distance, but also for average. He also missed the ball a near record number of times. Over the course of an 18-year career, the handsome slugger hit 536 home runs, batted .298, and fanned 1,710 times. Along with Harmon Killebrew, he amassed more strikeouts per home run than any other hitter of world class proportions.

The fleet-footed outfielder achieved superstar status in 1956, his fifth full season in the majors, when he walked off with the American League's triple crown, batting .353, with 52 home runs and 130 runs batted in. He batted over .300 ten times in his career, won three home run titles, and led the league in runs scored six times. In 1961, the year Roger Maris hit 61 home runs, the Mick chipped in with 54. When healthy, Mantle was a triple threat—as a hitter, a fielder, and a baserunner. He covered the outfield like a greyhound and had a strong, accurate throwing arm. He was timed at 3.1 seconds from home to first and was an excellent base stealer and baserunner. Unfortunately, the kid from Commerce was hobbled with bad legs during most of his career, limiting his defensive effectiveness and restricting his base-stealing efforts.

The Yankees participated in twelve World Series during Mantle's 18-year career, winning seven World Championships. The colorful switch hitter pounded out a record 18 home runs in Series play, three more than Babe Ruth. His career home run frequency of 6.62 percent ties him with Dave Kingman for fifth place on the all-time list. He averaged 36 home runs for every 550 times at bat and, most assuredly, got more distance per home run than any hitter in major league history. Mickey Mantle was a magnificent ballplayer to watch.

In spite of all the excitement and electricity generated by him in his 16 years in New York, however, Mickey Charles Mantle may have been the most lamentable figure ever to reign over the baseball arena. Sadly, the handsome Sooner's saga will always be remembered as "Paradise Lost" to his legion of fans. The Mick was blessed with almost unlimited talent. He could hit the ball farther, and with greater frequency, than any other major league hitter. He could also run faster, jump higher, and throw more accurately than his outfield peers. In short, Mickey Mantle could do it all. If he had disciplined himself better and had taken better care of his body, he might well have established batting records and home run totals that would last forever. The young slugger from the Dust Bowl went another route, however. Arriving in the big city at the reckless age of 19, Mantle soon teamed with fellow players, Whitey Ford and Billy Martin, to seek out the good life. The unholy triumvirate made the rounds of every glittering night club, and every noisy beer hall, in every American League city, across the United States.

Mickey Mantle destroyed his body and his reflexes over time, as surely as if he had taken a hammer to them. From a purely professional standpoint, his statistics reflect his self destruction. The powerful switch hitter slugged

The ferocity of a Mickey Mantle swing is reflected in this photo. The bulging biceps, developed by swinging a sledge hammer in a lead mine, sent baseballs hurtling great distances. Note the Mick's eyes still focused on the ball, even as it disappears in a blur (credit: Transcendental Graphics).

more home runs before the age of 30 (404) than any ballplayer in baseball history. Hank Aaron had hit 366 home runs before he turned 30 years old, while the Babe had banged out a meager 309 homers. But, where Ruth piled up a mighty 405 circuit blows between the ages of 30 and 40 and where Hammerin' Hank totaled 389 round trippers after the age of 30, a deteriorating Mantle could accumulate only 132.

Mickey Mantle's career was essentially history by the age of 30. He could still hit the ball a long way in his waning years, even though his home run average dropped from 38 homers a year to 33, but his other talents diminished noticeably. His batting average tailed off to a shadow of its former self. During the first half of his career, the "Commerce Comet" rapped the ball at a solid .309 clip. After the age of 30, however, he could muster only a mediocre .269 average. And even more telling, he missed more and more games, for one reason or another. Where he had averaged almost 500 at bats a year before the age of 30, he stepped up to the plate no more than an average of 368 times over his last six years. He was finally forced to call it quits at the age of 36, whereas Aaron went on until he was 42 and even the old profligate, Babe Ruth, managed to play until he was 40.

Granted, his bad legs contributed to some of his poor performances and to his reduced playing time. But that wasn't the whole story. As Mickey himself stated, he thought he was going to die young and, as a result, he lived for today, and to hell with tomorrow. When tomorrow came, as it usually does, Mickey Charles Mantle was not healthy enough to take advantage of it.

Another brilliant ballplayer, who happened to display his talents in New York at the same time as Mickey Mantle, was Willie Mays, the famous "Say Hey Kid." Together with Duke Snider of the Dodgers, Mantle and Mays gave the big city the greatest center field triumvirate in the annals of baseball. Mays, an enthusiastic graduate of the Negro leagues, made his debut in New York in 1951, the same year as the Mick. The five-foot-eleven, 187-pound dynamo was as flamboyant as Mantle was shy. Patrolling center field in the old Polo Grounds, Mays thrilled the patrons with his patented basket catches and strong, accurate throws.

Like Mantle and Snider, the native of Westfield, Alabama, was a dangerous baserunner. He pilfered 338 bases during his career, four times leading the league in that category. He batted .300 ten times, including .343 in 1954 when he won the National League batting title. He led the league in home runs four times and in triples three times. His great speed accounted for 140 career three-base hits. Twice in his career, the "Say Hey Kid" hit more than 50 home runs in a season, getting 51 round trippers in 1955 and 52 round trippers in 1965. Four other times, he exceeded the 40 mark. On April 30, 1961, the transplanted New Yorker, now wearing San Francisco black-and-orange, poled four home runs in a single game.

Over a period of 22 seasons, with one year out for military service, Willie Mays batted .302. His 3,283 base hits included 523 doubles, 140 triples, and 660 home runs. His home run total ranks third in major league history behind Hank Aaron (755) and Babe Ruth (714). His home run frequency of 6.07 percent ranks 13th all-time, averaging out to 33 home runs a year.

Willie Mays split his career between New York and San Francisco, two cities with distinctly different ballparks. The odd-shaped Polo Grounds presented the righthanded slugger an inviting, 279-foot left field foul pole; however, it quickly opened out into a 455-foot power alley and a ridiculously distant 483-foot center field wall. In Frisco, the "Say Hey Kid" took aim at a more conventional left field wall, 330 feet from home plate. The power alley was 397 feet to the wall, and the distance to dead center was 420 feet. A swirling wind in Candlestick raised havoc with fly balls almost constantly.

Mays's home run averages were basically identical in both parks. He averaged 35 home runs in six years in New York and 33 home runs in 15 seasons in California. During his most productive years (his last four in New York and his first nine in Frisco), his averages were 39 and 37, respectively.

His home and road statistics were also essentially the same. He averaged 35 homers a year at home and 32 homers a year away from home.

Willie Mays could do all the things required of a great baseball player: hit, hit with power, field, run, and throw. Many baseball experts consider him to be the greatest all-around baseball player of all time.

Henry Louis "Hank" Aaron, the quiet man with the big stick, battled his way from Mobile, Alabama, to Milwaukee, Wisconsin, in the early '60s destined to challenge Babe Ruth for the home run championship of the world. His epic journey included stops with the Indianapolis Clowns of the Negro American League and with Milwaukee Braves' farm clubs in Eau Claire, Wisconsin, and Jacksonville, Florida, en route to the Big Show. He began his pursuit of the Bambino at the age of 21.

Aaron's forte was consistency. He was not spectacular, and he did not fashion legendary seasons. His success was built on producing above-average batting statistics year in and year out. He did this for 23 long years. During that time, he set or tied many major league or National League records, including most consecutive years scoring 100 or more runs (13), most years hitting 40 or more home runs—NL (8), and most years with 100 or more RBIs—NL (11). Fifteen times, over a period of 17 years, the man from Mobile hit more than 30 home runs and knocked in 95 or more runs. Fourteen times in the same period, he batted .300 or better.

Aaron's home run totals were significantly influenced by his playing environment. The righthanded slugger spent twelve years in Milwaukee, then the next nine years in Atlanta. Although the distances in the playing fields were similar, the atmospheric conditions in Atlanta's Fulton County Stadium earned the park the nickname of "The Launching Pad." At 1,000 feet above sea level, it was the highest park, elevation-wise, in the major leagues. More home runs sailed out of Fulton County Stadium than any other National League stadium.

Aaron is truly deserving of the many accolades he has received over the years and is a worthy home run champion. His 755 career home runs is 41 more than Babe Ruth's total and is 95 better than the number three man, Willie Mays. On a frequency basis, however, his average of 34 home runs per year is no better than number twelve on the major league list, before even considering the candidates from the minor leagues, the Negro leagues, and the Japanese leagues.

Roger Maris, the man who broke Babe Ruth's single-season home run record, was born in Hibbing, Minnesota, on September 10, 1934. He came up to the big leagues with the Cleveland Indians as a 22 year old in 1957. Three years later, the big, 205-pound outfielder, then a member of the Kansas City Athletics, was traded to the New York Yankees. Teaming up with Mickey Mantle proved to be a distinct blessing for the likeable Maris. He batted third in the Yankee batting order, just ahead of the Mick, and,

Hank Aaron, the brilliant outfielder of the Milwaukee and Atlanta Braves, overtook the mighty Bambino, Babe Ruth, in April 1974, hitting his 715th home run off Al Downing of the Los Angeles Dodgers (credit: Transcendental Graphics).

as a result, got a much better selection of pitches to swing at. In 1960, Maris, who had never hit more than 28 home runs in one season, suddenly walloped 39 round trippers for the Bronx Bombers and led the American League with 112 runs batted in. One year later, he slammed 61 baseballs out of Yankee Stadium and other American League parks, to become the new Sultan of Swat. Once again, he showed the way in RBIs, this time with 142.

The big, blond slugger was born to be a Yankee. His uppercut swing and pull-hitting style of attack were made to order for the short, right field porch in Yankee Stadium. And batting third in the Yankee batting order, just ahead of Mantle, was icing on the cake. Maris put together three consecutive outstanding seasons from 1960 through 1962. His last great season as a Yankee was 1962, when he hit 33 homers and drove in 100 runners. His productivity declined after that, although he stayed in the majors another six years. Two mediocre seasons in New York and two more ordinary performances in St. Louis convinced the 34-year-old, lefthanded bomber that his gun was empty. He retired in 1968, ending an eventful 12-year career.

Maris was never fully appreciated during his major league career. Many people resented his breaking the home run record of the legendary Bambino. But Roger was a solid, if not spectacular, major league player. In addition to his power stats, Maris was a fine, all-around outfielder, with good speed and an excellent arm. He was also an adept baserunner.

Maris was never a high-average hitter, leaving behind a career batting average of only .260. His best year, average-wise, was 1960 when he hit .283. His 275 career home runs in 5,101 at bats average out to be 30 home runs a year. He was not in the same class, frequency-wise, as Babe Ruth or Ralph Kiner, but for one spectacular season, he was the world's greatest home run hitter. During the warm and glorious summer of 1961, Roger Maris was everybody's King of Swat.

The last half of the twentieth century produced a plethora of home run hitters who hit more than 500 circuit blows in their career. The list includes Frank Robinson (586), Harmon Killebrew (573), Reggie Jackson (563), Mike Schmidt (542), Willie McCovey (521), and Ernie Banks (512).

Of that group, the most prolific slugger was Killebrew. The stocky, six-foot, righthanded hitter pulverized American League pitching for 22 years. He led, or tied for the lead, in home runs six times. Eight times, he hit more than 40 home runs. Although not a high percentage hitter, the big first baseman drove in more than 100 runs in nine seasons, compiling a total of 1,584 RBIs in all.

Harmon Killebrew arrived in Washington to stay in 1959, having rotated back and forth between the minors and the big club for five years. The 23-year-old rookie immediately jumped to the head of the pack, topping the league in home runs with 42. Although he batted a slim .242, his home run total helped him knock in 102 runs. Five more times, over the next ten years, "Killer" won the home run title, with totals of 48, 45, 49, 44, and 49. He also hit 46 home runs in 1961 and 41 home runs in 1970. At one point in his career, the 210-pound power hitter was on course to break Ruth's record. At the age of 31, he had accumulated 380 home runs, 19 more than the Bambino at that age. Unfortunately injuries caught up with the husky slugger, and he played only four more full seasons. During his 22-year career, Killebrew bounced around from position to position, at one time or another playing the outfield, second base, third base, and first base. He was never a big average hitter, topping out at .288 in 1962. His career batting average was .256.

Harmon Killebrew broke into major league baseball with the Washington Senators as an 18-year-old second baseman in 1954. He went on to star for the Senators and their successors, the Minnesota Twins, for 22 years, smashing 573 career home runs, fifth on the all-time list (credit: Transcendental Graphics).

"Killer" was one of the few home run hitters who did not benefit from his home park. He played parts of seven seasons in Griffith Stadium in Washington, D.C., with its long 350-foot left field fence and its 435-foot center field barrier. He then played fourteen more years in Minnesota's Metropolitan Stadium, with dimensions of 344 feet, 430 feet, and 330 feet, left to right. His home and away home run averages were close in both ballparks. In Washington, he averaged 37 homers at home and 38 on the road. In Minneapolis, he hit 41 round trippers at home and 37 on the road. Unlike some other noted sluggers, Harmon Killebrew got his home runs the hard way—he earned them.

On a frequency basis, Harmon Killebrew was one of the top sluggers in major league history, averaging 39 home runs per 550 at bats, only 0.3 home runs less than Ralph Kiner. And he didn't have Kiner's Korner to assist him.

Reggie Jackson came out of Wyncote, Pennsylvania, in 1967 to become "King of Swat." The husky, lefthanded hitter was always his own best press agent. A graduate of Arizona State University, he helped the Oakland Athletics to four successive American League Western Division titles and three

Roger Maris fit the Yankees like a hand to a glove. Contrary to what his detractors claim, Maris did not benefit from the short right field porch in Yankee Stadium. In 1961, when he broke Babe Ruth's single-season home run record, he hit 31 of his 61 homers on the road (credit: Transcendental Graphics).

World Championships. Moving on to the Big Apple, Jackson powered the Yankees to four division titles and two World Championships.

Reggie Jackson had the reputation for being a hot dog, an egocentric showboat. The reputation was well earned. The six-feet tall, 215-pound slugger was a lumbering runner who was a defensive liability in the outfield. After taking one fly ball in the chest, Jackson almost got into a dugout brawl with manager Billy Martin. It made for great television entertainment, but it was far from good baseball.

Jackson was a free swinger, who fanned a record 2,597 times during his career, 661 times more than the runner-up. His strikeouts averaged out to mind-boggling 145 K's a year. It is no wonder, with all those whiffs, that his lifetime batting average was no higher than .262.

The man could hit a baseball a long distance, however, when he connected. Using a big, sweeping swing, which oftentimes left him sprawling in the dirt when he missed, Reggie Jackson hit some of the longest home runs seen in the American League in many years. And he had a flair for the dramatic. Playing in five World Series, the southpaw slugger hit ten home runs in 98 at bats, including five in one Series—a new record. Jackson's three home runs in game six of the 1977 World Series, joined him and Ruth as the only two players ever to hit three home runs in one Series game. And Jackson did it on three consecutive pitches off three different Dodger pitchers. His dramatic World Series performances earned him the title of "Mr. October."

When Reggie Jackson retired in 1987 after 21 years in the majors, he had played for 11 division winners, 6 pennant winners, and five World Champions. His 563 career home runs is the sixth best ever; however, his home run frequency of 30 home runs per year is far down the list.

Reggie Jackson was all flair and dramatics and electrifying excitement. He was not a well-rounded ballplayer, nor a slugger of the ilk of Ruth, Greenberg, or Kiner.

The year 1972 saw the introduction of one of the greatest third basemen in baseball history, Michael Jack Schmidt. The husky, righthanded hitter from Dayton, Ohio, protected the hot corner in Veteran's Stadium for 18 years, a National League record. Coming to the City of Brotherly Love as a 22 year old, he soon established himself as one of the top home run hitters in the National League.

In his first full season, Schmidt led the league with 36 home runs, while batting .282 and knocking in 116 runs. The following year, he once again led in homers with 38. He made it three in a row in 1976 when he slammed another 38 dingers.

In all, the slugging third baseman led, or tied for the lead, in home runs eight times. He followed his first three titles with five more, piling up totals of 48, 31, 40, 36 (tie), and 37. He also led the league in RBIs four times and in slugging five times. To prove he was not a one-dimensional player, he stole 174 bases during his career and captured 11 gold gloves.

Schmidt was a class act during his long tenure in Philadelphia. He was a pleasant breath of fresh air in an age of crass, loud, and ignorant ballplayers. The six-foot-two, 203-pound slugger sent 548 balls into orbit around the National League, the seventh highest total of all time. He was not aided by the comfortable dimensions of Veterans Stadium, either. In spite of a 330-foot left field foul line, a 371-foot power alley, and a 408-foot center field wall, Schmidt averaged 37 home runs at home, compared to 36 on the road.

Mike Schmidt's home run average of 36 home runs per year puts him in the upper echelon of home run hitters. He definitely deserves to take his place alongside the other big bashers of major league baseball.

One of the Los Angeles Dodgers' most feared enemies for more than a decade was a tall, powerfully built, lefthanded hitter nicknamed "Stretch." His baptismal name was Willie Lee McCovey, and he was born on January 10, 1938, in Mobile, Alabama. By the time McCovey reached the major leagues with the San Francisco Giants, he had grown to a full six-feet-four-inches and weighed a muscular 225 pounds. He did not punish the Dodgers alone, however; he got his licks in against every team in the National League.

The big first baseman slammed 521 home runs during his 22-year career. Playing in Candlestick Park was probably not a factor in his totals, one way or the other. The park's dimensions—330 feet to left, 420 feet to center, and 330 feet to right—are normal distances for modern, major league stadiums.

Mike Schmidt batting in a spring training game—1986 (credit: W. McNeil).

The crazy, swirling winds that sweep Candlestick from left center field to right center field might have given him some advantage in the home run department, but the cold temperatures probably offset any positive effect of the wind.

McCovey led the league in home runs three times, hitting 44 homers in 1963, 36 homers in 1968, and 45 homers in 1969. Seven times he hit more than 30 home runs in a season. His 521 career home runs are the most ever by a lefthanded batter in the National League. He also holds the league record for the most home runs by a first baseman (439) and the most grand slams (18).

Willie McCovey was a terrifying sight at the plate. When his finely tuned, six-feet-four body uncoiled, sending a high drive into the San Francisco night sky, the best of pitchers would shake their head in disbelief. McCovey made believers out of most of them. The big man's offensive statistics are world class: home runs (10th all-time), total bases (35th all-time), runs batted in (25th all-time), and slugging average (33rd all-time). His home run average of 35 home runs per year ranks with the best of them.

If Mike Schmidt was the hardest hitting third baseman of all time and if Willie McCovey was the hardest-hitting first baseman in National League history, then, without a doubt, Ernie Banks was the king of offensive short-stops. Banks, a lithe six-foot-one, 186-pound bundle of energy, went directly from the Negro leagues to the major leagues in 1953. Two years later, as a 24-year-old, he hit 44 home runs, drove in 117 runners, and batted a respectable .290.

Banks twice led the National League in home runs, hitting 47 homers in 1958 and slamming 41 round trippers in 1960. He holds the major league record for the most home runs by a shortstop in a season (47). He hit three home runs in a game four times. He led the league in RBIs twice, knocking in 129 runs in 1958 and 143 runs in 1959. In both 1958 and 1959, the handsome infielder walked off with league's Most Valuable Player honors.

Ernie Banks finished his career with many impressive statistics. He is 12th all-time in home runs, 18th in total bases, and 17th in RBIs. His 512 career homers average out to be 30 home runs a year, making him the most productive shortstop in major league history.

The handsome infielder also demonstrated his defensive capabilities by leading National League shortstops in fielding average three times in eight years.

One other slugger of note was big Dave Kingman, the six-six, 215-pound giant from Oregon. Kingman slammed 442 round trippers during a mediocre 16-year career. There was no doubt that "Kong," as he was called, could put the ball into orbit whenever he connected. The problem was, it was all or nothing at all with him. He didn't make contact very often. His 1,816 career strikeouts (150 per year), combined with a .236 lifetime batting average and leaky outfield play, caused him to be shuttled around from team to team. He played with seven teams in 16 years, four of them in 1977 alone.

The towering righthander smashed 35 home runs in 1986 at the age of 38. In spite of that, his defensive deficiencies, plus his antisocial behavior, brought about his exit from the major leagues. He ended his career with Phoenix in the Pacific Coast League the following year, hanging up his glove after just 20 games.

Still, Dave Kingman's great power rocketed him to the top of the major league sluggers' list. His home run average of 36 home runs a year is exceeded by only four men in major league history: Ruth, Kiner, Killebrew, and Williams.

Dave Kingman was the poor man's Babe Ruth.

It is interesting to note that, since Aaron and Mays retired in the 1970s, there has been a dearth of bona fide superstars in the major leagues—players who could hit, hit with power, run, field, and throw. Mike Schmidt came closest to meeting the criteria, but he finished his career with a modest .267 lifetime batting average, caused in part by his high strikeout ratio of one strikeout for every 4.4 times at bat.

During the 1930s, '40s, and '50s, outstanding hitters like Babe Ruth, Lou Gehrig, Jimmie Foxx, and Ted Williams consistently slugged 30 or more home runs a year, knocked in 130+ runs, and stung the ball at a torrid .340 pace. Williams was the last batter to do that on a consistent basis, in the late '40s. Willie Mays and Hank Aaron produced more modest numbers during the 1960s.

Most of the sluggers who surfaced in the '80s and '90s were free swingers like Schmidt, with high home run totals and high strikeout totals to match. Very few threatened a .300 batting average. Players like Reggie Jackson and Dave Kingman, had the home run averages to compete for the "King of Swat" crown, but they also had severe defensive liabilities, as well as problems making frequent contact with the ball.

One heir apparent did surface in 1987, when six-foot-five, 225-pound Mark McGwire strode onto the major league scene. The big 23-year-old rookie stunned the baseball world by smashing a league-leading 49 home runs, to go along with a .289 batting average and 118 runs-batted-in. Unfortunately, foot problems and a bad back have plagued the handsome redhead since his explosive debut. He has been on the disabled list six times in eleven years, missing all but 74 games during the 1993 and 1994 seasons.

In 1996, a reasonably healthy McGwire returned to the wars, to blast 52 homers in just 423 at bats, an average of one homer for every 8.1 bats. That performance broke Babe Ruth's major league record of one homer for every 9 at-bats, set in 1927. At the end of the 1996 season, Mark McGwire stood second to the mighty Bambino in career home run frequency, with an average of 43 home runs a year. The 34-year-old Californian still has time to reach the 500 homer level before he retires, and to solidify his position as one of baseball's all-time leading sluggers.

Other potential superstars have arrived on the big league scene from time to time. Players like Eric Davis, Darryl Strawberry, and Bob Horner flashed across the horizon with spectacular brilliance, then quickly faded and fell by the wayside, derailed by a myriad of problems. Davis averaged 35 homers a year during his first seven years in the National League before injuries curtailed his attack on Olympus. The "Straw Man" piled up 280 home runs by the age of 29, but personal problems turned his party into a nightmare. Bob Horner, another big boomer of the '80s, also went down under a barrage of injuries, leaving his destiny unfulfilled. The slugging third baseman banged out 32 home runs a year for the Atlanta Braves between 1978 and 1986. He also whacked 31 homers in just 303 at bats for the Yakult Swallows of the Japanese Central League in 1987.

There may be a rebirth coming in the '90s, but it is still too early to know for sure. Sluggers like big Frank Thomas, Ken Griffey Jr., Albert Belle, and

Mike Piazza have the potential to be great hitters, but only time will tell if they can sustain their early promise, staying healthy and motivated throughout their careers. Griffey, in fact, could be baseball's next superstar, if he can stay off the disabled list long enough.

One of the problems facing professional baseball today is the dilution of talent. In the "old days," prior to World War II, each major league had a total of eight teams, and there were dozens of minor league teams funneling talent up to the Big Show. Then, beginning in 1960, after the majors had spread their roots from coast to coast and from Texas to Canada, they began to expand. Today, there are 28 teams in the two major leagues, with more teams on the way.

Complicating the picture is the fact that baseball is no longer the only route out of the inner city. In fact, it is not even the most popular route. Professional football and professional basketball, nurtured at the breast of the new technological mother, television, have gradually siphoned off some of baseball's talent pool. Basketball, in particular, is an ideal sport for the street kids of the inner city: the only piece of equipment required is a basketball, and hoops are available in every schoolyard and every playground in the concrete jungle. Stickball lost some of its popularity when the city streets became too congested to use as ballfields. Unlike baseball of days past, basketball and football have also provided outstanding athletes with a free college education, as scholarships have become abundant throughout the land, from Notre Dame, Indiana, to Miami, Florida. Talented young men can pursue their athletic dreams, knowing that if they don't make it in the big time, they at least have a college education to fall back on.

Today, football and basketball are booming, while baseball is struggling to maintain its dwindling popularity advantage. Baseball also has a recent image problem brought about by too much money and too little dedication. It has gone from a sport to a business. Players today, even the journeymen, become overnight millionaires. Loyalty is a quality that is no longer affordable, as players follow the dollar from team to team through free agency. At the same time, the quality of the play has diminished drastically. Forty years ago, every team had a four-man pitching rotation, with the starters hurling complete games more often than not. Players played through their injuries, knowing that, as former St. Louis Cardinals catcher Joe Garagiola once said, "there were players waiting in Columbus [the Cardinals' farm team], to take our place if we couldn't play." Today, every team has a five-man pitching rotation, and if a pitcher can last six or seven innings a game, he is considered to be a quality pitcher.

Lost-time injuries are commonplace today, as athletes are reluctant to jeopardize their million-dollar potentials by playing hurt. Players are pampered by their managers, who rest them at the slightest sign of an illness or injury. Today, the inmates are running the asylum. Even so, there is evidence that there are more injuries now than there were forty years ago, some of them caused by artificial turf and others apparently resulting from a lack of conditioning. The future is uncertain. The disgraceful strike of 1994–95, reflected negatively on both the owners and the players. The only innocent victims were the fans. Players and owners alike insulted the integrity of the game.

Until such time as all those concerned realize that it's just a kid's game, and that it belongs to the fans, the old magic will not return.

Babe Ruth. Ralph Kiner. Harmon Killebrew. They are the home run kings of the lively ball era. There are few challengers on the horizon.

CHAPTER 4

THE JAPANESE LEAGUES

Baseball has been a favorite sport in Japan for more than a century. Although initially not as popular with the Japanese people as the centuries-old sumo wrestling, baseball developed an increasingly large and boisterous following over the years and is now considered the national sport. Horace Wilson, an American professor at Kaisei Gakko University in Tokyo, is credited with introducing the game to the Land of the Rising Sun in the early 1870s. Another American teacher living in Tokyo, Albert Bates, arranged the first organized baseball game in 1873, according to Robert Whiting in his book on Japanese baseball, *You Gotta Have Wa*.

In the ensuing 120 or so years, the level of skill on the diamond has increased to the point where Japanese professional teams are now very much competitive with American major league teams. Although not completely equal in skill, they can no longer be taken lightly by the touring Americans. In fact, a Los Angeles Dodgers squad limped home from a 1992 Asian tour after losing four of five games in Taiwan and Japan. The Daiei Hawks/Tokyo Giants all-stars took the Dodgers to task in two straight games, including a 16–1 shellacking in the finale in the Fukuoka Dome.

Baseball became a popular sport in Japanese collegiate circles following its introduction by Wilson. According to *Total Baseball*, the game was dubbed *yakyu*, or "field ball." Also *beisu boro*. The first recorded game between Japanese and American teams, as reported by Whiting, took place in Tokyo in 1896. Ichiko Prep School defeated an American team from the Yokohama Country Athletic Club by the lopsided score of 29–4. A rematch gave the same result. Ichiko won 35–9. The Americans demanded, and got, yet another rematch. This time, they recruited some sailors from one of the U.S. Navy ships anchored in Yokohama harbor, but the sailors weren't much help. Ichiko romped again, this time by a margin of 22–9, before several thousand excited spectators. The result of Ichiko's stunning success against the foreigners was to increase the popularity of the sport in Nippon.

Japan's entry into the world baseball arena was confirmed by a visit of the Waseda Imperial University baseball team to the United States in 1905. Waseda played 26 games on the west coast, defeating Los Angeles High

School and an amateur team of American Indians, while losing to several west coast colleges, including Stanford, USC, and Washington. In all, Waseda compiled a 7–19 record for their efforts, a creditable showing for a fledgling nine.

Four years later, the University of Wisconsin Badgers visited Japan as guests of the Athletic Association of Keio University. Keio defeated the Americans in three out of four games, but the Badgers triumphed over a Tokyo all-star team by scores of 10–0 and 8–7.

In 1910, the University of Chicago baseball team visited the island empire, taking Waseda University to task in three straight games by scores of 9–2, 15–4, and 20–0. These humiliating defeats weighed heavily on the mind of Waseda second baseman, Suishi Tobita, who vowed to develop a training regimen that would produce championship baseball teams, capable of defeating any team in the world. Over the years, Tobita, as coach of Waseda, developed a punishing baseball regimen, based on dedication and self sacrifice. He refined and modified his theories to the point where Waseda became the most successful college baseball team in the country.

The pinnacle of his career came in 1925 when his Waseda University baseball team rolled up a spectacular 36–0 season record, capped by a sweep of his old nemesis, the University of Chicago, by scores of 1–0, 1–0, 3–3, and 1–0.

Suishi Tobita's obviously successful training techniques, as demonstrated by his record at Waseda, were soon adopted by high schools and colleges all over the island nation. When professional teams came into existence, in 1935, they too adopted the Tobita plan.

Tobita, known as the god of Japanese baseball, believed that only through complete dedication to physical and mental development can a player reach his ultimate potential. His regimen, one of complete subservience to the team, its coaches, and its manager, is the foundation upon which the Japanese professional leagues have operated for the past fifty years. In Tobita's program, the game is all consuming. A player's personal life has no priority. Japanese players are not permitted to take time off for personal matters, such as the death of a parent, the illness of a wife, or the birth of a child.

In high schools and colleges, the brutal training regimen is a year-round experience. Students practice day-in and day-out, month after month, even during holiday vacations. They sacrifice their personal lives and their family relationships to the game of baseball. Their goal is to achieve spiritual, as well as physical, perfection.

The professional game is much the same. The merciless exercises begin in late winter, in the bitter cold, with teams spending all day on the practice field, running, throwing, and fielding. Evening sessions include meditation and indoor drills.

Training continues into the regular season, without a break. Players warm up on the field for hours prior to each game. It is a philosophy of mind over matter, a philosophy that has proven particularly destructive to pitchers. Injuries are not recognized. Players are expected to play through their difficulties. Pitchers, with sore arms, are expected to work the soreness out of their arms by frequent work. It is not uncommon for hurlers to pitch in up to 35 percent of their team's games. Needless to say, pitcher's careers are often of short duration and are characterized by severe overwork. Victor Starffin, a Russian national, was an early victim of this practice. The six-foot righthander set many Japanese pitching records during the late 30s and early 40s, including most victories in a season (42), most consecutive 30-win seasons (3), and most career shutouts (84). Over one six-year period, Starffin hurled more than 400 innings a season twice and more than 300 innings a season three other times. He averaged 30 wins a season during those six years and, for all intents and purposes, was burned out at the age of 26.

Baseball was introduced into Japan by Americans and was based on the American game. The two games, however, have developed independently over the years, particularly with regard to training philosophy and game strategy. Hard work, dedication, and submission to management are the heart and soul of the Japanese system. The game itself is much more conservative, in part due to the Japanese fear of making a mistake. In Japan, the greatest sin is to lose face. People have been known to commit hara-kiri after failing some task and bringing disgrace on themselves and their families. Baseball managers, fully aware of this dilemma, anguish over every decision during a game, no matter how small. The result is a slow-paced contest, with a minimum of risks being taken strategy-wise. The game usually evolves into one of bases on balls, sacrifice hits, stolen bases, singles, and squeeze plays.

Many people believe the United States and Japan will eventually become cofounders of a world baseball league, with the champions of the east and the champions of the west meeting every year in a true World Series. Others feel that such a scenario will never happen, emphasizing the drastic differences in philosophies between the two countries. LeRon Lee is one who doubts we will ever see such a union. This veteran of both the American and the Japanese major leagues says, in Whiting's *You Gotta Have Wa*, that "The Japanese and American games are running on parallel tracks. And they will never, ever, cross." He may be right.

The first American professional baseball tour of Japan took place in 1908, when the Reach All-Americans toured the island. The team, composed of a combination of major league reserves and players from the Pacific Coast League, rolled up an impressive 17–0 record against Japanese college teams. Five years later, the Chicago White Sox and New York Giants traveled the world together, playing exhibition games at the base of the pyramids in Egypt, on the cricket fields of England, as well as on homemade diamonds in the Philippines, China, and Japan. American players participating in the games included Tris Speaker, Buck Weaver, Hal Chase, and Christy Mathewson. These events attracted large crowds throughout the island empire, sparking the interest of the average Japanese in the game of baseball. Although most of the games were exhibitions between the Giants and the White Sox, a combined group from the two teams easily took the measure of the Keio University nine, by a count of 12–3.

A 1922 major league all-star team, composed of players like Herb Pennock, Waite Hoyt, and Casey Stengel, had the dubious distinction of being the first American professional team to lose a game to a Japanese squad, according to Whiting. The Mita Club of Shibaura, behind the southpaw slants of Ono, thrashed Hoyt, 9–3.

During the '20s and early '30s, a number of Negro league all-star teams conducted exhibition tours to Japan. In 1927, the Royal Giants, a team from the California Winter League, completed a tour of Nippon with a spotless 23–0–1 record. Five years later, the Royal Giants swept through the island again, losing only one game of a 24-game schedule. The Negro league players, including Bullet Joe Rogan, Newt Allen, Biz Mackey, Rap Dixon, and Crush Holloway, were equally as talented as their major league counterparts, and they spent many hours instructing their hosts in the finer points of the game. They also entertained the fans by putting on their fancy "shadow ball" demonstrations—infield drills without the benefit of a ball—and by engaging in a variety of baserunning and throwing contests.

Lefty O'Doul, one of the finest hitters ever to walk on a baseball field, accompanied an American all-star team to Japan in 1931. The major league team that included the likes of Lou Gehrig, Lefty Grove, Mickey Cochrane, and Al "Bucketfoot" Simmons swept 17 games from the Japanese, according to Richard Leutzinger. O'Doul led the awesome, major league hitting attack with an average of .600. One ironic footnote of that tour was an injury suffered by Lou Gehrig. "The Iron Horse" sustained a broken hand when he was hit by a pitched ball in game seven. The injury put the big first baseman on the shelf for the final ten games of the series. Fortunately for Gehrig, the injury occurred after the end of the regular American League season. If it had happened just two weeks earlier, Gehrig's consecutive game streak would have come to a sudden end at just over 1,000 games. His legendary record of having played in 2,130 consecutive games never would have reached fruition, and he never would have earned the sobriquet by which he is known, "The Iron Horse."

The smooth-swinging O'Doul established a lifelong friendship with the Japanese people. He was fascinated by both the people and their culture, and he returned to the island nation more than 20 times over the years, bringing major league all-star teams with him on occasion. He also conducted numerous baseball clinics around the country, teaching the fundamentals of the game to thousands of enthusiastic fans, both adults and children alike. He enjoyed working with the Japanese because he was impressed with their interest in the game and with their work ethic, which he considered to be far superior to that of American youngsters. Lefty O'Doul, perhaps more than any other person, popularized the modern game of baseball in Japan.

In 1934, baseball excitement reached a fever pitch in Japan when the immortal Babe Ruth made his first visit to the country, as a member of the Babe Ruth/Lou Gehrig All-Star team. The Sultan of Swat was a mythical figure in the Land of the Rising Sun, as he was in other countries around the world. As far as baseball fans everywhere were concerned, Babe Ruth and baseball were synonymous. The Babe and his teammates were welcomed to Tokyo with a rousing motorcade down the Ginza, witnessed by over one million enthusiastic fans. The following day, the American and Japanese teams drew an overflow crowd of 80,000 people to Meiji Jingu Stadium in the capital city. It was one of the largest crowds that any of the Americans had ever faced. The biggest major league stadium in the United States at the time, Cleveland's Municipal Stadium, held just over 78,000 people.

Over the next month, the Babe Ruth/Lou Gehrig All-Stars romped through an 18-game series in various Japanese cities, without suffering a single loss. The mighty Babe delighted his Japanese fans by slamming a total of 13 home runs, many of them prodigious blasts that left players and fans alike open-mouthed with amazement. Even the Babe's own teammates continued to be astonished by his awesome power.

The one bright spot for the Japanese was the pitching of 18-year-old Eiji Sawamura. The righthanded flamethrower, in a game played in Shizuoka, fanned the mighty Babe, Charlie Gehringer, Lou Gehrig, and Jimmie Foxx in succession. Unfortunately for him, a seventh inning home run by Gehrig sent him down to defeat, 1–0.

The following year, 1935, Matsutaro Shoriki, the publisher of the *Yomiuri Shimbun*, the nation's largest newspaper, fielded Nippon's first professional baseball team. The Tokyo Yomiuri Giants (or Kyojin), unable to find suitable opposition at home, made a lengthy 110-game exhibition tour of the States. They compiled an excellent 75–35 record against minor league opposition, much to the satisfaction of their owner.

By 1955, when the New York Yankees embarrassed their hosts with a 15–0–1 record, the unofficial win-loss record stood at 67-3 in favor of the Americans. Then things began to change as the quality of Japanese baseball gradually improved. When manager Walter Alston brought his world-champion Los Angeles Dodgers to the far east in 1966, winning was no longer a sure thing. In fact, the Dodgers barely eked out a series victory, winning nine games to the Japanese team's eight. Four years later, in 1970, Japan whipped the San Francisco Giants six games out of nine, giving them their first taste of victory.

One of the most embarrassing series for the Japanese occurred during the 1971 tour of the American League champion Baltimore Orioles. Earl Weaver's Birds, with Frank Robinson and Brooks Robinson, piled up a 12–2–4 record during the month-long tour. More significant, they humiliated the Yomiuri Giants of Oh and Nagashima—considered to be the greatest team in Japanese history—eight straight times. It was a long winter in Nippon that year.

Recently, the series has been played on more or less equal terms. In 1990, Japan took the measure of the visiting Americans, four games to three. Two important events highlighted that series. In game three, 21-year-old fireballer, Hideo Nomo, now a star pitcher for the Los Angeles Dodgers, stymied the major leaguers, 2–1. In the finale, Nomo's American League counterpart, six-foot-ten Randy Johnson of the Seattle Mariners, combined with Chuck Finley of the California Angels to no-hit the home team 5–0. Nomo took the loss.

Organized high school baseball began in Japan in 1915 and has thrived ever since. In fact, high school baseball is more popular in Japan than professional baseball. Every summer the nation studiously follows the national high school tournament being held regionally in 47 prefectures around the country. Over 4,000 high school teams enter the single-elimination tournament each year, with the 47 regional champions advancing to the finals in Koshien Stadium, near Osaka. The country literally goes baseball crazy during two weeks in August, as the finals begin. Over one million people cram their way into Koshien Stadium during the games, while most of the rest of the nation view it on television.

The national high school tournament is often the biggest single event in a boy's life. He attains a special place in Japanese society if his team makes it to the finals. Many of the players from Koshien go on to careers in the Japanese professional baseball leagues. Others are given lucrative positions with Japanese corporations so they can play for the company team in an industrial league. Even if they do not continue careers in baseball, the boys who participate at Koshien are honored throughout their life for their extraordinary achievement.

College baseball began its own league in 1925, and the six-team Tokyo Six University League now develops many players for the professional ranks. It is not as popular as high school ball, however, since most professional players still enter the Central or Pacific Leagues directly out of high school, foregoing college in their anxiety to begin a professional baseball career.

The first Japanese professional baseball league began in 1936. It consisted of seven teams, playing a total of three games each. As a portent of things to come, the Yomiuri Giants carried off the first championship trophy. The following year, a full schedule of games was played, with the season split into two halves: a spring half and a fall half. The Giants took the first-half title, with a record of 41–13; the Hanshin Tigers walked off with the second-half trophy with a record of 39–9. There was no playoff to determine an overall champion. In Japan, unlike the United States, the professional baseball teams are named after their owners, who are, for the most part, large corporations. Hanshin, for instance, is owned by the Hanshin Railroad Company of Osaka.

In 1950, with fan interest at an all-time high, the eight-team Central League was split into two separate leagues: the Central League and the Pacific League. Where originally there were 15 teams in the two leagues, there now are six teams in each league. Winning championships has become commonplace for the Giants over the years, as they have captured 35 Central League pennants in 52 years, a record that compares favorably with that of the old Bronx Bombers. Beginning with the formation of the Pacific League in 1950, a season-ending series between the winners of the two leagues has been held annually to determine the Japanese professional champion. The Yomiuri Giants have captured 18 Japan Series Championships in 45 years, through 1994. Their counterparts in the United States, the Yankees, have appeared in 33 World Series in 95 years, winning 22 World Championships along the way.

Legendary baseball players abound in Japan. Tetsuharu Kawakami was the first batting hero of the Japanese professional leagues. The rugged first baseman established many Japanese professional records over a period of 18 years, beginning in 1938, including the highest season batting average (.377) and the most home runs in a season (20). Naturally, as the years passed, most of his records fell by the wayside, but his name lives on in Japanese lore.

Kawakami, called "The Lord of Batting" by Yomiuri Giants fans, left a lifetime .313 batting average behind when he retired, at the time the highest average in Japanese baseball history. Although he wore glasses, the intense slugger insisted he could actually stop the ball in flight while batting. His great concentration was the result of his dedication to Zen meditation, which he practiced daily over the winter months in an isolated mountain retreat. When the Los Angeles Dodgers visited Japan in 1966, Kawakami was the hitting star for the home team, ripping the ball at a .364 clip with two home runs in 17 games.

The former all-star first sacker went on to an even greater career as a manager. He led the powerful Yomiuri Giants to eleven pennants in fourteen years. Amazingly, his teams won all eleven Japan Series they played in, including a record nine in a row. No professional team in the United States has come close to duplicating that record.

The first bona fide home run hitter in Japanese professional baseball was Katsuya Nomura, the lumbering catcher of the Nankai Hawks. Nomura, nicknamed "Moose" because of his slowness afoot, played 26 years in the Japanese Pacific League, winning nine home runs crowns during that time. He captured both the home run crown and the runs-batted-in title six consecutive years, from 1962 through 1967. Nomura's 657 career home runs, an average of 35 homers a year, were a Japanese record at the time. His 52 homers in 1952 established a single-season record, since broken. Both his single-season and lifetime home run totals are still the records for a catcher in professional baseball. Johnny Bench's 45 home runs in 1970 and his 389 career home runs, the American major league standards, pale by comparison to Nomura's numbers.

Nomura had a distinct home field advantage in his quest for home run immortality. He played in Japan's smallest park, Osaka Stadium, with its 280-foot foul lines and 350-foot claustrophobic center field fence.

Proving that he could hit for average as well as for distance, the muscular slugger won the triple crown in 1965, with a batting average of .320, to go along with 42 home runs and 110 runs batted in. In many respects, the Nankai backstop's career mirrored that of Brooklyn Dodger great, Roy Campanella. Their offensive statistics are eerily similar, as shown below. This table represents the career averages, per 550 at bats, for the two legendary catchers.

Name	AB	R	H	D	T	HR	RBI	BB	SO	BA
Katsuya Nomura	550	79	152	21	1	35	104	66	78	.277
Roy Campanella	550	82	152	23	2	32	112	70	65	.276

In addition to his offensive capabilities, Nomura was also recognized as an excellent handler of pitchers and as a top-notch defensive catcher. He was Campanella's equal in all departments, except in speed. Campanella had cat-like quickness around the plate. Where Nomura was a slow runner, the rotund Campanella was deceptively fast. A former high school track star, the Dodger receiver often beat runners down to first base on infield grounders.

The heavy-footed Nankai catcher was a durable receiver who seldom missed a game. One year he caught every inning of the 150 games the Hawks played. His career total of 2,918 games caught exceeds the American record of Carlton Fisk by 692 games.

Nomura outshone his American catching compatriots in almost every category. In addition to games played, season home runs, and career home runs, he also holds the world professional record for catchers in career hits (2,901), career runs scored (1,509), career RBIs (1,988), and number of seasons with 100 or more RBIs (7). And he did it all in 130-game schedules. By comparison, only Johnny Bench, with 45 homers in 1970 and 40 homers in 1972, won home run titles in the U.S. Ernie Lombardi won two batting championships in the National League, hitting .342 in 1938 and .330 in 1942. Bubbles Hargrave of Cincinnati took the batting title in 1926 with an average of .353.

The Japanese backstop's main competition for catching records came from the great Negro league catcher, Josh Gibson. Gibson captured two batting titles, hitting .521 for the Homestead Grays in 1943 and .479 in Puerto Rico in 1941. His .479 average is still the all-time, Puerto Rican season record after 55 years, in spite of challenges from the likes of Monte Irvin, Willie Mays, Tony Oliva, and Roberto Clemente. Gibson holds the record for most season home run championships won, with 12. He won nine home run titles in the Negro leagues, one in Cuba, one in Mexico, and one in Puerto Rico. Nomura is second with seven-season home run titles.

Nomura's statistics are extraordinary when you consider the day-to-day pounding a catcher absorbs. His record of catching for 26 years—and catching more than 100 games in a season, twenty one times—may never be equaled.

The Japanese miracle man retired in 1980, at the age of 47.

Futoshi Nakanishi played outfield for the Nishitetsu Lions for 18 years, sparking them to three consecutive championships over the powerful Tokyo Giants, from 1956 through 1958. In the run to the 1958 victory, the miracle Lions made up an 11-game deficit to the Nankai Hawks during September to capture the Pacific League crown. Nakanishi finished off the Hawks with a game winning home run in their final meeting. The compact, five-foot-eight, 180-pound slugger hit both for power and average. He led the Pacific League in home runs five times and, in 1953, hit a monstrous clout that was measured at 530 feet, the second longest home run ever recorded in Japan.

Although Nakanishi played 18 seasons in the Pacific League, he had only seven healthy, full-time years. He sat out from 1959 to 1960 with injuries, returning as a part-time player for the next nine years. His highest home run mark was 36 in 1953. At the time of his retirement, he had accumulated a total of 244 round trippers to go along with his .307 batting average.

Isao Harimoto, a Japanese born Korean, starred in the Pacific League for 23 years, beginning in 1959. The hard-hitting outfielder consistently rapped out 29 home runs a year, in addition to hitting for a high average. In 1970, he flirted with the magic .400 mark most of the season, but eventually settled for a Japanese professional record of .383. It was one of his nine batting titles. He won four consecutive batting championships, from 1967 through 1970, with averages of .336, .336, .333, and .383.

The Toei Flyers outfielder sparked his team to their only Pacific League title and Japan Series championship in 1982, with a league-leading .336 batting average, 31 home runs, and 99 runs batted in.

During his career, he accumulated a record 3,085 hits, the only player in Japanese history at the time, to surpass the 3,000 hit barrier. He was never an out-and-out power hitter. He was a spray hitter, who hit to all fields and had decent power. His .319 lifetime batting average is the third highest average ever recorded in Japan, and his 504 home runs trail only Sadaharu Oh,

Shigeo Nagashima was a Hall-of-Fame quality third baseman for the Yomiuri Giants of the Japanese Central League, from 1958 until 1974. During that time, he sparked the Giants to five league titles and three "world championships." His career statistics include a .305 batting average and 444 home runs (credit: Transcendental Graphics).

Katsuya Nomura, and Koji Yamamoto. The sweet-swinging righthanded batter was one of the most illustrious hitters in Japanese professional baseball and is still Korea's most renowned baseball player.

Perhaps the most popular player ever to step on a baseball diamond in Japan was third baseman Shigeo Nagashima of the Yomiuri Giants. A teammate of Sadaharu Oh's, the handsome Nagashima could do it all. A stellar defensive third baseman, Nagashima also wielded one of the most dangerous bats in the Central League. He could hit for average, had explosive power, and was considered to be the greatest clutch hitter in Japanese professional baseball.

Nagashima joined the Yomiuri Giants in 1958 out of Rikkyo University. The 21-year-old phenom immediately walked off with Rookie of the Year honors after leading the league in home runs (29) and runs batted in (92). It was only the beginning of a magical journey. Over a storied, 17-year career, the charismatic slugger captured two home run titles, five RBI crowns, six batting titles, and five Most Valuable Player awards.

Known as "Mr. Giant," Nagashima's most memorable day occurred on June 26, 1959. Playing against the Hanshin Tigers in the celebrated Emperor's Game, before His Imperial Majesty Emperor Hirohito, Nagashima slugged a game-winning, ninth-inning home run, considered to be the most dramatic hit in Japanese baseball history.

The righthanded slugger, who had the advantage of batting cleanup in the Giants lineup, just behind Sadaharu Oh, compiled a lifetime batting average of .305. His 444 home runs average out to 30 home runs for every 550 at bats. Nagashima and Oh, known popularly as the "O-N Cannons," carried the Tokyo team to eleven Japan Series championships, nine of them in succession. Nagashima was voted the Most Valuable Player in the Central League five times and won the Japan Series MVP four times.

Koji Yamamoto was a slugging outfielder for the Hiroshima Carp during the 1980s. He teamed with third baseman Sachio Kinugasa to convert the Carp from a mediocre baseball team into a world champion. The former college hero sparked the Hiroshima "Red Helmet" club to five Central League pennants and three Japan Series championships. He won four home run titles in six years, between 1978 and 1983, with 43, 44, 43, and 36 home runs respectively. His league leading RBI totals from '79 through '81 were 113, 112, and 103. He also captured a batting championship in 1975, with an average of .319, as he propelled the Carp to their first Central League title. Yamamoto retired after an 18-year career, with a .290 career batting average and a total of 536 home runs, the third highest total in Japanese history. His home run average of 37 homers for every 550 at bats ranks third, behind Sadaharu Oh and Hiromitsu Ochiai.

One of the most heroic figures in the annals of Japanese professional baseball was Sachio Kinugasa, the third baseman of the Hiroshima Carp.

Kinugasa, the offspring of a Japanese mother and a African-American G.I. father, was one of the major proponents of the Suishi Tobita's work ethic. He believed it was the duty of every baseball player to be ready to play every game, regardless of his physical condition. As a result, Kinugasa punished his body year after year, adhering to that principle.

Sachio Kinugasa became a regular of the Carp in 1970, at the age of 23, and he played every game for the next 17 years. Over that period, he played whether he was healthy or not. Five times, he played through broken bones. He played with the flu, stomach problems, contusions, and sprains. Finally, on June 13, 1987, the tough little infielder's determination was rewarded, when he broke Lou Gehrig's record of playing in 2,130 consecutive games. When he retired at the end of the season, his total stood at 2,215 games. Cal Ripken Jr. broke Kinugasa's record in 1996.

Kinugasa was a free spirit, who loved fancy clothes and big cars. He was a party animal, who whiled away the nights in revelry. But through it all, he never neglected his training—and he never missed a game. Robert Whiting tells of one incident that epitomizes the third baseman's dedication to his vocation. According to Whiting, Kinugasa returned to his dormitory one morning as the sun was coming up, feeling no pain after his night's entertainment. He was intercepted in the hallway by his coach, Junzo Sekine, who proceeded to put his student through his bat-swinging drills until the exhausted player passed out. Kinugasa's dedication helped the Hiroshima Carp win five Central League titles and three Japan Series championships. The victories were all the sweeter because they came at the expense of their Central League adversaries, the hated Yomiuri Giants.

The five-foot-nine, 160-pound infielder, used a free swinging approach to batting, much to the chagrin of his coaches. His 23-year career was sprinkled with 1,587 strikeouts, but it also produced 504 home runs, fourth all-time in Japan, 2,000+ base hits, and a .271 career batting average. In 1984, Kinugasa hit .300 for the only time in his life and led the league with 102 runs batted in, en route to the Central League Most Valuable Player award. His performance propelled the Carp to their third Japan Series championship in six years.

The king of Japanese baseball, however, without a doubt, was the powerful first baseman of the Yomiuri Giants, Sadaharu Oh. The son of a Chinese father and a Japanese mother, Oh was big by Japanese standards, standing five-feet-eleven-inches tall and weighing 174 pounds. The 19-year-old rookie joined the Giants directly out of Waseda Jitsugyo High School in Tokyo. Originally a pitcher, he was quickly converted to a first baseman to take advantage of his superior power.

It took the handsome infielder three years to become a full fledged offensive threat, but once he got his batting stroke synchronized, he became the most dangerous hitter in Japanese professional baseball. Batting third in

Yomiuri's lineup, just ahead of Shigeo Nagashima, the lefthanded power hitter sent 38 balls screaming into the Japanese sky in 1962, to win the home run championship of the Central League. It was the first of thirteen consecutive home run titles captured by Oh. In 1964, at the age of 24, Sadaharu Oh established a new, single-season Japanese home run record with 55 circuit clouts in 140 games. That would equate to 64 home runs in the American 162-game major league schedule. Twice more in his career, he hit 50 or more home runs in a season, smashing 51 circuit blows in 1973 and putting 50 balls in orbit in 1977.

Oh played professional baseball for 22 seasons. During that time he won five batting championships, as well as 15 home run titles. He led the league in runs scored 15 times, in hits 3 times, doubles once, total bases 12 times, and runs batted in 13 times. He won two triple crowns, back to back, (.355, 51, 114 in 1973) and (.332, 49, 107 in 1974). He was voted the league's Most Valuable Player an unprecedented nine times, as he led the Yomiuri Giants to 14 Central League titles and 11 Japan Series Championships. Proving he was not a one-dimensional player, the steady first baseman won nine gold gloves in 22 years.

One of Oh's greatest attributes was his extraordinarily precise batting eye. He never swung at a bad pitch, preferring to take a base on balls rather than expand his strike zone. As a result, he set the professional record for career bases on balls with 2,504, an average of 113 walks per year. Five times, Oh exceeded 140 walks in a season, with a personal high of 166 in 1974. He led the Central League in walks an unprecedented 19 times, with 18 of those coming in succession, from 1962 through 1979. When the big first baseman did swing at the ball, however, he put it in play consistently, striking out only 1,319 times during his career. In five seasons, he had more home runs than strikeouts, a figure exceeded only by Joe DiMaggio.

Oh passed Hank Aaron's professional record of 755 home runs in 1978. Two years later, he called it quits with the astronomical total of 868 home runs, an average of 52 home runs for every 550 at bats—the highest average in professional baseball—at the AAA level or above.

Like Hank Aaron before him, Sadaharu Oh's numbers were significantly affected by the unique features of the baseball stadiums he played in. Most Japanese parks, including Korakuen Stadium, the home of the Yomiuri Giants, measured approximately 297 feet down the foul lines, and a convenient 387 feet to straight-away center. That compares with the average major league park, which measures approximately 330 feet down the lines and 405 feet to the deepest part of center field.

Hiromitsu Ochiai is the present heir to Oh's throne. The outspoken outfielder of the Lotte Orions has dominated the Japanese leagues for the past 16 years. The scholarly looking Ochiai burst upon the Japanese professional baseball scene in 1981, when he captured his first batting championship, with an average of .326. The following year, he walked off with the triple crown, batting .325, with 32 home runs and 99 runs batted in. The big slugger subsequently won two other triple crowns, back to back, in 1986 and 1987. In '86 he hit a sizzling .367, with 52 home runs and 146 runs batted in. Both his home run and RBI totals are Pacific League single-season records, his 52 home runs tying Katsuya Nomura's record. In 1987, Ochiai banged out a .360 average, hit 50 circuit blows, and knocked in 116 teammates.

The righthanded-hitting slugger teamed with American LeRon Lee to give the Orions the most devastating one-two punch in the Japanese leagues since the famous "O-N Cannons," Sadaharu Oh and Shigeo Nagashima, roamed the field for the Yomiuri Giants. Lee's .320 batting average and 32 home runs a year, complemented Ochiai's .316 average and 40 home runs.

Hiromitsu Ochiai was traded to the Chunichi Dragons in 1987. His $812,500 salary with the Dragons was the highest salary ever paid to a Japanese player up to that time. Ochiai, now a member of the Yomiuri Giants, was still active in 1996, at the age of 43. His home run average of 39 homers a year is second only to Oh's 52 in the annals of Japanese professional baseball. His career total of 505 home runs presently ranks fifth all-time in Japan.

Since 1950, many foreign baseball players have demonstrated their talents on the playing fields of the island nation. Some 400 American players have graced the various rosters of Central and Pacific League teams over that period. Many of them have shown superb skills in all aspects of the game, but their primary attraction has been their ability to drive the ball long distances, especially in the smaller parks found in Japan.

One of the first Americans to play in Japan was pitcher Leo Kiely. The tall southpaw, who went on to a seven year career in the United States, pitched for the Mainichi Orions in 1953. He compiled a perfect 6–0 record with a 1.80 earned run average. The first bona fide slugger to strut his stuff in Japan was Daryl Spencer. The big, righthanded slugger had spent ten years in the National League, finishing with a .244 batting average and 105 home runs in 3,689 at bats, an average of 16 homers for every 550 at bats. His seven-year stats for the Hankyu Braves of the Pacific League showed a .275 batting average and an average of 37 home runs a year.

During the 1970s and 1980s, more and more Americans made their way to Japan. The lure of big dollars beckoned to former major leaguers who wanted to extend their careers and to minor league players with little hope of making the majors. In order to prevent the game from becoming too "Americanized," league officials restricted the number of foreigners to two per team.

Some American players, particularly former minor leaguers, became sports heroes in Japan. The Lee brothers, LeRon and Leon, were prime examples. The two young sluggers endeared themselves to the Japanese fans, not only by their outstanding baseball skills, but also by their interest in Japanese culture, their efforts to speak the language, and their exemplary conduct on the playing field.

Leon Lee completed a fine, ten-year career in Japan in 1987. His career totals included a .308 batting average and 268 home runs, an average of 32 home runs a year. His brother LeRon, spent eight years in the major leagues as a utility outfielder, compiling a .250 batting average with 11 home runs a year. In Japan, LeRon became a legend.

The six-foot, 196-pound, lefthanded hitter found the short fences in Japanese ballparks to his liking. Over an 11-year period, LeRon established a new Japanese professional career batting mark of .320, while averaging 34 home runs a year. Lee batted over .300 ten times, falling to .272 in his final year. He led the Pacific League in home runs in 1977 with 34, and in 1980 he showed the way in batting with a .358 average.

Other American sluggers also performed brilliantly on the island. Players like Orestes Destrade, Warren Cromartie, and Cecil Fielder all smoked the ball at a 40+ home run average during limited careers. Destrade averaged 51 home runs a year over a four-year period, leading the Pacific League in home runs three times. He smashed 42 circuit blows for the Seibu Lions in 1990, 39 in 1991, and 41 in 1992.

Warren Cromartie sparkled during a seven-year career in the Land of the Rising Sun. The big, lefthanded-hitting first baseman rapped the ball at a .321 clip in the Central League, 41 points higher than his major league average. His 32 home runs a year for the Yomiuri Giants exceeded his American average by 23. In 1989, he walked off with the batting title, spanking the ball at a .378 clip, the fourth highest season average in Japanese professional baseball history.

Cecil Fielder used the visibility of the Japanese leagues to catapult himself into a rewarding major league career. The huge first baseman bounced around the minor leagues for five years in the late '80s; then he spent four years as a bit player in Toronto. Disenchanted with his long-term prospects, Fielder signed a contract with the Hanshin Tigers of the Japanese Pacific League. During his one-year stint in the Land of the Rising Sun, the righthanded slugger smashed a home run every ten times at bat, winning him a trial with the Detroit Tigers. He immediately won two American League home run crowns and three RBI crowns for Sparky Anderson's team. The six-foot-three, 250-pound power hitter compiled 219 total home runs in six years in the Steel City, an average of 37 homers a year. His home run average in Japan was 54 homers a year, while his minor league average was a modest 29 homers a year. His .259 major league batting average is 43 points less than his average with Hanshin.

Two players with extended careers in Japan also hit with exceptional power. Clarence "Woody" Jones holds the distinction of being the only player to hit more than 200 home runs in both the Japanese leagues and the American professional leagues. Jones smashed 246 home runs in the Japanese Pacific League in eight years, an average of 43 homers per 550 at bats, and 211 home runs in the American minor leagues, an average of 30 homers per year. The lefthanded hitter averaged 8 home runs in a short major league trial.

Greg "Boomer" Wells, a journeyman ballplayer in the United States, had an outstanding, ten-year career in Japan. Joining the Hankyu Braves after brief trials with the Toronto Blue Jays and the Minnesota Twins in the American League, the six-foot-five, 250-pound first baseman ripped the ball at a .317 clip while averaging 34 home runs a year. He won the triple crown in Japan in 1984 with a .355 batting average, 130 runs batted in, and 37 home runs, carrying his team to the Pacific League title in the process. He also won another batting title, two more RBI crowns, and a home run title for the Hankyu Braves and Orix Braves. The towering slugger is credited with hitting the longest home run in the annals of Japanese baseball, a 532-foot shot in 1988.

Dick Davis, a six-foot-three, 190-pound outfielder, played briefly in the major leagues during the late '70s and early '80s, averaging .265 with 12 home runs. In Nippon, the righthanded-hitting slugger walloped 38 homers a year with a .331 batting average. Tony Solaita, another 200 pound basher, hit 47 home runs a year during his four years in Japan. Twice, he hit four home runs in a row. His American averages were 30 homers a year in the minors and 21 homers a year in the majors.

Two other Americans, in addition to Destrade (51) and Fielder (54), averaged more than 50 home runs a year in the Japanese leagues. Both Randy Bass (50) and Ralph Bryant (53) showed exceptional power across the ocean. Other impressive career home run performances in Japan included the aforementioned Woody Jones (43), Charley Manuel (49), Lance Parrish (44), Adrian Garrett (43), Reggie Smith (43), and Mike Diaz (42).

The undisputed king of American sluggers was Randy Bass, a six-foot-one, 210-pound first baseman from Lawton, Oklahoma. The big, lefthanded hitter had brief trials with five major league teams between 1977 and 1982, but came up short every time. When he moved to the Japanese Central League in 1983, he suddenly blossomed into a hitter extraordinaire. His six-year career included a .337 batting average and 202 home runs. His batting average is the highest ever recorded in Japanese professional baseball, but he did not accumulate enough at-bats to qualify for the official record. Bass twice won the triple crown with the Hanshin Tigers—showing the way first in 1985 with a .350 batting average, 54 home runs, and 134 runs batted in, and again in 1986 with totals of .389, 47, and 109. His .389 average is the highest season batting average in Japanese baseball history.

Randy Bass was the victim of an unfortunate incident in 1985 that prevented him from becoming more of a legend in the island empire. On his way to the triple crown, the handsome slugger had piled up 54 home runs in 125 games, trailing Sadaharu Oh's season home run record of 55 by a single homer. The Hanshin Tigers played the Tokyo Giants, managed by Oh, on the final day of the season. In a regrettable display of poor sportsmanship, Giant pitchers walked Bass on four consecutive at bats, thereby preventing him from challenging the record.

Bass did get even, however. His great offensive production carried the Tigers to the Central League pennant over Oh's Giant team. They then went on the capture the Japan Series in six games over the Nishitetsu Lions.

A review of the present status of Japanese professional baseball indicates that the Japanese leagues are still slightly behind their American major league neighbors in caliber of play. One of the problems in Japan is the lack of a substantial minor league farm system. It is still commonplace for players to enter the Japanese major leagues directly out of high school, something that is almost unheard of in the United States. A few of them, like Sadaharu Oh and Hideo Nomo have the ability to make the jump satisfactorily, but most players need several years of minor league ball in order to develop their talents. Unfortunately, there are only two minor leagues in Japan at the present time, an Eastern League and a Western League. Each major league team has one farm club, consisting of about 25 players. The entire minor league system totals about 300 players, compared with 15 to 20 minor leagues and some 4000 players in the United States. As a result, Japanese players do not have the luxury of developing their skills in a progressive manner. They are often forced to compete on a major league scale long before they are ready.

The quality of play in Japan at present seems to vary with the position. The pitchers and the infielders are ahead of the outfielders and the hitters. The Japanese leagues have some of the finest defensive infielders in the world. They also have excellent pitchers who are capable of competing on an equal footing with anybody. Hideo Nomo has recently confirmed this opinion. After five outstanding years with the Kintetsu Buffaloes of the Japanese Pacific League, Nomo led the Los Angeles Dodgers to the 1995 National League Western Division title, with a 13–6 record. His achievements included a league-leading 236 strikeouts and the National League Rookie of the Year award.

Japanese outfielders, by contrast, are not at the present time up to major league standards defensively. They have average range, but are penalized by weak throwing arms. Catchers have the same problem. They are capable defensively, and they are good handlers of pitchers, but they do not have major league throwing arms. The hitters are good contact hitters, with a firm grasp of the basics. They can hit-and-run, drag bunt, sacrifice, and work the count with effectiveness, but they lack the power of their American counterparts.

The gap between the two countries continues to narrow, however. It has been gradually getting less and less since 1950. If the Japanese can develop more depth in their farm system and if the individual players continue to develop physically, that gap will disappear completely in a few short years.

CHAPTER 5

THE NEGRO LEAGUES

The names of the great home run hitters in organized ball are familiar to baseball fans everywhere. Most enthusiasts of the game have heard about minor league sluggers Joe Bauman and Dick Stuart. They are familiar with the exploits of Sadaharu Oh in Japan. Big league sluggers like Babe Ruth, Hank Greenberg, Ralph Kiner, and Hank Aaron are household names. However, many of these same baseball experts are ignorant of the fact that professional baseball of major league caliber was played outside the realm of organized ball for over sixty years.

Black ballplayers were banned from playing organized baseball from the mid 1890s until 1945, when Branch Rickey signed Jackie Robinson to play ball for the Brooklyn Dodger farm club at Montreal. That gross injustice did not prevent blacks from participating in the sport, however. It just forced them to play their games outside the umbrella of organized ball. Black baseball teams played some of the most exciting baseball seen in the United States during the first half of the twentieth century. Some of the most glorious ballplayers ever to grace a diamond were spawned in this environment, legendary figures whose heroics have been passed down by word of mouth from generation to generation.

Blacks started playing baseball around the same time their white counterparts did, in the 1850s and '60s. During the Civil War, integrated baseball games were played in army campgrounds up and down the east coast, as well as in both Union and Confederate prisons, where southerners were first introduced to the game.

Shortly after the Civil War, the first black baseball team was formed. As reported by Jules Tygiel in *Total Baseball,* two black teams, the Uniques of Brooklyn and the Excelsiors of Philadelphia, met on the field of battle in the City of Churches in October 1867 to determine the "colored champion." The Excelsiors defeated the Uniques in a spirited contest by the score of 37–24.

When professional baseball began in 1871, it was not a segregated sport. As a matter of fact, more than 100 blacks played professional ball during the nineteenth century. John W. "Bud" Fowler was the first known black in organized ball, breaking in as a pitcher with Lynn, Massachusetts, of the International Association in 1878. He later converted to second base, where he excelled for more than 18 years. He was considered by many baseball experts of the time to be one of the best second baseman, black or white, in the entire country. The righthanded hitter could also pound the ball with authority. During his ten-year organized ball career, he batted over .300 six times, including .350 with Binghamton in the International League in 1887, .332 with Galesburg in the Inter State League in 1890, and .331 with Adrian-Lansing in the Michigan State League in 1895. When he left organized ball in 1895, a victim of professional baseball's unofficial segregation policy, he left behind a career batting average of .309. Fowler went on to play with all-black teams, such as the Cuban Giants, and the Page Fence Giants for another nine years.

Moses Fleetwood Walker is well known to baseball aficionados as the first black player to play major league ball. Fleet Walker was one of the first blacks to play minor league ball, as well. The slender catcher joined the Toledo Blue Stockings of the Northwest League in 1883. He had the reputation of being a good defensive catcher, with a strong throwing arm. He was not much of a hitter, however, batting only .251 with one home run in 235 at bats.

In 1884, Toledo joined the American Association, a major league, and Walker was a member of the team. His brother Welday was also on the roster and saw limited action in the outfield. According to *The Ballplayers*, Walker was the regular catcher and was also a decent singles hitter, his .263 batting average being 23 points higher than the league average.

When the Toledo club folded after the 1884 season, Walker joined the Cleveland ballclub of the Western League. He later played with George Stovey at Newark before finishing his career with Syracuse of the International League in 1889.

George Stovey was one of the outstanding pitchers in baseball in the late 1880s, and was on his way to major league stardom when discrimination scuttled his hopes. The big southpaw compiled a record of 34–14 with the Newark Little Giants of the International League in 1887, pitching in 48 games and holding opponents to a meager 2.46 earned run average. His 34 victories are still an International League record. Stovey was scheduled to pitch against the Chicago White Stockings in an exhibition game in July of 1887, but Chicago manager Cap Anson refused to let his team take the field against a black. Anson was also instrumental in finalizing the unofficial segregation policy that kept blacks out of organized ball for almost fifty years.

Other nineteenth-century, black baseball stars included Charlie Grant and Frank Grant. Charlie Grant, a sensational second baseman, was so good that manager John McGraw of the Baltimore Orioles tried to pass him off as an American Indian in order to add him to his roster. When the plot was exposed by Charles Comiskey, president of the Chicago White Sox, "Chief Tokohama" went back to playing ball with the Negro teams.

Ulysses S. "Frank" Grant was born in Pittsfield, Massachusetts, in 1865. Named after the Union army's great Civil War leader, Frank Grant was the first genuine home run hitter in black baseball history. The five-foot-seven, 155-pound infielder was generally regarded as the best second baseman in America during the 1880s. Unfortunately, his dreams of playing baseball in the major leagues vanished when Cap Anson and the major league club owners voted to ban blacks from the league. Grant languished in the minor leagues for six years before the unofficial segregation policy devoured that outlet also. Playing for Buffalo in the International League, the little second baseman hit a blazing .353 in 1887 and led the league in home runs with 11. He also chipped in with 26 doubles and 10 triples. The next year, the righthanded slugger hit another 11 home runs, while stroking the ball at a .346 clip.

In addition to his hitting, Frank Grant was a slick-fielding second baseman with exceptional range and a strong throwing arm. He was also an accomplished baserunner, once stealing home twice in the same game. Sportswriters around the east compared Grant to Fred Dunlap, the all-star second baseman of the St. Louis Cardinals.

From 1889 through 1891, there were several all-black teams competing in organized ball. The Cuban Giants represented Trenton, New Jersey, in the Middle States League in 1889, the York Monarchs in the Eastern Interstate League in 1890, and Ansonia in the Connecticut State League in 1891. Grant played with the Cubans in '89 and '91, In 1890, he was with Harrisburg in the Atlantic Association, where he batted .333 and hit a league-leading five home runs.

Sadly, as the major league segregation policy took hold, blacks were gradually eliminated from all organized baseball teams. The Acme Colored Giants, as members of the Pennsylvania Iron & Oil League in 1898, were the last African-Americans to play organized ball for more than 47 years. After recording a dismal 8–41 record during the first two months of the season, the team disbanded in July. The next time a black player represented a team in organized ball was when Jackie Robinson took the field for the Montreal Royals of the International League in 1946.

Frank Grant eventually slipped out of organized baseball altogether, spending his final years with various touring black clubs. He was a member of the Cuban Giants in 1889, moving on to the Big Gorhams of New York and the Page Fence Giants in later years. He finished his career with the Philadelphia Giants in 1902.

Frank Grant left behind an exceptional record in professional baseball, including a .337 batting average for six years in white leagues, with an average of nine home runs a year. After retiring from baseball, he moved to New York City where he worked as a waiter until his death in 1936.

Ulysses S. "Frank" Grant was the greatest black baseball player of the nineteenth century.

Many outstanding Negro teams barnstormed up and down the east coast during the first years of the twentieth century, showcasing the superb black baseball players of the era. These included the New York Lincoln Giants, the Brooklyn Royal Giants, the Chicago Leland Giants, and the Cuban X Giants. The Philadelphia Giants were, perhaps, the best black team of the time, with such standouts as William Monroe, Grant "Home Run" Johnson, Charlie "Tokohama" Grant, Spot Poles, Pete Hill, and Rube Foster.

Andrew "Rube" Foster, known as the "Father of Negro Baseball," was an outstanding screwball pitcher shortly after the turn of the century. He has been credited with teaching his pet pitch to the New York Giants' Christy Mathewson in 1903. The Giant ace won a whopping 30 games that year, after compiling a mediocre 13–18 record in '02. According to many of his major league contemporaries, such as Honus Wagner, Foster was one of the greatest pitchers of his time. He was also a dynamic baseball executive and was the founding father of the Negro National League in 1920. Foster was inducted into baseball's Hall of Fame in Cooperstown, New York, in 1981.

Smokey Joe Williams was another magnificent pitcher of the 1915 era. He was considered by many baseball experts of the period to be the fastest pitcher in the country. Williams faced major league teams thirty times in exhibition games over the years and came away with a record of 22–7, plus one tie game. The tall righthander counted Chief Bender, Rube Marquard, and Grover Cleveland Alexander among his many victims. He bested Walter Johnson 1–0 in a stirring pitchers' duel in 1917. That same year, he threw a no-hitter at the National League Champion New York Giants, fanning 20 men in 10 innings, only to lose 1–0 on an error.

There were not only outstanding pitchers displaying their wares around the Negro circuits in those days. There were great hitters as well. Spotswood Poles (called the black Ty Cobb), Pete Hill, Jimmy Lyons, and Louis Santop gave opposing pitchers fits with their bat handling talents.

The first great, black home run hitter of the twentieth century was Grant "Home Run" Johnson, the slugging shortstop of the Page Fence Giants. Johnson played professional baseball for 27 years, from 1895 through 1921. The righthanded hitter was not big as sluggers go, standing five-foot-ten in height and weighing around 170 pounds, but he had tremendous power, lightning quick wrists, and the ability to wait on a pitch until the last instant before committing himself. In 1910, Johnson played for the Havana Reds in an exhibition series against Hughie Jennings's mighty Detroit Tigers, with Ty Cobb and Wahoo Sam Crawford. Cobb, who had just won the American League batting championship with a .420 average, socked the ball at a .369 clip in the eight-game series, but was outhit by three members of the Havana team, including Johnson, who recorded a sizzling .412 batting average.

The Findlay, Ohio, native began his professional baseball career in his home town in 1894. Playing for the Findlay Sluggers, along with Fleetwood

Walker, Grant Johnson hit 60 round trippers against various opponents and, thereafter, was known as Home Run Johnson, according to James A. Riley in his Negro baseball epoch, *The Biographical Encyclopedia of the Negro Baseball Leagues*. In 1895, Johnson and Bud Fowler founded the Page Fence Giants. That year, Johnson, the team captain and shortstop, hit a resounding .471 as the Giants rolled up an incredible 118–36 record

Johnson played with many different black clubs over the next 16 years, including the Cuban X Giants, the Lincoln Giants, and Rube Foster's famous 1906 Philadelphia Giants. In the City of Brotherly Love, he teamed with John Henry Lloyd, arguably the greatest shortstop (and greatest all-around player) in Negro league history. Johnson also played winter ball in Cuba, where he starred for six years. Riley reports that the right-handed power hitter put together a .319 career batting average in Cuba, with a one-season high of .424.

The all-star shortstop retired from the Negro leagues in 1921 at the age of 47, but he continued to play with amateur teams around Buffalo, New York, until he could no longer bend over and touch the ground. He was 58 when he packed his glove away for good.

Grant "Home Run" Johnson was an outstanding shortstop, a

Grant "Home Run" Johnson was the Negro league's most fearsome slugger at the turn of the century. He was nicknamed "Home Run" after walloping 60 home runs for the Findlay Sluggers in 1894 (credit: Dick Clark).

Pete Hill was black baseball's first superstar. The lefthanded batter could hit for average or could slam the long ball, as the situation warranted. He also was the league's most outstanding outfielder, with great range and a strong, accurate throwing arm (credit: Dick Clark).

world-class long ball hitter, and a contact hitter who hit for a high average year after year. His Negro league average, according to partial statistics published by Riley, was .389. Someday, Johnson's bust may grace the wall of the baseball Hall of Fame in Cooperstown, New York. He certainly deserves the honor.

Hill, Lyons, and Santop were contemporaries during the first three decades of the twentieth century. Preston "Pete" Hill was the first bona fide superstar in Negro baseball. He hit for average, hit with power, fielded flawlessly, had a strong throwing arm, and ran like a deer. The fleet-footed centerfielder began his baseball career with the Pittsburgh Keystones in 1899, at the age of 19. Most of his career, however, was spent playing for Rube Foster, first with the Chicago American Giants and later with the Detroit Stars.

J. Preston "Pete" Hill was always the key player on a Foster team—and for good reason. He patrolled the outfield like a gazelle. He had great range and, with the large open fields that existed at the turn of the century, he was able to run down many a ball that had looked like an extra base hit when leaving the bat. Once he had the ball in his possession, Hill was even more dangerous. He had a cannon for a throwing arm and dared baserunners to take an extra base on him. Very few took him up on the challenge.

Standing six-feet-one-inch tall and weighing about 215 pounds, Hill could circle the bases in record time. But it was at the plate where he gained his greatest notoriety. Pete Hill was a great hitter. He had a smooth, graceful swing that almost always found the ball. He seldom struck out. Cum Posey, one of the patriarchs of Negro baseball, claimed that Hill was the most consistent hitter he ever saw. Over one prolonged period in 1911, the Giants star hit safely in 115 out of 116 games.

Pete Hill was a member of Rube Foster's 1910 Leland Giants, one of the great black teams of the twentieth century. The lefthanded slugger rapped the ball at a .428 clip that year, as the Giants won 106 out of 113 games. The following year, with the team now called the Chicago American Giants, Hill batted an even .400. In 1912, he came back with a solid .357 average.

Hill played baseball in the United States for 28 years, retiring in 1926. He was a line-drive hitter, who sent extra base hits to all parts of the field. His career batting average in the Negro leagues was .326, according to Riley. The speedy outfielder also played winter ball in Cuba for six years, racking up a .307 career average. He won the Cuban League batting championship in 1911, swatting the ball at a .365 gait. In an era when a home run was a rarity, Pete Hill averaged about nine a year, on par with Frank "Home Run" Baker of the old Philadelphia Athletics.

Jimmy Lyons has been called the fastest man ever to play Negro league baseball. Certainly the five-foot-eight, 175-pound dynamo could run with the best of them. He succeeded Pete Hill as the centerfielder of the Chicago American Giants, and he led the Giants to pennants in each of the first three years of the Negro National League. Known more for his speed than his power, the lefthanded hitter still managed to slug nine home runs a year during his career.

One of the premier home run hitters of the old, dead ball days was Louis Santop of the Hilldale Daisies in the Negro National League. Santop was born in Tyler, Texas, on January 17, 1890. He began his baseball career with the Fort Worth Wonders in 1909. By that time, Santop had grown to full stature. He stood a towering six feet and four inches in height, a gigantic figure in those days, and he topped the scales at a mighty 240 pounds, all of it muscle.

During his 18-year career, Santop was primarily a catcher, the first Hall-of-Fame-quality catcher in Negro baseball history. The big Texan had a strong throwing arm and, with his enormous bulk, was an expert at blocking the plate. As good as he was defensively, however, he was even better offensively.

Known as "Big Bertha" for his cannonading of opposing pitchers, the lefthanded slugger hit many legendary blasts out of ballparks all across eastern America. The original "Big Bertha" was a mammoth, long-range cannon that the German army used during World War I to spew death and destruction over long distances. Louis Santop also spewed death and destruction over long distances. One legendary Santop home run was said to have been

Louis Santop, nicknamed "Big Bertha" because of his cannonading of opposing pitchers, was the Home Run King of the Negro Leagues from 1909 to 1926. He reportedly hit 400-foot home runs frequently during the dead ball era, with one blast carrying well over 500 feet (credit: Noir Tech Sports, Inc.).

in excess of 500 feet, a mighty wallop in the days before the lively ball. Sporadic statistics credit Santop with an average of ten home runs a year during the dead ball era, the highest average in Negro league baseball.

But Santop didn't stop with home runs. He also hit for a high average, putting together some astronomical seasons of .470, .422, .429, .455, .373, .358, .364, and .389, according to James A. Riley. His career batting average for 18 years was .364, a figure exceeded only by six other players in Negro baseball history.

Louis "Big Bertha" Santop was the top hitter and premier slugger of the early days of black baseball. He was also the greatest catcher of his day —a true Hall-of-Famer.

With the advent of the Negro National League in 1920, the achievements of the black baseball players began to be documented. And with the introduction of the lively ball, celebrated ·home run hitters emerged from these players' midst. Most black players played baseball year-round. They played in the Negro leagues during the summer, toured the country with major league all-star teams in the fall, and played winter ball in Cuba, Puerto Rico, or the Dominican Republic from December through March.

When the Eastern Colored League was formed in 1923, as a competitor of the Negro National League, it was only natural that the two groups would square off in a World Series. In 1924, the Kansas City Monarchs, with Bullet Joe Rogan, Heavy Johnson, and Dobie Moore, defeated the Hilldales, with Judy Johnson, Louis Santop, and Biz Mackey, in the first Negro World Series, five games to four, with one tie. The first of the three subsequent Series was won by the Hilldale Daisies; the Chicago American Giants won the second and third. Willie Foster, perhaps the greatest lefthanded pitcher in Negro league history, (and also Rube's kid brother), sparked the Giants to their two titles. In 1926, the 22-year-old fireballer won two series games without a loss, including a 1–0 shutout in the finale. The following year, the six-foot-one, 195-pound hurler won two more series games, including the decisive 11–4 clincher.

The Eastern Colored League folded after the 1928 season, ending the Negro league World Series temporarily. Several other ill-fated leagues followed, but none of them lasted long. Finally, in 1937, the Negro American League came into existence, and competed successfully with the Negro National League for the next eleven years. The World Series was reinstituted in 1942 and continued until the demise of the Negro National League in 1948. Jackie Robinson's entrance into major league baseball spelled doom for the segregated Negro circuits. The Negro National League was first to go, folding in 1948. The Negro American League held on for another 12 years, before calling it quits in 1960.

Many outstanding ballplayers graced the rosters of the first Negro National League clubs, including several of the top home run hitters of the period. Edgar Wesley was one of those players. The lefthanded-hitting first baseman joined the Chicago American Giants in 1918, moving to the Detroit Stars the following year. The big, burly slugger teamed with Turkey Stearnes to give the Stars a powerful, one-two clout for eight seasons. According to James A. Riley, Wesley had batting averages of .277, .290, .344, .338, .266, .424, .300, and .421 from 1920 through 1927. His .424 average gave him the batting championship in 1925. He also captured three home run titles, with 10 home runs in 1920, 17 in 1923, and 18 in 1925.

The tall, muscular Wesley was a good fielder as well as a slugger, and he was an aggressive baserunner. Some opponents even referred to his temperament as "mean." In any language, Edgar Wesley was a winner. He hated to lose.

Incomplete records compiled by John Holway credit Wesley with a .324 batting average for his 14-year career in the Negro professional leagues. His 84 home runs in 1,629 at bats give him a home run average of 28 home runs a year, the seventh highest home run average in Negro league history.

Another of the early sluggers was shortstop John Beckwith. Known as "The Black Bomber," the big, 230-pound slugger hit some of the longest shots seen in the old Negro leagues during his 20-year career. Playing for the Chicago Giants in 1921, the 19-year-old rookie became the first player to hit a ball over the left field fence in Cincinnati's Redland Field. It landed on the

John Beckwith, the "Black Bomber," hit some of the longest balls in Negro league history. He averaged 30 home runs a year over his 22-year career, with a .356 batting average. In 1930, he led the Eastern League in batting with a .480 average, while smashing 19 home runs in 50 games, to lead in that category also (credit: Noir Tech Sports, Inc.).

roof of a laundry behind the fence, a mammoth, 440-foot shot. He batted .398 that year.

Beckwith won two home run crowns during his career, with 19 home runs in 1930 and 9 home runs in 1931, in the abbreviated Negro league season. Although he consistently hit for a high average, several times exceeding the .400 mark, he won only one batting title, taking the coveted honor in 1930 with an average of .480.

In addition to playing shortstop, the talented Beckwith also played third base, catcher, and the outfield, and he played them all admirably. It didn't really matter where he played defensively, however. His bat did all the talking, and it spoke loud and clear. He hit the ball often, and he hit it hard. According to many of his contemporaries, he hit longer home runs than Mule Suttles, Turkey Stearnes, or Josh Gibson. Legend has it that he slugged one ball in Washington's Griffith Stadium that hit a sign behind the left field fence, 460 feet from home plate and 40 feet above the ground.

In spite of his enormous talent, however, the righthanded pull hitter was in constant trouble with his managers. He was a troublemaker who fought with opponents and teammates alike. As a result, he was shuttled around from team to team, playing with as many as ten teams in 20 years.

When John Beckwith retired in 1938, he left behind some very impressive batting statistics. His career batting average of .356 is exceeded by only seven men in Negro league history. His home run average of 31 home runs a year ranks up there with Suttles, Chino Smith, and Stearnes. His personality may have been deficient, but his baseball talents were second to none.

Another mighty slugger of the '20s was Oscar "Heavy" Johnson, a Bunyanesque outfielder with the Kansas City Monarchs, Baltimore Black Sox, and Memphis Red Sox. Standing six-feet tall, Johnson topped the scales at a blubbery 250 pounds. Defensively, he was a serious liability to his teams, but at the plate, he tattooed the ball with monotonous regularity. The big, righthanded slugger could hit either for distance or for average as the situation warranted. In 1923, Johnson sparked the Monarchs to the Negro National League pennant with a .380 batting average and a league-leading 18 home runs in just 80 games. The Monarchs, with a 57–23 win-loss record, finished ten games ahead of their nearest rivals, the Detroit Stars.

Heavy Johnson played in the Negro leagues for 12 years, finishing with a lifetime batting average of .363. His home run totals have not yet been assembled; but when they are, Johnson will be ranked in the top echelon of Negro league sluggers.

The most renowned of the fabled, early black sluggers was Charles "Chino" Smith, a stocky, five-foot-six, lefthanded hitter who played for the Brooklyn Royal Giants and the New York Lincoln Giants from 1925 through 1930. Called "Chino" because of his oriental features, the diminutive demolition expert hit vicious line drives to all sections of the ballpark. He was a dangerous contact hitter who seldom struck out. Twice he led the Negro National League in batting. In 1929, he tattooed the ball at a .461 clip, leading the league with 28 doubles as well as 23 home runs. The following year, he again showed the way in hitting with an average of .429.

Smith had great wrist speed and outstanding bat control. He usually hit the ball where it was pitched, but he could be a dangerous pull hitter when the situation called for it. He participated in the first Negro league game ever played in Yankee Stadium. Stationed in Babe Ruth's spot in right field, and hitting third in the batting order, little Chino put on a Ruthian exhibition. In four at bats, he pulled two homers into the right field stands, tripled to left field, and drew a base on balls. He finished the day three for three with six RBIs.

Smith had the utmost confidence in his hitting ability. He also had little regard for pitchers, often bragging to them before the game, how he was going to punch out two or three hits that day. If the opposing crowd was particularly boisterous when he came to bat, little Chino, in the ultimate act of contempt, would often watch two strikes go by, spitting at the ball as it crossed the plate. Then he would line the next pitch back through the box, clotheslining the pitcher on its way to center field. Once he had reached first base, the little hitting machine would wave to the crowd and smile at the pitcher, with one last taunt—"Made you duck."

Chino Smith's talents were not restricted to playing against Negro league teams. He played ten games against major league opponents, and treated them just like he treated everyone else. He ripped the likes of Adolfo Luque and Ed Rommel for a sizzling .405 batting average, with one home run in 37 at bats. He also played ball in Cuba for five years, averaging .335. Tragically, the native of Columbia, South Carolina, contracted yellow fever in Cuba during the winter season of 1930-31. He died in that island nation on January 16, 1932. He was not yet 30 years old.

He left behind batting records that may never be broken. He is the all-time Negro league batting champion with a lifetime average of .428, which is 50 points higher than Larry Doby and 66 points higher than Josh Gibson. Many Negro league veterans, including Satchel Paige, called Smith the greatest hitter the Negro leagues ever produced.

Not only could Smith hit for average, he could hit for distance as well. Over his abbreviated, six-year career, the young slugger walloped an average of 33 home runs a year (based on 550 at bats), putting him in select company. How he compared with his major league counterparts will be examined later, when the necessary adjustments are made to put the various leagues on an equal basis.

The first decade of the lively ball and the first decade of the professional Negro leagues coincided. In addition to the renowned long ball hitters mentioned above, the 1920s produced two of the greatest home run hitters in baseball history, the aforementioned Norman "Turkey" Stearnes and George "Mule" Suttles. Stearnes, one of the all-time great Negro league outfielders appeared on the scene in 1923. The slim, 168-pound bundle of dynamite is often considered to be the greatest centerfielder in Negro league history, Oscar Charleston and Cool Papa Bell not withstanding. Stearnes could do it all: hit, hit with power, run, field, and throw. In 1923, as a 22-year-old rookie with the Detroit Stars, the speedy ballhawk stung the ball at a .353 clip and led the league in home runs with 16 in 232 at bats. In all, the Nashville, Tennessee, native captured home run honors seven times. He hit 10 homers in 231 at bats in 1924, 18 homers in 324 at bats in 1925, 21 homers in 313 at bats in 1927, 24 homers in 310 at bats in 1928, 8 homers in 131 at bats in 1931, and 5 homers in 137 at bats in 1932. He also hit 20 homers in 301 at bats in 1926 but lost the home run race to Mule Suttles's 26 round trippers. Stearnes also won the Negro National League batting championship in 1935 with an average of .430.

The lefthanded-hitting outfielder was at his best in postseason play. In three league playoffs and one World Series, he stung the ball at a .474 clip, with 11 extra base hits in 38 at bats. Four of his blows were home runs. He also played in 14 games against major league competition after postseason play had ended, hitting against pitchers like Sloppy Thurston, Larry French, and Bucky Walters. He hit a respectable .313 against the big boys, with three doubles and four home runs in just 48 at bats.

Turkey Stearnes played in the Negro National League for a total of 14 years, never hitting less than .299. His career mark of .352 ranks in the top ten in Negro league annals, and his 181 career home runs is second to Mule Suttles's 190. These numbers may change as more Negro league data is developed. At the present time, all Negro league records are incomplete due to poor record keeping, lack of newspaper coverage, etc. However, dedicated researchers, like John Holway and other members of SABR, are continuing to search the media records in an effort to reconstruct a complete statistical summary of the Negro leagues.

In addition to being a big home run hitter, the fleet-footed center fielder could fly around the bases, as evidenced by his extra base hits. He ranks third in career doubles in the Negro leagues with 201 and first in triples with 107. He averaged 33 doubles and 18 triples per year. In the long ball department, Turkey Stearnes averaged 30 home runs a year, the fourth best in Negro league history, behind Josh Gibson, Mule Suttles, and Chino Smith.

Norman Turkey Stearnes was a true superstar.

George "Mule" Suttles, a husky, six-foot-six first baseman, entered the Negro National League the same year Turkey Stearnes did, in 1923. The 230-pound slugger was a mediocre fielder, but with a bat in his hands, he took back seat to no one. The rugged, righthanded batter swung one of the heaviest bats in baseball, a mammoth 50 ounce model. He waved that big wand from the heels on every pitch, hitting towering home runs wherever he played. Unlike Josh Gibson, who hit line drives into the seats, Suttles uppercutted the ball, sending it into orbit, much like Babe Ruth. No one hit a ball any higher or farther than Mule Suttles.

Mule's titanic blasts are legendary, not only in the Negro leagues, but in Cuba, where he played winter ball, and around the major leagues as well. Suttles played Negro league ball for 22 years, compiling a lifetime batting average of .329. He is the all-time Negro league home run leader with 190 circuit clouts to his credit. These numbers will probably change as new statistics are added to the history of the Negro leagues.

Mule Suttles had a career season in 1926. The 27-year-old slugger led the league with 19 triples, 26 home runs, and a .418 batting average. He also laced out 25 doubles in just 342 at bats. In 1929 he hit 20 home runs in 320 at bats, and in 1930 he smashed 20 homers in only 203 at bats. He set one record in 1930 that will probably never be broken—perhaps not even tied. In one inning, the big righthander hit three home runs.

The strapping first baseman took special pleasure in punishing major league hurlers. He played 29 times against the top white teams over a period of eleven years, facing pitchers like Earl Whitehill, Bobo Newsome, and Lefty Grove. He tagged George Uhle, Newsome, Bucky Walters, and Larry French for home runs over the years, piling up 11 circuit blows in all. His .374 batting average in 99 at bats included four doubles and five triples, in addition to the 11 homers.

When Suttles stepped to the plate, particularly if the game was on the line, the chant of "kick, Mule, kick" would reverberate through the stands. More often than not, Mule would respond with a colossal blast into the upper atmosphere.

Mule Suttles averaged 34 home runs a season in the Negro leagues, second only to Josh Gibson. It is too bad that most of the baseball fans of America never had the chance to see Mule in action. His kick was something to behold.

One modern-day slugger who graduated from the ranks of the Negro leagues to star in the majors was Luke Easter. Big Luke stood six-foot-five and weighed a prodigious 240 pounds. When he planted his feet in the batter's box, and waved that big bat of his, not many pitchers were inclined to let go of the ball.

Easter started his baseball career late in life, joining the Negro league Cincinnati Crescents at the ripe old age of 30. The lefthanded slugger spent three years in Negro ball, posting a solid .336 batting average and slamming 23 home runs in 434 at bats. His Negro league home run average, based on 550 at bats, was 29, putting him in sixth place in Negro league history.

The Cleveland Indians obtained Easter's contract in 1949 and sent him off to San Diego in the Pacific Coast League for seasoning. A .363 batting average and 25 homers during the first half of the PCL season convinced Cleveland manager Lou Boudreau that the big man was ready, and he was quickly promoted to the big club.

Luke Easter, the 34-year-old rookie, cracked 28 home runs in 1950, with 107 runs batted in. He went on to spend three full seasons in a Cleveland uniform, holding down first base and driving in runs in bunches. The towering lefty walloped a total 93 home runs in 1,725 at bats for the Indians, an average of 30 home runs per year. He followed his rookie season with 27 homers and 103 runs batted in 1951, then hit 31 homers with 97 RBIs the following year.

The aging veteran drifted down to the minors during the '54 season, and he thrilled the crowds in the International League for another eleven years, before hanging up the spikes for good in 1964 at the age of 49.

Luke Easter was one of the premier sluggers in the Negro leagues during his abbreviated three-year career, and he was near the top of the pack in the American League as well. His minor league career was even more impressive. In 13 years in AAA ball, the big, likable slugger tattooed opposing

George "Mule" Suttles was one of the greatest sluggers in Negro league history. His 190 career home runs are the most yet recorded in the Negro league. Statistics for the league are still incomplete, and change frequently as more box scores are discovered (credit: John B. Holway).

pitchers for 36 home runs a year, while posting a .296 batting average and driving in an average of 121 runs.

If Luke Easter had started plying his trade early in life, instead of beginning his baseball career at an age when other players are thinking of retirement, there's no telling what he might have accomplished. His potential was unlimited.

There were other talented sluggers in the Negro leagues, players like Martin Dihigo, Cristobal Torriente, Oscar Charleston, and Buck Leonard, but none of them were in the same class as Beckwith, Suttles, Stearnes, and Smith.

And none of the above power hitters were in the same class with Josh Gibson, at least not on a frequency basis. Some of them, like Suttles and Beckwith, may have hit the ball as far as the jovial giant did, but none of them ever came close to hitting them as often as he did. Gibson was on another level.

Physically, Joshua Gibson was a magnificent specimen, having grown to six feet in height and tipping the scales at more than 200 pounds by the age of 16. The former amateur swimming champion played semipro baseball for four years before catching on with the Homestead Grays of the Negro National League in 1931.

The teenage slugger immediately made his mark on the Negro leagues, ripping the ball at a .368 clip and leading the league in home runs with six in just 32 games. The following year, he led the league in homers again, this time with seven. In all, the husky catcher showed the way in home runs nine times in 17 years. His best year was 1946 when he slugged 18 round trippers in 119 at bats.

Gibson played baseball 12 months a year, traveling to Cuba, Mexico, and the Dominican Republic during the winter months. In 1938, he led the Cuban Winter League with 11 home runs in just 186 at bats. He topped both the Mexican League and the Puerto Rican League in home runs in 1941, totaling 46 round trippers in 481 at bats between the two countries.

According to those who knew him, Josh Gibson was the strongest man in baseball. He smashed some of the longest home runs ever hit out of major league parks. He is reputed to be the only batter ever to hit a fair ball out of Yankee Stadium. He hit two of the three balls that went over the left field wall in Washington's Griffith Stadium. The other was hit by Mickey Mantle.

Gibson was more than just a home run hitter, however. He was a dangerous contact hitter with quick wrists. His short, compact stroke allowed him to hit a ball anywhere around the plate, making him a difficult batter to fool. He seldom struck out. Like Joe DiMaggio and Ted Williams, Josh Gibson had years where he had more home runs than strikeouts. Although Negro league records are sparse, John Holway uncovered two years in Mexico that typified Gibson's strikeout/home run ratio.

Year	AB	H	SO	BB	HR	BA
1940	92	43	6	16	11	.467
1941	358	134	25	75	33	.374

Only a handful of batters in the history of baseball can match these statistics.

Josh Gibson was not a one-dimensional player. He had all the superstar qualifications, including above-average foot speed. The big man led the Negro league in triples three times and averaged 14 triples for every 550 at bats over his career. He even showed the way in stolen bases once.

Defensively, "Big Boy" as he was affectionately called, worked hard at his trade to become a first-class receiver. He always had a strong, accurate throwing arm and was a good handler of pitchers, but he had to overcome

Josh Gibson (right) led the Puerto Rican league in batting (.480), slugging percentage (.957), and home runs (13 in 123 at bats), in the 1941-42 season. Here he accepts his most valuable player trophy from Luis Rosario Jr., Sports Director of El Imparcial *newspaper (credit: Luis Alvelo).*

an early weakness on high pop flies. As with everything else he tried, he mastered that with time.

When Josh Gibson died prematurely of a stroke in 1947, he left behind a legacy for future generations to shoot at. His .362 lifetime batting average is fifth on the all-time Negro league list. His home run total of 146 trails only

Mule Suttles and Turkey Stearnes. When you realize that Gibson had only half as many at bats as his two adversaries, his home run totals suddenly assume immense proportions. Based on an average of 550 at bats per year, Gibson's home run average was 48, far exceeding the averages of either Suttles (34) or Stearnes (30).

In the entire annals of Negro baseball, no hitter ever dominated the sport as completely as did Josh Gibson. On the mound, Satchel Paige had serious competition from Smokey Joe Williams, Bullet Joe Rogan, and Cannonball Dick Redding for the title of the world's greatest pitcher, but no one challenged Gibson for the title of the world's greatest home run hitter.

Josh Gibson was a legend in his own time. And his stature as a world class slugger grows larger with each passing year.

CHAPTER 6

COMPARISON OF LEAGUES

The greatest home run hitters of all time have been established within their own leagues. They include:

Charley Jones
Sam Thompson
Dan Brouthers
Roger Connor
Tilly Walker
Gavvy Cravath
Babe Ruth
Ralph Kiner
Harmon Killebrew
Joe Bauman
Dick Stuart
Bobby Crues
Sadaharu Oh
Josh Gibson
Mule Suttles
Chino Smith
Turkey Stearnes

On a strictly statistical basis, the leading sluggers in professional baseball history, those few players to hit an average of 40 or more home runs a year are

Joe Bauman (American Minor Leagues) . . . . 54 home runs a year
Sadaharu Oh (Japan Major Leagues) . . . . 52 home runs a year
Josh Gibson (Negro National League) . . . . 48 home runs a year
Babe Ruth (American Major Leagues) . . . . 47 home runs a year
Dick Stuart (American Minor Leagues) . . . . 46 home runs a year
Bobby Crues (American Minor Leagues) . . . . . . 40 home runs a year

In order to identify the greatest individual home run hitter of all time, baseball's King of Swat, the performances of the top players had to be evaluated on the same level. That required comparing one league with another and then making certain adjustments to put all individual playing records on an equal basis. The major leagues were used as the base point. All statistics from the minor leagues, the Japanese leagues and the Negro leagues were adjusted to a major league level. Within the major leagues themselves, the lively ball era was considered the norm. Statistics from the dead ball era and from the nineteenth century were adjusted to the lively ball era as closely as possible.

It should be noted up front that this exercise neither was nor is intended to be a scientific study. Far from it. It is solely an introduction to the subject matter, an attempt to stimulate interest in the relative accomplishments of the foremost sluggers around the world, some famous and some who toiled in relative obscurity. Hopefully, in future years, more in-depth studies will be conducted concerning this same topic. A detailed statistical analysis will either verify or contradict the findings of this rudimentary work. Eventually, purely scientific results will give credence to the relative positions in their chosen field of such famous names as Josh Gibson, Babe Ruth, Sadaharu Oh, and Joe Bauman.

Actually, before embarking on the comparison phase of the study, there are a number of misconceptions that should be cleared up. To begin with, certain minor league parks and leagues have been denigrated as "home run havens." These include the parks that fell victim to the four-base assaults of Joe Hauser, Dick Stuart, Joe Bauman, and Tony Lazzeri. The facts concerning these records bear repeating one more time. Joe Hauser hit 63 home runs for Baltimore in the International League in 1930. In 41 years, only three other Baltimore players hit more than 50 home runs in one season, and none of them exceeded 54. With Minneapolis in the American Association, Hauser sent 69 balls screaming skyward in 1933, a new professional baseball record at the time. Over a 31-year period, only four International League players hit 49 or more home runs. Joe Hauser did it twice. Ted Williams played for Minneapolis in 1938, and the best he could do was 43. Dick Stuart smashed 66 homers for Lincoln in the Western League in 1966. As was noted earlier, teams representing Lincoln participated in professional baseball over a period of 56 years, but no other Lincoln player even hit as many as 50 home runs in a single season. Tony Lazzeri walloped 60 home runs for the Salt Lake City Bees in the Pacific Coast League in 1925. He accomplished that feat over a 200-game schedule. Adjusted to a 154-game schedule, his home run total would have been a modest 44. In total, only 7 players hit over 50 home runs in the PCL in 89 years, even with the longer schedule, and, except for Lazzeri, no one hit more than 56. Joe Bauman almost single-handedly destroyed the Longhorn League in the early '50s, hitting 50 or more homers three years in a row, with a record high of 72 in 1954. The Longhorn League was in existence for only nine years, and Bauman led the league in home runs during four of those years. The home run leader, during the other five years, averaged 37 homers a year, which is similar to the leading home run averages in the National League, the International League, the American Association, and the Pacific Coast League. The American League average is 41.

So much for home run havens. It is time to give the home run kings their due. Hauser, Stuart, and Bauman were presented with an opportunity, and they took advantage of it. Thousands of other players had the same opportunities, but couldn't pull the trigger.

A review of the great home run hitters in professional baseball history revealed that to date there have been 59 hitters who have hit 50+ home runs in a single season. Nine of those men had multiple 50-homer seasons, led by the inimitable Babe Ruth with four such years. Sadaharu Oh had three 50+ seasons, as did Joe Bauman. Broken down by league classification, there were twelve 50-homer seasons in the American League, seven in the National League, five in the Japanese Central League, three in the Japanese Pacific League, seven in the Pacific Coast League, four in the International League, three in the American Association, three in the Longhorn League, and five in the West Texas–New Mexico League.

A further breakdown, by decade, shows that the period from 1930 through 1959 was the peak period for the long ball hitters. From 1930 through 1939, the 50-home run barrier was broken 14 times. From 1941 through 1949, it was broken 15 times. And from 1951 through 1959, it was broken 19 times — at least once in all league classifications. It seems as if everyone wanted to get into the act during the '50s. The appendix identifies all the culprits in these heinous crimes against defenseless pitchers.

One of the major reasons for the sudden explosion of home runs appears to have been related to a rapid increase in the popularity of minor league baseball. The history of the minor leagues has been one of wild fluctuations in the number of operating leagues. From a modest beginning in the late 1800s, the number of leagues grew to 52 in 1910. By 1919, there were only 12 leagues still in existence, and by 1930 the number was 23. Then another boom period set in, with the number of leagues increasing to 44 in 1939, then up to 59 in 1949. Ten years later, the minor league membership had dwindled once again, this time to 21. It has remained relatively stable for the past 36 years.

The rapid increase in minor league baseball in the '30s, '40s, and '50s, was a great boon to talented home run hitters. They, more than anyone else, took advantage of the thin pitching staffs to deposit record numbers of balls over the fences and into the distant grandstands. When stability returned to professional baseball in the late '50s, the era of the 50+ home run hitter came to an end. Since 1957, a period of 39 years, there have been only 21 players who hit 50 or more home runs in a year. Eight of those players performed in the Japanese leagues, seven in the major leagues, and only six in the American minor leagues. A breakdown of the minor league totals show that, of the six 50+ home run hitters, three players accomplished their feats in the Mexican League, where the rarefied air still gives balls a big boost. The other three minor league sluggers played in the Pacific Coast League, and only one of them can be considered "legitimate." Bill McNulty of Sacramento belted 55 round trippers in 144 games in 1974. His teammate Gorman Thomas chipped in with 51. It should be noted that the Sacramento team hit a total of 305 home runs that year (a professional baseball record), thanks to the friendly, 233-foot left field fence in Hughes Stadium. Eight years later, Ron Kittle of Edmonton whacked 50 home runs. He is the last minor leaguer outside Mexico to perform that feat. Jack Pierce of Leon was the last Mexican Leaguer to hit 50+ home runs when he smacked 54 in 1986. The only professional players to reach the 50-home run plateau since 1986 are American Leaguers Cecil Fielder of Detroit, Albert Belle of Cleveland, Mark McGwire of Oakland, and Brady Anderson of Baltimore.

Information on the 50+ home runs hitters and on the breakdown by league classification and decade can be found in the appendix. The present home run leaders in many of the league classifications, from Roger Maris in the American League to Ken Guettler in the Texas League, can also be found there.

Major Leagues: The Game Pre–1920

The first step in the establishment of a major league base point, was to compare nineteenth century baseball with twentieth century baseball and the dead ball era with the lively ball era. We identified the foremost long ball hitters of the nineteenth century as Charley Jones, Sam Thompson, Roger Connor, Dan Brouthers, and Harry Stovey.

It was extremely difficult to evaluate the relative skills of these players and of any players whose careers predated 1893. Prior to that time, the game was in a constant state of flux, with playing rules and field dimensions changing almost every year. Many primitive rules were in effect during the early years of the National League. The batter could call for the type of pitch he wanted to hit, high or low, until 1887. More than four balls were required for a base on balls and more than three strikes were required for a strikeout until 1889. The pitcher was restricted to throwing the ball underhand until 1881. It was 1884 before he was allowed to pitch overhand.

The ballparks themselves were poor cousins of today's stadiums. In the nineteenth century, most baseball fields had strange shapes, with short foul lines and unrealistically long center field fences. Many of the fields were used for other athletic activities, such as bicycle races, track and field events, polo matches, etc. As a result, many fields were oblong nightmares, not unlike today's Los Angeles Coliseum.

A representative sampling of such fields is listed below.

| | | Distance, Feet | | |
Baseball Park		LF	CF	RF
West Side Pk., Chicago	1885–1891	216	500	216
West Side Grounds, Chicago	1894–1915	340	560	316
League Park II, Cinc.	1894–1901	253		
Nat'l League Pk. II, Cleve.	1887–1890	410	420	410
League Pk. I, Cleve.	1891–1909			290
Eclipse Pk. I, L'ville	1882–1893	360	495	320
Polo Grounds IV, N.Y.	1890–1911	277	500	258
Philadelphia BB Grounds	1891–1909	500		310
Exposition Pk. III, Pitts.	1891–1909	400	450	400
Sportsmans Pk. I, St. Louis	1882–1892	350	460	285
Union Grounds, St. Louis	1884–1886	285		285
Average Distance to Fences		339	484	309

Two things are immediately apparent. First, as noted previously, most parks had spacious outfields, making home runs hard to come by. There were never any home runs hit over the center field fences in those parks. Secondly, many parks favored lefthanded hitters, as can be seen by the short, right field foul lines, which averaged 30 feet less than the left field foul lines. This inequity has also continued throughout most of the twentieth century and is just now being corrected.

Most home runs were either hit close to the foul lines or were inside-the-park home runs past the outfielders. This wide open expanse of outfield explains the high number of triples that were hit during the first fifty years of the major leagues' existence.

Very few home runs were recorded during the first forty-four years of major league play. Other than Ned Williamson's 27 homers in 1884, only four other batters hit as many as 20 home runs in a single season, from 1876 through 1918. They were Sam Thompson (20 in 1889), Buck Freeman (25 in 1899), Frank Schulte (21 in 1911), and Gavvy Cravath (24 in 1915). Triples were another story. Thirty-eight players hit 20 or more triples in a season through 1918. Two even surpassed the 30 mark. The top nine major league leaders in career triples played during the dead ball era. The leader was Sam Crawford with 312 three baggers.

Other differences in the nineteenth century game centered around the pitcher. Until 1881, the distance from the pitcher's mound to the plate was only 45 feet, and the pitchers had to throw underhand. In 1881, the pitching distance was extended to 50 feet, and the pitcher was allowed to throw sidearm. Three years later, the pitcher was permitted to throw overhand. Finally, in 1893, the pitching distance was lengthened to its present 60 feet and 6 inches.

As noted earlier, the ball in use during the first 45 years of professional baseball was a far cry from today's ball. It was almost entirely handmade, resulting in mediocre construction, ball-to-ball variation, and a soft product by modern standards. Since only one ball was used during a game, it became badly discolored, misshapen, and spongy in the late innings.

It is almost impossible to measure the effects of the various changes on the home run percentages of the individual players. A study of several dozen players whose careers covered the years prior to, and after, the 1893 pitching change indicates that the longer pitching distance had no effect on the number of home runs hit in the league, but that it had a significant effect on the batting averages, as might be expected. Once pitchers had to throw the ball from a distance of 60 feet instead of 50 feet, the hitters dug in and tattooed the ball at a livelier pace. Batting averages increased approximately 35 points over the last seven years of the decade.

Individually, some ballplayers did see an increase in their home run production after 1892. Big Sam Thompson led the way, jumping his home run totals from 10 to 14 per year. Roger Connor's average increased from 9 to 11, but Dan Brouthers dingers went down from 8 per year to 7. The fact that Brouthers was 35 years old when the change took place may have had something to do with the decrease. Some players, like Harry Stovey, completed their careers before the pitching distance was lengthened.

Other averages of interest include Ed Delahanty's, and Billy Hamilton's. From strictly a batting average standpoint, both Delahanty and Hamilton experienced significant increases in their batting averages, which was to be expected. As far as home runs were concerned, Billy Hamilton, who was a Punch-and-Judy-type hitter, continued to rack up his three home runs a year. Big Ed Delahanty, on the other hand, increased his homer output from four to eight after 1892.

The hitting philosophy in the dead ball era was to protect the plate at all costs and to make contact with the ball. It was strictly a defensive philosophy. The inferior baseball in use at the time made it unproductive to try for home runs, particularly in the large ballparks that were then in vogue. As a result, batters carried warclubs to the plate: large, cumbersome weapons that were heavy to carry and unwieldy to swing. The average bat weighed in the neighborhood of 40 ounces and was 35 inches long. Some bats weighed more than 50 ounces.

Major league hitters of the dead ball era didn't strike out much. They choked up on the bat, giving them good bat control, and they slapped at the pitch, hitting it where it was pitched—but they seldom got enough snap in their swing to drive the baseball out of the park. The best they could hope for was a "gapper" that would split the outfielders for extra bases. At the same time, pitchers discolored the balls so badly with tobacco juice, licorice, and dirt that it was hard to see the pitch after an inning or two. It was definitely a pitcher's game.

During the first decade of the twentieth century, club owners discouraged batters from hitting the long ball. Many owners felt that long ball hitters were a brutish lot, who relied on sheer muscle power at the expense of brain power. They generally hired small, fast, quick-thinking individuals who could field and make contact with the ball consistently. Players like Sam Thompson and Dan Brouthers were considered oafish louts by many in baseball's inner circle.

The average number of home runs per team, over the first quarter of a century after the legalization of overhand pitching, is shown in the table below.

Years	Home Runs Per Team, Per Year
1884–1892	39
1893–1899	36
1900–1909	19

As can be seen, the lengthening of the pitcher's mound to a 60-foot-6 inch distance from the plate did not increase the number of home runs hit in the league. In fact, the averages show a slight decrease, although that was probably coincidental.

The game, at the turn of the century, was one of pitching, defense, and close-to-the-vest strategy. Games were normally low-scoring affairs, with few home runs. The outcome was, more often than not, decided on singles, bases on balls, sacrifice hits, hit-and-run plays, stolen bases, and squeeze plays. Home run averages plummeted after 1900. Teams had averaged approximately 36 home runs a season during the "Gay Nineties," as shown above, but after 1900 that number dropped to a minuscule 19.

A new, cork-centered ball was introduced into the major leagues around 1910, reviving interest in the long ball. National League home runs jumped up from 19 per year per team to an almost normal 31. New sluggers emerged from the bushes wielding their lumber with abandon. Still, the home run averages remained modest, with Gavvy Cravath's 24 circuit blows in 1915 being the record for the period from 1910 through 1918—and being only the third time a player had exceeded the 19 home run mark.

In 1919, things began to change. A pitcher-turned-slugger by the name of Babe Ruth suddenly began to hit baseballs to legendary distances. His 29 home runs in only 432 at bats for the Boston Red Sox broke the all-time major league home run record of 27, set by Ned Williamson 35 years previously, and instilled a new excitement and interest in the national sport.

In 1920, the owners, desirous of cultivating this new curiosity, took steps to improve the batter's chances of hitting home runs, making the game more offensive-minded at the same time. First, they inserted a jacked-up baseball into the game to give hitters a better shot at driving the ball out of the park. Second, they took away some of the advantage that pitchers had enjoyed over the previous decade by outlawing trick pitches such as the spit ball, emery ball, and shine ball. They also changed balls more frequently during the game, once again aiding the batter by giving him a livelier ball to swing at in the late innings.

The incomparable Babe Ruth was the major benefactor of all the changes. His home run total suddenly exploded from his record 29 homers in 1919 to an unbelievable 59 homers in 1920. The New York strongman seemed to hit the baseball twice as far as any other player in professional baseball. In fact, no other player in the major leagues hit more than 19 home runs that year.

As the years passed, more and more players disdained the choked-up batting grip—a la Ty Cobb—and converted to Babe Ruth's hold-the-bat-at-the-end-and-swing-for-the-fences philosophy. Major league home run production jumped from 447 in 1919 to 1,093 in 1928. In 1950, it broke the magic 2,000 home run barrier, with 2,073 circuit blows being recorded: 1,100 in the National League and 973 in the American League.

The home run performances of more than a dozen long ball hitters who took dead aim at the new lively ball during the transition period from the dead ball, from about 1910 to 1930, were studied in detail to determine the effect the lively ball had on home run averages. The results of this study are shown below.

Average Home Runs Per Year

Player	Pre-1920	From 1920
Rogers Hornsby	7	25
Zack Wheat	6	12
Cy Williams	10	29
Ken Williams	7	24
Ty Cobb	5	7
Frank Baker	8	16
George Burns	6	6
Jack Fournier	6	18
Harry Hooper	3	9

Player	Pre-1920	From 1920
Baby Doll Jacobson	5	9
Stuffy McInnis	2	1
Emil Meusel	9	13
Ed Roush	4	6
Babe Ruth	24	50
George Sisler	4	7
Tris Speaker	4	9
Bobby Veach	3	9
Max Carey	4	5
Tilly Walker	7	23
Harry Heilmann	6	16
Total	130	294
Average	7	15

These averages indicate a doubling of home runs after the lively ball came into play in 1920. The actual factor from the above table is 2.14. In fact, the total number of home runs for both leagues increased by a factor of 2.51 from 1910 through 1929. From 1910 through 1919, the American and National Leagues hit a total of 4,007 home runs. Over the next decade, after the introduction of the lively ball, the two leagues sent 10,042 balls into orbit.

Individually, some players benefited more than others. Some players, like Ty Cobb, showed modest increases, while other players realized tremendous improvement. Rogers Hornsby's home run totals jumped up from 7 per year to 25; Cy Williams's totals went from 10 to 29; Ken Williams's totals went from 7 to 24; and Tilly Walker's totals increased from 7 to 23. The Babe, of course, led the way with an increase from 24 homers per year all the way up to 50 homers per year.

Like most of the batters in the dead ball era, Ruth swung a big, heavy bat, usually a 44 ounce model, 35 and a half inches long. Occasionally, he hefted a bludgeon that tipped the scales at an unbelievable 54 ounces. The difference between Ruth and the other players, however, was that Ruth held his bat down at the knob and swung for the fences on every swing. His cuts were sheer theatre, with gigantic misses and prodigious home runs mixed indiscriminately. Until the modern era of Mantle and Reggie Jackson, the Babe owned the major league career strikeout record with 1,330 K's in 8,397 at bats.

The two standout sluggers in the 1900-1919 era were Gavvy Cravath and Tilly Walker. Cravath, who led the National League in home runs six times between 1913 and 1919, averaged 17 homers a year in an 11-year career during the dead ball era. Using the factors calculated above, Cravath's totals would have been approximately 43 home runs a year in the modern era, making him a definite world-class slugger, perhaps second only to Babe Ruth.

Tilly Walker, whose career began in the dead ball era (1911) and ended in the lively ball era (1923), averaged 13 home runs a year. Interestingly, in his last full season in the majors, with the Philadelphia Athletics in 1922, the 35-year-old righthander smashed 37 home runs, second in the American League to Ken Williams and two ahead of Babe Ruth. Based on the dead ball era conversion factors, Tilly Walker would have pounded out 33 home runs a year, in the modern era, a figure that would make him one of the top 15 home run hitters in major league history.

The top sluggers of the pre–1900 era are more difficult to evaluate. In fact, it is impossible to predict with any certainty how they would have performed alongside the likes of Ruth, Cravath, Killebrew, or Kiner. The most significant rules change in the nineteenth century was the aforementioned lengthening of the distance from the pitcher's mound to home plate from 50 feet to sixty feet-six inches in 1893. According to National League statistics, the change had a major effect on batting averages, but did not impact home run production to any great extent.

The player who capitalized the most on the longer pitching distance was "Big Sam" Thompson of the Philadelphia Phillies. Big Sam's home run output increased from 10 home runs a year to 14 home runs a year after 1892. Considering the additional advantage of the lively ball, it is safe to say that Thompson would have hit 30–35 home runs a year in the modern era.

As awesome as Thompson's power was, he was not even considered the premier slugger of the nineteenth century. That honor belonged to Big Dan Brouthers, who played with several teams from 1879 through 1904. Brouthers's home run averages were impressive for his day, but would not put him in the upper echelon of today's big bombers. His home run average of 8 homers a year would give him a total of somewhere between 17–20 homers a year in today's game.

It was his overall slugging prowess that made Brouthers the most feared hitter of the nineteenth century. In addition to his home run output, Big Dan averaged 36 doubles and 17 triples a year, giving him an average of 61 extra base hits a year, one ahead of Harry Stovey. Thompson and Connor both averaged 55 extra base hits a year, and Charlie Jones chipped in with 48. Brouthers also led all his competitors in singles with 124 a year.

Brouthers extra base hit percentage was 11.3 percent, tops in the nineteenth century. His performance does not compare to the averages of the players who performed during the lively ball era, but it does put him ahead of Gavvy Cravath (11.0 percent) and Tilly Walker (10.5 percent). Additionally, Brouthers's career slugging average of .519 is the highest of any major league player prior to 1920. Big Sam Thompson and Ed Delahanty, with slugging percentages of .505 each, were the only other players prior to 1919 who had a slugging percentage over .500. By comparison, Gavvy Cravath had a slugging average of .478 and Tilly Walker had a slugging average of .427.

Although the numbers do not give a clear-cut prediction as to Brouthers's home run production in the modern era, it is safe to assume that he would have been in the 30+ homer class. The other long ball hitters of the nineteenth century—Charlie Jones, Roger Connor, and Harry Stovey—probably would have been pushing the 30-home run mark themselves. Big Ed Delahanty, another nineteenth-century slugger of note, might also have challenged the magic 30-home run average.

Neither Brouthers nor Thompson can be considered for the King of Swat title because their achievements cannot satisfactorily be evaluated on the same scale as modern day players. They do, however, deserve a special niche in the Home Run Hall of Fame, as the greatest sluggers of the nineteenth century. It is a toss up as to which one of them was the King of nineteenth-century sluggers. Let's call it a draw.

Major Leagues—The Lively Ball Era

From 1920 to about 1940, baseball was played under, more or less, uniform conditions. The big home run hitters, as noted previously, were Babe Ruth with an average of 50 home runs a year, Jimmie Foxx with 36, Hank Greenberg with 35, and Larrupin' Lou Gehrig with 34.

As the game moved into the modern, post–1940 era, it presented a variety of new distractions and inconveniences to the ballplayers. It also created many new changes, from a hitting standpoint, some that penalized the players and some that benefited them. The major differences between the modern era and the pre–1940 era included the standardization of the overall dimensions of the major league ballparks, the advent of night ball, air travel, major league expansion—with the resultant dilution of talent, the geographical increase in the major leagues—covering the entire United States and parts of Canada, and the increase in the physical size of the players.

The game gravitated toward standardization as the twentieth century progressed, particularly in the design of the baseball stadiums. During the first 50 years of major league play, as noted before, ballparks were vast areas of land favoring lefthanded batters. This inequity continued unabated into the 1950s. With the construction of new stadiums in Milwaukee, Houston, Los Angeles, and San Francisco, though, major league stadiums began to take on a more uniform look. The right and left field foul lines were essentially the same distance from the plate, favoring neither the righthanded nor the lefthanded hitter. The center field fence was a realistic 400-foot distance from the plate. The following table shows the changes in the dimensions of the major league ballparks over the first 100 years of play.

Distance, Feet

Time Period	LF	CF	RF
19th Century	339	484	309
1900–1910	353	492	332
1910–1920	355	440	327
1994	332	405	329

The old ballparks of the nineteenth century, such as West Side Park in Chicago and Sportsmans Park I in St. Louis, gradually gave way to new stadiums, made of steel and concrete. Sportsmans Park III, Ebbets Field, Shibe Park, Comiskey Park, Griffith Stadium, and Yankee Stadium began to show some conformity regarding the dimensions of the playing field, although some oddities like the Polo Grounds V, with its 256-foot right field fence, still remained.

In the 1950s baseball began to expand beyond its confined borders. Until that time, the isolated boundaries of big-time baseball consisted of Boston in the north and east and St. Louis in the south and west. In 1953, the Boston Braves uprooted their wigwams and moved to Milwaukee, Wisconsin. Within four years, the Dodgers abandoned Brooklyn for sunny California, as did the New York Giants. Soon, major league baseball was being played in such widely separated places as Seattle, Washington; Montreal, Canada; Atlanta, Georgia; Miami, Florida; and Denver, Colorado.

With expansion came uniformity in stadium design. Most modern ballparks now average about 330 feet down both the left and right field foul lines and 400 feet to dead center. Expansion resulted in the dilution of available talent as the original 16 major league teams increased to 28 by 1993. Theoretically, the big major league sluggers should have benefited from this thinning out of the talent pool. In 1961, there was some evidence that that had happened. When Los Angeles and Minnesota were added to the eight-team American League, the league home run totals shot up by 41 percent. Roger Maris led the bombardment with 61 homers, breaking Babe Ruth's 34-year-old season record. Mickey Mantle was second in the league with 54 homers, while four other players hit 40 or more. Not all the changes were beneficial to the hitters, however. Expansion also resulted in geographically widespread distances between cities. Long, tiring, two-week road trips had negative effects on a player's stamina. Prior to the 1950s, road trips were relatively comfortable excursions by railroad, from one-hour jaunts to Boston and New York to relaxed overnight trips to St. Louis and Chicago. With expansion, more cities had to be covered in the same amount of time. A team might play a game in Boston today, then jump a jet for a quick flight to Detroit for a game tomorrow.

The problems were further complicated by the increase in night baseball.

The first night game was played in Cincinnati in 1935. By the 1980s, most games were played under the lights. This condition caused many problems, some of them still unknown. Certainly, it created more of a physical drain on the players. Hopscotching from one city to another often resulted in playing a day game in one city after a night game in another city, with a hectic jet flight in between.

The heavy air associated with night games did, in most people's opinion, reduce the number of home runs that were hit, compared to day games. In addition, the damp, cold air caused more muscle-related injuries than when the game was played only in the warm sunlight. Expansion aggravated that even more by shuttling teams from one extreme climate to another and forcing them to play a game before their bodies became acclimated to the new conditions. It was possible to play in Montreal, Canada, one day, then hop a flight to Miami, Florida, for another game the following day. That 1,800 mile jaunt could result in a temperature swing of 50 or 60 degrees, with a correspondingly serious shock to the body's circulatory system.

One new factor that increased the potential for home runs was the physical size and conditioning of the athletes. In the nineteenth century, most players were in the range of five-foot-eight and 160 pounds. By 1950, an average player was about five-foot-ten and weighed in the neighborhood of 180 pounds. A few players like Williams and DiMaggio topped the six-foot mark by several inches, but very few of them went more than 200 pounds. As the 1980s progressed, more and more big men entered the game. Physical fitness became a fad throughout the United States, with an increase in body building through the use of weights and Nautilus equipment. Jose Canseco stands six-foot-three tall and weighs 240 pounds. His former teammate on the Oakland Athletics, Mark McGwire is six-foot-five and 225 pounds. Juan Gonzalez at six-three and 210 pounds and Frank Thomas at six-five and 257 pounds have become typical big leaguers, rather than anomalies.

It is difficult to measure all the changes that have taken place in major league baseball over the past 50 years, much less to determine if they have had an overall positive or negative effect on home run production. Perhaps the pros and cons have canceled each other out. For the purpose of this study, all statistics after 1920 were treated equal.

The evaluation of individual players, even within their own era, is complicated by the previously mentioned variability in stadium dimensions. John Thorn and Pete Palmer, in their book, *Total Baseball*, cover this thorny problem in some detail. In fact, they assigned a factor, called the HRF, or "home run factor," to every ballpark that has ever been used for major league baseball. An HRF of 100 is normal, and indicates that the same number of home runs are hit in that particular ballpark as are hit on the road. It should be noted that the HRF is not a quick fix when evaluating a baseball stadium, or a particular batter. In order for the HRF to be truly representative, the ballpark must be symmetrical, with equal distances down both foul lines, and equal distances to the power alleys. It must also be located in such a manner that the direction of the wind does not favor either the righthanded or lefthanded batters. This is not the case in many parks. For instance, the HRF for Yankee Stadium is given as 102. A close examination of individual batters, as we shall see, indicates that the HRF for "The House That Ruth Built" is more like 110 for lefthanded batters, and 71 for righthanded batters. In summary, the HRF is a valuable piece of information, but it must be used with discretion.

In a perfect world, all baseball stadiums would have an HRF of 100. Since this is not a perfect world, and probably never will be, HRFs will always be of interest to the studious baseball fan. As an example, Lake Front Park in Chicago, the home of the Chicago White Stockings, had a left field fence that stood only 180 feet away from home plate. Ned Williamson took advantage of that anomaly to establish a new home run record in 1884, by depositing 25 baseballs over that fence. He hit only two homers on the road. A quick check of the HRF explains the situation conveniently. The home run factor for Lake Front Park was 480, meaning that there were 4.8 times as many home runs hit in Lake Front Park as in the average park in the league. Lake Front's 480 HRF is the highest HRF in major league history.

The highest HRF in existing major league stadiums is 143 for Atlanta's Fulton County Stadium. That may soon be surpassed, however. The early results from Coors Field in Denver, Colorado, indicate an HRF in the neighborhood of 161 for baseball's newest park, which is not surprising when you consider the 5,176 foot altitude. The Rockies' big hitters took advantage of that HRF when four of them each smashed over 30 homers in 1995, tying a 17-year-old major league record, set by the Los Angeles Dodgers in 1978. Looking back on it, the Dodger mark was quite a feat, considering the fact that Dodger Stadium has an HRF of only 86, approximately half that of Coors Field. And both parks are basically symmetrical, favoring neither righthanded nor lefthanded batters.

The HRF is not a cure-all, however. As noted previously, the HRF of 102 for Yankee Stadium in New York is misleading because of the unusual design of the playing field. Until 1976, the Stadium was death on righthanded hitters, with a 402-foot left center field power alley and a 457-foot center field wall. Right field, on the other hand, has always been a tempting target for the likes of Ruth, Gehrig, Mantle, and Maris. The close-up, 296-foot right field foul pole opens up to a comfortable 344-foot shot to the right of the bullpen in right center field.

A study of the performances of a few of the Yankee sluggers will give a better understanding of the "true" HRF for the "House That Ruth Built." The Babe averaged 50 home runs in the Stadium and 47 home runs on the road. That converts to a home run factor of 106. Lou Gehrig's home run totals give credence to that number. Larrupin' Lou socked 36 homers in New York and 32 on the road, for an HRF of 113. It would appear therefore that left-handed batters had a decided advantage hitting in Yankee Stadium, significantly above the published factor of 102. From the other side of the plate, it was a different story. Joe DiMaggio hit an average of only 24 home runs a year out of the cavernous left field pastures in Yankee Stadium, but on the road, he walloped 34 circuit blows, giving him an HRF for Yankee Stadium of only 71.

It is obvious that significant differences exist, even within a particular ballpark, for hitting home runs. The HRFs of different stadiums will be discussed during this study, but there will be no attempt made to adjust home run totals, to standardize the performances of the individual players. That is beyond the scope of this study. It would be impossible to utilize HRFs in any case, since none exist for the minor league parks, the Japanese league parks, or most of the old Negro league parks.

The legendary Babe Ruth towered over major league baseball like a colossus. No player has been able to sustain a serious challenge to Ruth's home run frequency over an entire career. The Bambino's average of 47 homers for every 550 at bats remains one of the most secure records in professional baseball.

The Babe's nearest challengers in the major leagues were Harmon Killebrew and Ralph Kiner. Both righthanded sluggers averaged 39 homers a year during their careers, eight homers a year behind Ruth. In reviewing the home park advantage, it would appear that the New York slugger did not benefit from the short right field porch in Yankee Stadium. A closer look at the Babe's statistics, however, gives fascinating insight into his home run totals. Over a 22-year period, Ruth averaged 47 home runs a year at home and 46 home runs a year on the road. Those totals cover three different ballparks. If we look behind the numbers, we discover that Ruth, in fact, had a significant home field advantage in certain parks—and a significant disadvantage in others. During his first six years in the league, the powerful lefty played his home games in Boston, where he was hampered by Fenway Park's distant right field stands. He averaged only 11 home runs a year in Fenway, compared with 35 homers a year on the road. These totals do not approach his later statistics because they were accumulated during the waning days of the dead ball era; however, they do show a decided 3–1 home run advantage for Babe when he played away from Beantown.

His New York stats are eye popping. During Ruth's first three years in the big city, the Yankees played their home games in the Polo Grounds, since Yankee Stadium was not built until 1923. The Babe took advantage of the cozy, 256-foot right field foul line in the Giants' ballpark by slamming an astounding 63 home runs a year over the wall. He complemented that with 54 round trippers a year on the road. His Yankee Stadium home run averages, home and away, from 1923 through 1934, were 50 and 47, respectively. His total home run average, after the advent of the lively ball, was an even 50 home runs a year. There is no question that Babe Ruth was indeed in a class by himself when it came to hitting the long ball. However, if he had played his entire career in Boston, it is likely that his career home run totals would have been closer to 639 than 714. If, on the other hand, he could have played all his home games in the Polo Grounds, his home run total would have been a glittering 886. And, if he had played all his games, both home and away, in the Polo Grounds, his home run totals would have reached a staggering 962!

As for Killebrew, he experienced some benefits from his team's move from Griffith Stadium in Washington, D.C., to Metropolitan Stadium in Minneapolis, Minnesota. "Killer" whacked 36 homers a year out of Griffith Stadium with its 388-foot left field wall, but was able to propel 42 homers a year over Metropolitan Stadium's friendlier 340-foot barrier. If he had played in Minneapolis his entire career, his home run average of 42 would still have left him a good distance behind the immortal Ruth. His career home run totals would have increased a modest amount, from 573 home runs to 622.

One point of interest, for those who like to consider a player's home run potential from all perspectives—if Harmon Killebrew had played all his games, home and away, in Atlanta's Fulton County Stadium, with its home run factor of 143, instead of in Metropolitan Stadium in Minneapolis, with its 110 HRF, his home run average would have been an eye-popping 55, eight more than Hank Aaron's Atlanta average. He would not have passed Babe Ruth however. Using the same criteria, the Sultan of Swat would have sent 67 balls a year into the Atlanta firmament!

Ralph Kiner played most of his career in Forbes Field in Pittsburgh. In its early days, during the time Josh Gibson performed there, Forbes Field was a formidable target for righthanded batters. Left field usually measured a hefty 365 feet from home plate. The home run factor for Forbes Field was 75 for 1946, meaning that there were only 0.75 home runs hit in Forbes Field for every home run hit away from Forbes Field.

When the Pirates added rookie Kiner to their roster in 1946, and obtained Detroit slugger Hank Greenberg in 1947, they reduced the left field distance to 335 feet by adding a chicken-wire fence along the left field wall. Originally called "Greenberg Gardens," it was renamed "Kiner's Korner" after Greenberg retired following the '47 season. The addition of the fence effectively increased the Forbes Field home run factor from 75 to 121, giving Kiner a decided advantage in the National League home run derby. Realistically, it gave Kiner an 61 percent increase in home park home runs, strictly as a result of playing field design.

In 1946, Kiner hit 23 home runs in 502 at bats—adjusted to 25 homers for every 550 at bats. The following year, with Kiner's Korner in place, the

Pittsburgh slugger hit a league-leading 51 homers in 565 at bats—adjusted to 50 per 550 at bats. His home run average improvement of 100 percent can be attributed to an actual improvement of 56 percent (from 25 to 39) and an adjustment of 28 percent due to the new Forbes Field home run factor. Without the benefit of Kiner's Korner to aid him in 1947, Kiner would have hit an estimated 40 home runs, not 51!

Over the course of his 7+ year career in Pittsburgh, the California slugger hit 175 home runs in Forbes Field, compared with 126 home runs on the road. That equates to an HRF of 1.39, slightly higher than the actual Forbes Field HRF. During his Pittsburgh tenure, his home run average of 43 home runs a year was composed of 25 home runs a year in Forbes Field and 18 home runs a year on the road.

Prior to the construction of Kiner's Korner, over a period of 38 years, there were 41 percent more home runs hit on the road than were hit in Forbes Field. During the Kiner years, the home run average shifted dramatically in favor of Forbes Field, with 21 percent more homers hit there than on the road. In 1954, after Kiner was traded to Chicago, the chicken wire fence was torn down, and the left field distance was once again returned to 365 feet. Home run production dropped immediately back to its pre-Kiner ratios, with the road home runs outnumbering the Forbes Field home runs more than one and a half to one.

Ralph Kiner's career is another example of a ballpark being tailored to a hitter's strength. Billy Cox, a notorious singles hitter, pounded out 15 round trippers in 1947, after hitting only two the year before. Wally Westlake, a big, righthanded hitter, averaged 26 home runs a year when he played in Pittsburgh, but saw his average drop to 16 a year after he left the friendly confines of Kiner's Korner.

In fairness to Kiner, it should be pointed out that the 335-foot distance to the left field foul pole in Kiner's Korner, was not an unusually short distance by today's standards. In fact, most new major league baseball stadiums are approximately the same distance. Also, the center field wall remained a distant 435 feet from the plate. He did have an advantage in the left center field power alley, however, which was reduced from 406 feet to just 355 feet, a short chip shot for a slugger like Kiner. He also benefited from the atmospheric conditions around Pittsburgh, particularly the thin air at the 1,000-foot elevation. All things considered, Ralph Kiner's Pittsburgh home run totals appear to have been inflated by 21 percent over the totals for an average major league stadium, thanks to the natural advantage of the geography of the area, plus the installation of Kiner's Korner.

Two other sluggers who loved to play at home were Hank Aaron and Jimmie Foxx. As stated earlier, Hammerin Hank had a distinct home field advantage, averaging 47 home runs a year in Atlanta's Fulton County Stadium, 17 more than his average in Milwaukee's County Stadium. His on-the-road home run average was 32 in Milwaukee and 34 in Atlanta. A study of the statistics indicates that the move from Milwaukee to Atlanta added 79 home runs to Aaron's career totals. If Aaron had played all his games on the road, he would have accumulated 742 home runs, just slightly less than his actual numbers. If, on the other hand, he had played all his home games in Milwaukee, he would have hit just 674 homers, dropping him to second place in the major league home run derby, behind Babe Ruth. Conversely, if he had been able to flex his muscles in Atlanta's Fulton County Stadium for 23 years, he would have piled up the astounding total of 1,057 round trippers, surpassing the world record of Sadaharu Oh by some 289 circuit blows.

Hank Aaron's on-the-road home run average of 33 home runs per year is normal, based on the major league parks' home run factors. Therefore, his career home run total of 755 home runs is an accurate reflection of his capabilities. Aaron deserves his ranking as the number one career home run hitter in major league history.

Old Double-X profited from both of his home parks: Philadelphia's Shibe Park with its 334-foot left field fence and Boston's Fenway Park with the famous Green Monster hovering over the left fielder, only 315 feet from home plate. As discussed earlier, Foxx averaged 39 home runs a year in Shibe Park and 43 home runs a year in Fenway. His road average was 32 home runs a year. Since Foxx's most productive years were behind him by the time he was traded to Boston, one can only wonder what might have happened had he been able to play his entire career in Beantown. Old Double-X might have given the Bambino a run for his money.

Foxx's Shibe Park HRF of 126 exactly matches that calculated by Thorn and Palmer, which it should since Shibe Park is a symmetrical stadium. His Fenway Park HRF of 134 is significantly higher than the published one of 112, as would be expected in that misshapen facility. Actually, averaging Foxx's HRF for left field (134) and Ted Williams's HRF for right field (90) gives an average HRF for Fenway Park of 112, once again a match.

Some players appeared to enjoy a slight home field advantage, but not enough to significantly affect their career stats. Lou Gehrig hit 36 home runs at home and 32 away, while Willie Mays showed a 35–32 edge at home. Mickey Mantle's statistics were essentially the same, 37 homers in Yankee Stadium and 36 homers on the road.

Two famous long ball hitters were actually penalized by their home ballparks. They were Ted Williams and Joe DiMaggio. Williams, a lefthanded hitter, had to shoot at a right field area that opened up rapidly from 302 feet at the foul pole to 380 feet, a short distance away. Joltin' Joe's power alley in left center field was a monumental 402 feet from home plate. Since the two slugger's careers coincided, there were constant rumors that they would be traded for each other so they could practice their art in a stadium more designed to their physical qualifications. Nothing came of the rumors, however, and both Williams and DiMaggio finished their careers in the same parks they began playing in.

The statistics show that both were penalized by their home fields from a home run standpoint, although Williams was a better average hitter at home. "The Splendid Splinter" averaged 39 home runs a year on the road during his career, but only 35 home runs a year at Fenway. On the other hand, his .361 career batting average in Boston was 33 points higher than his road average. Joe DiMaggio's home run disparity was even greater than Williams's. The "Yankee Clipper" slugged 34 home runs a year away from Yankee Stadium, but could muster only 24 round trippers a year in the Bronx. His batting averages were .315 at home and .333 on the road.

The averages of the major league's foremost homerun hitters are presented below.

Player	AB	H	D	T	HR	BA
Babe Ruth	550	188	33	9	47	.342
Harmon Killebrew	550	141	20	2	39	.256
Ralph Kiner	550	153	23	4	39	.279
Ted Williams	550	189	38	5	37	.344
Jimmie Foxx	550	179	31	8	36	.325
Mickey Mantle	550	164	23	5	36	.298
Dave Kingman	550	130	20	2	36	.236
Mike Schmidt	550	147	27	4	36	.267
Willie McCovey	550	148	24	3	35	.270
Hank Greenberg	550	172	40	8	35	.313
Hank Aaron	550	168	28	4	34	.305
Lou Gehrig	550	187	37	11	34	.340

Note: Babe Ruth's home run average during the lively ball era, from 1920 through 1935, was 50 home runs a year. That's a full 28 percent more than his nearest competitors.

Other world class sluggers, and their average home run totals, include Hank Sauer (33), Willie Mays (33), Eddie Mathews (33), Frank Robinson (32), Roy Campanella (32), Reggie Jackson (31), Duke Snider (31), Ernie Banks (30), and Mel Ott (30).

No matter what criteria is used, Babe Ruth is in another league when compared with any other major league slugger. His best home run average was 63 homers a year in the Polo Grounds. By comparison, Ralph Kiner's average in Forbes Field was 49 homers a year. Hank Aaron's average in Atlanta was 47 homers a year. Jimmie Foxx hit 43 dingers a year in Boston. Harmon Killebrew averaged 42 homers a year in Minnesota. No one else exceeded 39.

In the matter of total extra base hits, Babe Ruth still led the way, averaging 89 extra base hits a year during his career. He was followed by Hank Greenberg with 83, Lou Gehrig with 82, and Ted Williams with 80.

Minor Leagues

There were a handful of minor league sluggers whose prodigious wallops left spectators gasping and researchers thumbing frantically through the record books. Joe Bauman, the minor league's all-time home run king, averaged 54 home runs for every 550 at bats during his much-interrupted, 16-year career, most of it spent in the Class C Longhorn League in New Mexico. In addition to having the highest career home run average in professional baseball history, he also holds the single-season mark of 72 home runs, set with the Roswell Rockets in 1954.

The Longhorn League was in existence for only nine years, from 1947 through 1955. It consisted of eight teams from the New Mexico–Texas border region, including Roswell, Artesia, Big Spring, Odessa, Midland, San Angelo, Sweetwater, and Vernon. During the first five years of play, the season home run leader averaged 37 home runs a year, a figure comparable to the numbers generated in the higher minor leagues, as well as in the major leagues. Joe Bauman led the league in home runs for the last four years of its existence, hitting 50, 53, 72, and 46 home runs, for an average of 55 homers a year, 49 percent more than previous league leaders.

Dick Stuart, another big boomer, split his time between the minor leagues, the majors, and the Japanese leagues. He played six years of minor league ball, nine years of major league ball, and two years of Japanese ball. His minor league average of 46 home runs per year included 66 home runs with Lincoln in the Class A Western League in 1956. Stuart's average of 31 home runs per year in the majors gives some indication of the relationship between the major leagues and the minor leagues from a home run standpoint.

Putting Stuart's 66 home run feat at Lincoln in perspective: Lincoln participated in several different professional leagues over a period of 56 years. Twenty six of those years were in the Western League. Over that period, only four league players hit 40 or more home runs in one season, and no one exceeded 44. No Lincoln player ever hit as many as 40 home runs in one year. Dick Stuart was in a class by himself.

Bobby Crues, the Amarillo Cannon, dominated the southwest territories during the late '40s and early '50s. His career home run average of 40 is exceeded only by Joe Bauman and Dick Stuart. Crues held a share of the all-time, professional-baseball, single-season home run record, with Joe Hauser, for six years, until Bauman topped it in 1954.

Joe Hauser, "Unser Choe" to thousands of Milwaukee fans, had distinguished careers in both the major leagues and the minor leagues. He was a star first baseman for the Philadelphia Athletics before a knee injury ended his big-league career in 1925. During the early '30s, Hauser was the scourge of the high minors, leading the International League or American Association in home runs four years in succession. Along the way, he became the only player in baseball history to hit 60 or more homeruns in one season, twice. Like Stuart, his statistics give a comparison between major league home run averages and minor league home run averages. Hauser averaged 21 home runs per year during his seven-year major league career and 34 home runs per year during his 19 years in the minors.

Analyzing Joe Hauser's mighty home run feats in the International League and the American Association provides strong evidence of his superiority in the slugging field. Over a period of 30 years, from 1930 through 1960, the individual home run leader in both leagues averaged 36 home runs a year. That compares favorably with the major league averages of 36 home runs in the National League and 41 home runs in the American League over that same period.

Joe Hauser hit 63 home runs for Baltimore in 1930. Only three other International League players exceeded 50 home runs in one year, Buzz Arlett (54 in 1932), George Puccinelli (53 in 1935), and Howie Moss (53 in 1947). Hauser's feat of hitting 69 home runs with Minneapolis in 1933 left his challengers far behind. Nick Cullops's 54 homers in 1930 and Tom Winsett's 50 round trippers in 1936 were the closest anyone could come to his level. Hauser's 49 homers in 1932 are still fourth on the all-time AA list. Again, like Stuart and Bauman before him, Joe Hauser was always on a higher level than his contemporaries in the high minors.

In 119 years of professional baseball, only 64 players have hit 50 or more home runs in one season. Just 12 sluggers have surpassed the 60 mark. The major leagues have had 17 players smash 50 or more homers, the last being Albert Belle of Cleveland in 1995. Babe Ruth and Roger Maris are the only big leaguers to break the 60 home run barrier.

In the high minors (AAA), a total of 14 players hit 50 or more home runs. Three hit more than 60—Joe Hauser twice and Tony Lazzeri once. The records show that four International League players hit 50 or more homers, three American Association players broke the magic barrier, and seven Pacific Coast League players piled up more than 50 homers in a single season.

The PCL was not the homer haven it was reported to be. The statements that the PCL was easy pickings does not stand up under close scrutiny. Tony Lazzeri was the only player to hit 60 home runs in one year in the 91-year history of the league, and he accomplished that feat over a long, arduous, 200-game schedule. On the same basis as the major leagues, figuring a 154-game schedule, Poosh-em-up Tony's home run total would have been only

44. In fact, no one in the PCL would have hit more than 53 home runs in one year over a normal, major league schedule.

In the lower minors, Class AA through Class D, 33 players hit 50 or more home runs over a 100-year period. Joe Bauman did it three times. Seven players exceeded the 60 homer mark, including Stuart and Bauman. But only one man ever broke the magic 70 home run barrier. Joe Willis Bauman.

The accomplishments of Joe Bauman, Dick Stuart, and Joe Hauser should not be taken lightly. There have been more than 500,000 professional baseball games played in the United States over the last 119 years, with more than 60,000 players participating. Games have been played in large stadiums and in tiny ballparks, at sea level and at high altitudes, with favorable winds and with swirling headwinds. Some players have been of small stature and some players have been large and muscular. Yet, in all that time, in all those parks, and under all those playing conditions, only one man has hit more than 70 home runs in one year—Joe Bauman. And only one man has hit 60 or more home runs in a season twice—Unser Choe Hauser. And only one man other than Bauman averaged 46 or more homers during his minor league career—Dick Stuart. These three men are the Sultans of Swat of minor league baseball.

It is obvious that minor league statistics do not carry the same prestige as major league statistics. Base hits and home runs are easier to come by in the bush leagues, for many reasons. To begin with, the quality of the opposition is less than in the majors. Most of the players in the minors do not have major league potential and can never hope to make it up to the Big Show. The talented players take advantage of this situation to pad their credentials.

One significant difference between the major leagues and the minors over the years has been the relative strengths of their respective pitching staffs. In the big time, teams have carried 10 or 11 pitchers, each with specific responsibilities. Some pitchers have been starters, others closers, and still others have been middle-relief specialists. In the minors, the lower minors particularly, there may have been only six pitchers on the staff, with the four starters pitching as often as possible. As a result of this lack of depth, starting pitchers often stayed in a game long after their effectiveness had disappeared. Also, when a game was out of reach or when the pitching staff had been depleted, another member of the team, such as an outfielder or an infielder, may have been called in to finish the game. In fact, Joe Bauman's record setting 72nd home run was hit off Artesia's regular center fielder Mickey Diaz, according to Bob Rives.

The dimensions of the ballparks, their elevations, and prevailing wind conditions have been given as other reasons for inflated minor league offensive statistics. In some cases, particularly with regard to the elevation in the western part of the country, that inflation was true, but, as we have also seen, many major league parks have similar idiosyncrasies. And, to be fair, the minor leagues have their disadvantages, as well as their advantages. The lighting systems in most minor league parks is inferior, making it difficult to see the ball clearly. Also, many minor league games begin at dusk, when visibility is particularly bad. Travel conditions are notoriously poor. Bus rides are long and hot, hotels are second rate, and the food is, more often than not, a Burger King special.

Minor league play may have some advantages, as far as the quality of the opposition is concerned, but it is a tough life, with few of the modern conveniences. And it puts a strain on a player's physical, as well as emotional, well-being.

Putting minor league accomplishments on a major league plane is not easy. Since this study involved the old Negro leagues and the Japanese leagues, as well as the American major and minor leagues, statistics from all those leagues were used to compare one league with another. Those players who played in both the Negro and the major or minor leagues and players who played in both the Japanese and the major or minor leagues were used to adjust the statistics from the Japanese leagues, Negro leagues, and minor leagues to a major league base point.

In order to determine the correlation between the high minor league performances and the major league base point, the experience of the group of Negro league players who successfully advanced from Negro league ball to the major leagues was studied. Most of the Negro league players began their professional careers in the American high minors, so it was possible to obtain a direct comparison from the Negro leagues to AAA ball and from the Negro leagues to major league ball. Those comparisons, in turn, provided a correlation between the major leagues and the high minor leagues as well.

The players studied included Luke Easter, Roy Campanella, Jackie Robinson, Larry Doby, Sam Jethroe, Monte Irvin, Bob Boyd, Ernie Banks, Willie Mays, Elston Howard, Junior Gilliam, Hank Thompson, Minnie Minoso, and Sandy Amoros. The averages of some players were not utilized because of their limited at bats or, in the case of Ernie Banks and Willie Mays, because it was felt their Negro league experience was not representative of their capabilities due to their young age. Averaging in Banks's and Mays's major league home run totals would have skewed the numbers in an unrealistic manner.

The players selected accumulated a total of 32,117 at bats in the high minors, 8,246 at bats in the Negro leagues, and 47,102 at bats in the majors. The relative differences between the leagues is shown below.

League	AB	H	D	T	HR	BA
Major Leagues	550	143	25	6	19	.260
High Minor Leagues (AAA)	550	157	26	6	20	.287

The above statistics were derived from the tables in the appendix, most notably from the comparison of the Negro leagues to the major leagues and from the comparison of the Negro leagues to the high minor leagues (AAA). The batting averages have been adjusted to give a major league basepoint of .260. The source of the home run totals for both the Negro leagues and the major leagues can be found later in this chapter, in the Negro league section.

The same procedure was used to study the lower minors (AA–C). In this instance, the Japanese experience was studied since many American players have divided their baseball careers between various American leagues and Japanese leagues. Some of the players studied, to compare the lower minor leagues with the major leagues, included Orestes Destrade, Adrian Garrett, Woody Jones, Stan Palys, Jack Pierce, Dave Roberts, Jose Vidal, and George Wilson. These players accounted for 11,475 at bats in the Japanese leagues and 41,936 at bats in the lower minor leagues in the United States. A total of 64 American players who played both in the American major leagues and for at least one full year in Japan was also studied. A sampling of these players reads like a "Who's Who" in American baseball. It includes Willie Davis, Reggie Smith, Clete Boyer, Roy White, and Cecil Fielder. The 64 players in the study accumulated 82,674 at bats in the Japanese leagues and 156,378 at bats in the major leagues.

The results of the two studies, combined, showed the following relationship between the major leagues and the lower minor leagues.

League	AB	H	D	T	HR	BA
Lower Minor Leagues (AA)	550	168	28	5	31	.306
Major Leagues	550	143	25	6	19	.260

Averaging all the minor league data, from both the higher minor leagues and the lower minor leagues, gave the following correlation.

League	AB	H	D	T	HR	BA
Minor Leagues	550	163	27	6	26	.296
Major Leagues	550	143	25	6	19	.260

The West Texas–New Mexico and Longhorn Leagues were reviewed independently. Since the thin air in the southwest did seem to contribute to an increase in home runs in both leagues and since the professional-baseball, single-season home run king, Joe Bauman, played in those leagues, it was decided to study them separately.

The above stats show an average difference of 36 points in batting average between the minor leagues and the major leagues, although, admittedly, this relationship is a broad generalization. There is an obvious difference between playing ball in the AAA Pacific Coast League and playing ball in the Class C California League. In this study, players who played most of their minor league ball with AAA teams were measured against the AAA stat. Players who spent most of their careers in the lower minors were measured against the AA stat. Those players who bounced around between all levels of minor league competition were measured against the "average."

Based on the above comparisons, all AAA minor league home runs were factored by the ratio of $^{19}/_{20}$ (0.95), and all lower minor league home runs were factored by the ratio of $^{19}/_{31}$ (0.61). Minor league averages that represented a more-or-less balanced blend of the higher classification and the lower classification were factored by a ratio of $^{19}/_{26}$ (0.73), to determine their predicted major league equivalent.

Testing the factors on Joe Hauser's and Dick Stuart's averages brought the following results. Hauser actually averaged 34 home runs a year in the minors and 21 home runs a year in the majors. Using the factor, Unser Choe's minor league average of 34 home runs, multiplied by 0.73, would give him 25 homers a year in the major leagues, only four above his actual numbers. Dick Stuart's 46-home run average in the minors, multiplied by 0.73, would give him a 34-home run average in the majors, three more than his actual totals.

There is one nineteenth-century minor league slugger who should be recognized at this point for his mighty wallops. Edward L. "Home Run" Breckenridge was a long ball-hitting first baseman for a number of minor league teams between 1888 and 1899. As noted earlier, Breckinridge slammed an average of 20 home runs a year in the minors. Converting those numbers to the lively ball era gave some startling results. Utilizing the lively ball era/dead ball era factor of 2.5, Breckenridge's home run output could be expected to skyrocket to 50 home runs a year in the minors, using today's juiced-up ball. That would put him near the top of minor league sluggers, only four homers a year behind the renowned Joe Bauman. Going one step further, if Breckenridge's numbers were adjusted to the major league standard, he could be expected to hit approximately 31 home runs a year in the Big Show.

Data on the West Texas–New Mexico and Longhorn Leagues is particularly sparse since there were few players who made the jump from those leagues to the majors. Most notable, though, were Ed Stevens, Zeke Bonura, Ed Carnett, Tom Jordan, and Mervyn Connors. Other players moved around from those southwestern leagues to other minor leagues, and that data was also analyzed to obtain relative comparisons between the various leagues.

A comparison of the West Texas–New Mexico and Longhorn Leagues to the major leagues is presented below. The relationship was not drawn entirely from a direct comparison between the southwest leagues and the major leagues, due to the paucity of data; it was also based on a comparison of the southwest leagues to other minor leagues, given the approximate relationship between the other minor leagues and the majors.

League	AB	H	D	T	HR	BA
WT-NM, Longhorn	550	177	—	—	32	.321
Major Leagues	550	143	25	6	19	.260

Using the above statistics, Joe Bauman could be expected to have hit approximately .276 with 32 home runs (54 × $^{19}/_{32}$) in the major leagues. If he were able to actually duplicate these numbers, he would have been one of the most prolific home run hitters in major league history.

As noted earlier, this exercise is not intended as a scientific study, but only as an introduction to the relative relationship of the various professional baseball leagues around the world. It may be that the adjustments for the West Texas–New Mexico and Longhorn Leagues are overly generous in favor of those leagues. If that is the case, attribute it to literary license.

Japanese Leagues

Professional baseball has been played in Japan since 1936, a period of 58 years. During that time, Japan has produced some notable sluggers, such as Katsuya Nomura, Isao Harimoto, Koji Yamamoto, Shigeo Nagashima, Hiromitsu Ochiai, and Sadaharu Oh. Nomura, the husky catcher for the Nankai Hawks of the Japanese Pacific League, hit 657 career home runs, second only to Oh. Harimota, the first man to accumulate more than 3,000 career base hits in Japan, accounted for 504 home runs during his 23-year career. Yamamoto, a powerful outfielder for the Hiroshima Carp during the 1970s, led his team to two pennants while smashing a total of 536 home runs. Shigeo Nagashima, the great third baseman of the Tokyo Giants, slugged 444 home runs during his glorious 17-year career. Ochiai, whose career is still active, has hit a total of 505 home runs through 1996. Sadaharu Oh, the all-time, professional-baseball home run king, piled up an incredible 868 home runs in 22 years. He surpassed the major league's all-time leader, Hank Aaron, by 113 homers.

The overall quality of play in Japan is very high. Many of the players, including those mentioned above, are of major league caliber. They know the fundamentals; they execute all the plays with great skill and precision; and they are outstanding defensively. Physically, however, the average Japanese is of small stature, compared to his American counterpart. Many of the Japanese players are in the neighborhood of five-feet-six-inches tall and weigh between 130 and 150 pounds. They do not possess the strength and power of most modern American players; therefore, they do not usually hit the ball as far.

Naturally, the early baseball stadiums in Japan were designed and constructed to accommodate the Japanese professional ballplayers. Most stadiums were built with a classic symmetry, with the right and left field foul lines being equal in length and the center field wall being proportionally farther from the plate. The distances in Japanese stadiums were, however, necessarily short in order to be within reach of the leagues' leading sluggers. In general, the right and left foul lines were only 297 feet from home plate, while the center field wall was an inviting 387 feet away. As noted previously, Osaka Stadium, the home field of slugger Katsuya Nomura, was only 280 feet down the foul lines and a short chip shot of 350 feet to the center field fence.

These small parks have cast some doubt on the validity of Sadaharu Oh's prodigious home run feats. Would he have been able to maintain his amazing, 52-home runs per year average in the United States, or would he have hit a lesser number of circuit clouts? Fortunately, there was an excellent way to compare the relative home run potential of the Japanese players with their major league counterparts.

Over the past 35 years or so, more than 400 foreign players have displayed their talents on Japanese baseball diamonds, even though Japanese league rules restrict the number of foreigners who can play at any one time. Currently, each team in the Central League and the Pacific League is allowed up to three foreign players on its roster. As discussed earlier, in the chapter on Japanese sluggers, many talented baseball players over the years have made the long trip from the United States across the Pacific Ocean to compete in the Japanese professional leagues. There are generally three types of players who choose this route: the aging major league player who wants to prolong his career another year or two and who can command a generous salary, the promising minor league player who hopes a short stint in Japan will bring him to the attention of the major league owners back home, and the career minor league player who does not have the talent to reach the major leagues but who can earn a comfortable living in Japan. Some examples of these three different types of players include: aging major leaguers like Clete Boyer, Reggie Smith, Dick Stuart, Matty Alou, Larry Parrish, and Willie Upshaw; promising minor leaguers like Cecil Fielder, Terry Whitfield, and Orestes Destrade; career minor leaguers like Randy Bass, Boomer Wells, and Woody Jones.

By far the most popular category was the aging major leaguer who tried to hang on to his career for another year or two while he accumulated a financial nest egg. There was a considerable amount of data available comparing the Japanese leagues with the American major leagues. For this study a total of 66 American players with both Japanese league experience and major league experience were evaluated. (See appendix.) These 66 players accumulated a total of 90,332 at bats in the Japanese leagues compared to 170,380 at bats in the major leagues. Although there were over 400 foreign players who have played in the Japanese leagues, many of them were not Americans; and of the American players, many had no major league experience in the United States, while others played only a few games in Japan. The 66 players used in this study had considerable experience in both Japan and the United States.

A comparison of the leagues is as follows:

League	AB	H	D	T	HR	BA
Japanese Leagues	550	152	21	1	31	.283
Major Leagues	550	143	25	6	14	.265

The results are, I believe, what you might expect. The players in the Japanese leagues, probably because of the smaller ballparks, hit more home runs but fewer doubles and triples. Triples are almost nonexistent because of the limited outfield space in the Japanese leagues: there is not enough open territory to allow a batter to make it all the way around to third base before a hit can be returned to the infield. The Japanese players, like the Negro leaguers, play a very conservative style of ball. They play for one run at a time. The bunt, the hit and run, and stolen bases dominate the game. For the most part, they are contact hitters, who rarely strike out and who go for average rather than for home runs. Only a very few players, like Yamamoto, Nagashima, and Oh, tried for home runs. Most Japanese players were content to hit singles time after time.

American players are brought into the league to add the power that is missing from all–Japanese lineups. As shown in the statistics above, and in the individual breakdown in the appendix, the American players do exactly that, in grand style. In fact, many of them have challenged Oh's season average of 52 home runs per 550 at bats. In one brief season in Japan, Cecil Fielder averaged 54 home runs a year, two more than Oh. With Detroit, he averaged 37 homers a year over a four year period. Orestes Destrade, who played four years with the Seibu Lions before returning to the States, averaged 51 home runs a year in Japan. In 1993, he hit 20 home runs for the Florida Marlins. Warren Cromartie averaged 32 homers a year in Japan, after averaging only 9 homers a year in the majors. Reggie Smith's averages were 50 and 25, respectively, while Larry Parrish's were 44 and 21, George Altman's were 35 and 18, and LeRon Lee's were 34 and 11.

Using the above table, home runs hit in the Japanese professional leagues would have to be multiplied by $^{14}/_{31}$, a factor of 0.45, to convert a player's Japanese League home run average to a major league equivalent. Using this equation, the all-time world home run champion, Sadaharu Oh of the Yomiuri (Tokyo) Giants, would have taken a major plunge in the statistics department.

Oh averaged a mighty 52 home runs a year in the Japanese leagues, well ahead of his American rivals, Hank Aaron and Babe Ruth. Taking into account the relative differences between playing conditions in the leagues, would however, make a drastic change in Oh's home run averages. Using the previously determined factor of 0.45, the Japanese slugger's home run average would plummet from 52 homers a year in the Japanese leagues to a modest 23 homers a year in the major leagues. His batting average would be an above-average .283.

Comments from various American baseball players who observed Sadaharu Oh in action would seem to corroborate the statistical evidence. In the book, *Sadaharu Oh* by Oh himself and David Falkner, former major leaguers like Frank Howard, Frank Robinson, Don Baylor, and Hal McRae all feel that Oh would have been a superior major league player, capable of hitting 30 to 40 home runs in any given year. Howard further declares, "He would play in any league, any time, including our own major leagues, and he would star in any league. Make no mistake about it. He's a champion." Tom Seaver estimates that Oh would have hit 20–25 home runs a year in the majors— exactly what this study predicted.

If the Japanese league to major league adjustments are correct, Sadaharu Oh's career batting statistics would compare favorably with the statistics of two famous, former major league first basemen, Steve Garvey of the Los Angeles Dodgers and Gil Hodges of the Brooklyn Dodgers. During their long careers, both American players were noted long ball threats and clutch hitters. The averages of the three players, based on 550 at bats, is as follows:

Name	AB	H	D	T	HR	BA
Sadaharu Oh	550	156	30	6	23	.283
Steve Garvey	550	162	27	3	17	.294
Gil Hodges	550	150	23	4	29	.273

Sadaharu Oh would still be a Hall-of-Famer.

Although the home run totals of the Japanese players would plummet in American parks, many of them, in addition to Oh, would still be major league stars. The following players would all be candidates for induction into baseball's Hall of Fame in Cooperstown, New York, in spite of reduced home run totals. Katsuya Nomura, the great catcher of the Nankai Hawks, a Campanella clone, would still have been a dominating backstop and a dangerous hitter. He would have been a .300 hitter when he was healthy, with 25–30 homers a year. Like Campanella, his offensive statistics would have suffered when he was hurt, but, like Campanella, he would have continued to play— hurt or not. And his remarkable durability would still have allowed him to establish career records for a catcher in most offensive categories.

Shigeo Nagashima also had a mirror image in the major leagues—Brooks Robinson. Both were defensive geniuses, and both were clutch hitters with good power. In fact, Nagashima's offensive numbers would have been somewhat superior to Robinson's. His .287 batting average would have been 20 points higher than Robinson's, while his home run total would have been the same (14). In any given season, Nagashima would have been capable of producing batting averages in the neighborhood of .335–.340 in the major leagues, with 25–30 home runs and 100+ runs batted in.

Other potential Hall-of-Famers would include "Lord of Batting" Tetsuharu Kawakami, Isao Harimoto, and Hiromitsu Ochiai. Kawakami, with an adjusted career batting average of .298, would have been capable of reaching the .360 mark in any given year, and would probably have won several batting championships in the American major leagues. His outstanding batting eye, with just 31 strikeouts a year, and his great speed would have made him adept at advancing baserunners and keeping out of the double play. He would also have been a dangerous stolen-base threat in the majors.

Harimoto would have been a lifetime .301 hitter in the majors, with good speed and good RBI potential. His knack of winning batting championships, nine in the Japanese Pacific League, would carry over into the majors. The Toei Flyers ballhawk would also have presented a stolen-base threat in the United States, making him doubly dangerous offensively.

Ochiai would also have threatened the .300 level, with a projected career average of .298. He had the skills to have hit in the .350 range on any given year, with as many as 25–30 home runs. He would have been a threat to win the batting championship, if not the home run crown, every year.

Negro Leagues

The Negro leagues have produced some mighty sluggers in the twentieth century, from Home Run Johnson of the old Page Fence Giants to Josh Gibson of the Homestead Grays. Many of the great slugging feats attributed to Gibson have taken on almost mythical proportions over the years. He has been credited with hitting 84 home runs in one season, with hitting the only fair ball out of Yankee Stadium, and with hitting home runs of up to 700 feet in length. It is often impossible to separate fact from fiction when discussing the fabled sluggers of the old Negro leagues.

Until recently, it was impossible to evaluate the relative talents of Negro league players because there were very few statistics available on the Negro leagues. The leagues were a loose confederation of teams whose owners were more concerned with survival than they were with seeing box scores in the newspapers. The players themselves were always on the move from one town to the next. They didn't have the time nor the interest to scan the morning papers looking for the write-up of the previous day's game.

Fortunately, thanks to John Holway, Dick Clark, Larry Lester, and a host of researchers with the SABR, the actual Negro league statistics are being developed for all the players who participated in the leagues onwards from 1920. These statistics are still incomplete, to be sure, but they do give us a measurement of the quality of play in the old world of black baseball. Previously, all that was known of the Negro leagues were the myths that were passed around by word of mouth, primarily about players like Satchel Paige and Josh Gibson. In Gibson's case, the amazing stories centered around the prodigious number of home runs he was credited with: 84 in one year, according to the word on the street, and 76 in another.

Scientific research has revealed that Josh Gibson's official Negro league season home run totals were modest by professional standards. The most home runs he ever hit in any one year in the United States was 18, for the Homestead Grays in 1946. He also hit 16 for the Grays in 1939. Those numbers were achieved, however, in only 119 and 72 at bats, respectively, so his frequency was astronomical. The rumors of his 84 home runs in one year were probably based on a 12-month schedule. Most Negro league players played ball year-round, with many of their games coming against amateur teams all across the United States. It is estimated that Gibson and his cohorts played as many as 200 games a year.

Still, as the numbers became available, it has been apparent that, despite the myths promulgated about Josh Gibson, the big catcher was an exceptional home run hitter in his own right. So too, were Mule Suttles, Chino Smith, John Beckwith, and Turkey Stearnes.

Some of the available Negro league averages are eye popping. For instance, little Chino Smith is credited with a lifetime Negro league batting average of .428, with 50 doubles, 8 triples, and 33 home runs per year. Josh Gibson hit .362 with an average of 48 home runs. Mule Suttles had 34 home runs and a .329 batting average, while Norman "Turkey" Stearnes pounded the ball at a .351 clip with 30 homers a year.

The slugging statistics of the old Negro league stars are impressive. The question is, how do they compare to major league averages? And under what conditions were the averages produced? To begin with, since the Negro leaguers played their league games in many of the major league stadiums, including Yankee Stadium, Forbes Field, Comiskey Park, and Griffith Stadium, the park should not have had any effect on their relative statistics.

Many of the individual players, including Gibson, were penalized by playing their home games in large parks with outlandishly long foul lines. Josh was at a particular disadvantage. He had to contend with the left field fences in Griffith Stadium (402 feet from home plate), Forbes Field (365 feet away), and Greenlee Field (350 feet away). The center field walls were 421 feet, 435 feet, and 400 feet distant, respectively—and Josh still averaged 48 homers a year, a monumental feat under the circumstances.

In general, the mentality in the Negro leagues seemed to focus on making contact with the ball, rather than on trying to hit a home run every time up, as in the majors. The Negro leaguers went for batting average and speed on the bases. They were satisfied to earn their runs one at a time, rather than sit around waiting for the big, three-run homer.

Playing conditions, for the most part, were substandard in the Negro leagues. It was not unusual for teams to play three games in a single day, in three different cities. There is at least one recorded instance where four games were played in one day. The mode of travel was usually by bus, and in those days, before superhighways and air conditioning, trips were often long, miserably hot, and exhausting. The players frequently hung their sweat-drenched uniforms out the bus windows to dry between cities, while trying to catch a quick cat nap before the next game. Sleep was, more often than not, achieved in a sitting position, squeezed tightly between other players and equipment.

Other problems associated with the difficult travel schedules were related to sleeping accommodations and food. The Negro leaguers were banned from most of the first-class hotels in many cities, due to the hotels' "whites only" rules. Many of the players were forced to stay in fleabag hotels, in the most run-down sections of the city. Some players reported they slept with the lights on to discourage the roaches. A fortunate few found lodging with friends in clean houses, with comfortable beds and bathtubs.

Restaurants were also a problem for the ballplayers, as many eateries would not serve blacks. As a result, food was often obtained on a "take-out" basis and consumed on the bus. Needless to say, the diet left a lot to be desired. There are many stories of players subsisting on cheese and crackers, bread and peanut butter, and hamburgers for days at a time. Very seldom was there the time or the opportunity to enjoy a fine restaurant dinner in a relaxed atmosphere.

As far as the talent on the individual teams were concerned, many of the old Negro league players, like Double Duty Radcliffe and Buck O'Neil felt there were many Negro league teams over the years that could have competed on an equal footing in the major leagues. They also felt that certain teams, like the Pittsburgh Crawfords or Homestead Grays of the Satchel Paige-Josh Gibson era, were of world-championship caliber. The problems with the Negro league teams did not lie with the starting nine. The problems were generally associated with a lack of depth on the bench. Most Negro league teams carried only 14 or 15 players. Teams didn't have the luxury of pitching specialists, like the major league teams. There were no middle relievers or closers, only starters. The starters were expected to finish what they began. And when they weren't pitching, they earned their keep by playing other positions in the field.

Negro league teams carried five or six pitchers, compared to the ten or eleven pitchers on major league rosters. That was a decided advantage for the hitters, because they often batted against a tired pitcher late in the game or against a non-pitcher who was brought in to mop up. The general consensus was that, because of the lack of depth on Negro league teams, particularly of pitching depth, the overall quality of play was probably equivalent to a triple-A minor league team.

That may be true, but the lean and mean Negro league teams did produce one type of athlete not often seen in the major leagues—a good hitting pitcher who could field his position. Since Negro league pitchers played other positions between starts, they developed into competent hitters and reliable fielders. In some cases, they became outstanding hitters. Bullet Joe Rogan, one of the top four or five pitchers in Negro league history, was an awesome hitter. Rogan often played center field when not on the mound; occasionally, he played one of the infield positions. But he always batted cleanup. His career stats reflect his ability with the lumber—a .343 lifetime batting average and 16 home runs a year. He was also regarded as one of the best fielding pitchers in Negro league ranks. Martin Dihigo, a Hall-of-Fame pitcher, was also an all-star second baseman and an outstanding outfielder. Over the course of a 25-year career in the United States, Mexico, and Cuba, "El Maestro" accounted for over 250 victories on the mound and hit a lusty .319, while averaging 25 round trippers a year. Dihigo is the only baseball player who is in baseball halls of fame in three different countries. He has been honored with that recognition in the United States, Mexico, and Cuba.

The Negro league legacy of good hitting pitchers carried over into the major leagues, with players like big Don Newcombe and Dan Bankhead of the Brooklyn Dodgers. Bankhead hit a home run in his first major league at bat. Newcombe batted .359 for Brooklyn in 1955, with seven home runs in 117 at bats. He also ran up a 20–7 win-loss record on the mound.

Under the atrocious playing conditions outlined above, it is difficult to see how the quality of play in the Negro leagues could compare with the quality of play in the major leagues. The big leaguers were pampered compared to their compatriots in Negro ball. There was, however, one way to obtain a direct comparison between the two leagues. After Jackie Robinson made the jump from the Negro leagues to the major leagues, many of the Negro league's top stars followed him into organized ball. Those players, entering the majors between 1947 and 1955, were the cream of the crop in the Negro leagues and were young enough to have comparable careers in both the Negro leagues and the majors.

The players studied included Easter, Campanella, Jethroe, Irvin, Gilliam, Thompson, Minoso, Doby, Mays, Banks, Howard, Al Smith, and Boyd: the top players in Negro league ball. A total of 12,154 at bats were recorded in the Negro leagues for those players, compared to 64,808 at bats in the majors. The home run comparisons for the different players is listed below.

Home Runs Per 550 at Bats

Player	Negro Leagues	Major Leagues
Luke Easter	29	30
Sam Jethroe	8	15
Roy Campanella	13	32
Monte Irvin	21	22
Jackie Robinson	17	15
Junior Gilliam	3	5
Hank Thompson	18	24
Larry Doby	27	26
Minnie Minoso	8	16
Bob Boyd	5	5
Sandy Amoros	16	18
Al Smith	10	17
Total	175	225
Average	15	19

Ernie Banks, Willie Mays, and Elston Howard were not included in the calculation of the home run averages because it was felt that their statistics would skew the final results in an unrealistic manner. These three players began playing professional baseball in the Negro leagues while they were still teenagers. They had not yet developed physically and were still several years away from becoming the long ball hitters they became in the major leagues.

The comparison of the batting averages for those players who had significant playing careers in both the Negro leagues and the major leagues can be found in the appendix. The overall statistical comparison between the Negro leagues and the major leagues is shown below, based on an average, 550 at-bat season. The actual batting averages for the two groups is slightly different than that shown in the appendix because they have been adjusted to the major league base point (as part of the total comparison of major leagues, minor leagues, Japanese leagues, and Negro leagues). The important number, however—the difference in batting average between the two leagues—is the same, at 51 points.

League	AB	H	D	T	HR	BA
Negro Leagues	550	173	24	8	15	.311
Major Leagues	550	143	25	6	19	.260

Consistent with the general batting philosophy in the Negro leagues—to make contact with the ball—the players in the study produced higher batting averages in Negro league ball than they did in major league ball, but hit fewer home runs. Based on these numbers, in order to evaluate the home run prowess of Negro league players for the sake of this study, the player's Negro league home run average should be multiplied by ¹⁹/₁₅, a factor of 1.27.

In addition, the home run averages for Negro league players who plied their trade in the old dead ball days has to be multiplied by a factor of 2.5 to bring their statistics up to the major league base point. When this is done, the home run averages for the top black sluggers of the late nineteenth and early twentieth century increase to impressive proportions. Unfortunately, it is not possible to evaluate Grant "Home Run" Johnson here, since no statistics of his career have yet come to light. Several other big bashers of the late nineteenth and early twentieth century, however, can receive their due.

Ulysses S. "Frank" Grant, the most renowned black slugger of the nineteenth century, after the adjustments would have a home run average of 29 home runs a year. Pete Hill, the first black superstar, would ring in with a solid 28 round trippers. So would his outfield compatriot, Jimmy Lyons. But the king of the dead ball era, based on the early stats, would be Big Bertha, Louis Santop, with an average of 32 home runs a year.

The home run averages of the top sluggers in the Negro leagues during the lively ball era is as follows:

Josh Gibson . . . . 48 home runs per 550 at bats
Mule Suttles . . . . 34 home runs per 550 at bats
Chino Smith . . . . 33 home runs per 550 at bats
Turkey Stearnes . . . . 30 home runs per 550 at bats
John Beckwith . . . . 30 home runs per 550 at bats

When these averages are adjusted to major league levels, the results are astonishing. For instance, John Beckwith, the slugging shortstop of the Chicago Giants, checks in with an average of 38 home runs a year, putting him into fifth place on the all-time home run list, behind Ruth, Cravath, Killebrew, and Kiner.

Beckwith didn't stay in fifth place for long, however. Turkey Stearnes tied Beckwith's record, with an average of 38 home runs of his own. They were both outshone by little Chino Smith and Mule Suttles. The tiny outfielder of Brooklyn's Lincoln Giants would have smashed 42 homers a year according to the statistics, one behind Gavvy Cravath and five behind the immortal Babe. Suttles did Chino one better, tying Cravath's record of 43 homers and holding down second place on the all-time sluggers list, only four homers from the top.

Only one man stood between Babe Ruth and the home run championship of the world. That man was the legendary catcher of the Homestead Grays, Josh Gibson. Babe was a legend in his own right, but he couldn't beat the happy-go-lucky kid from Pittsburgh. When Gibson's home run feats were adjusted to the major league level, they predicted the big righthander would have hit an average of 61 home runs a year in the majors, if he had shared billing with Ruth and his contemporaries.

It is almost unbelievable to think that any human being could smash as many as 61 homers a year over a protracted period of time. Roger Maris hit 61 home runs in 1961. No other man has ever hit as many as 61 homers in one season, let alone averaged that over a long career. But Gibson's numbers do not lie. For 17 long years, winter and summer, the 200-pound masher from Pittsburgh, Pennsylvania, hit them farther and more frequently than any other baseball player in the world.

Babe Ruth was a legendary figure. Josh Gibson remains a myth.

CHAPTER 7

THE KING OF SWAT

This study has identified the foremost home run hitters in professional baseball history. It has included all professional leagues: the major leagues, the minor leagues, the Japanese leagues, and the Negro leagues. The accomplishments of the leading sluggers were all adjusted to a major league base point. Based on the results, the greatest home run hitters of all time are listed below, in order of their home run frequency.

Home Runs Per 500 at Bats

Josh Gibson	61	Negro League
Babe Ruth	50	Major League
Gavvy Cravath	43	Major League
Mule Suttles	43	Negro League
Chino Smith	42	Negro League
Harmon Killebrew	39	Major League
Ralph Kiner	39	Major League
Turkey Stearnes	38	Negro League
John Beckwith	38	Negro League
Ted Williams	37	Major League
Jimmie Foxx	36	Major League
Mickey Mantle	36	Major League
Dave Kingman	36	Major League
Mike Schmidt	36	Major League
Ed Wesley	36	Negro League
Sam Thompson	35	Major League
Tilly Walker	33	Major League
Joe Bauman	32	Minor League
Dick Stuart	31	Major League
Bobby Crues	26	Minor League
Sadaharu OH	23	Japanese League

It is interesting to note that of the 21 home run hitters listed above, eleven were major leaguers, six performed in the Negro leagues, three starred in the minors, and one played his entire career in the Japanese leagues.

It is true that most of the world-class home run hitters in professional baseball were assisted by the playing conditions in their home park. In his quest for baseball immortality, Joe Bauman, at Roswell, had the benefit of light air at the 3,500 foot elevation, as well as a short, 380-foot center field fence. As he chased Hank Aaron's career home run totals, Sadaharu Oh took aim at the short, 297-foot right field porch in Korakuen Stadium, as well as at the other "friendly" parks around the Japanese leagues. Even Hammerin' Hank Aaron himself had the friendly confines of "The Launching Pad" in Atlanta to help him on his way to 755 career home runs.

Babe Ruth had the advantage of shooting at the 295-foot right field fence in Yankee Stadium. Over the course of his career, the Bambino crushed 347 home runs at home, for a home average of 47 a year, and 367 home runs on the road, for a road average of 46 a year. Those totals, however, include the six years he spent in Boston, trying to hit the dead ball. His career with the Yankees coincided with the introduction of the lively ball, which the big, easygoing outfielder made the most of. During his 15 years in the Bronx, Ruth put 50 balls a year out of the stadium. On the road, his average was 47 home runs a year.

Roger Maris, the major leagues' all-time, single-season home run king, had the same friendly target to shoot at—the cozy, 295-foot right field porch in Yankee Stadium.

Two world-class sluggers did not have the advantage of favorable home run parks to hit in. Harmon Killebrew played in two cavernous stadiums, Griffith Stadium in Washington, D.C., and Metropolitan Stadium in Minneapolis, Minnesota. Both parks had left field foul lines of 340 feet or more, with greater than 420-foot center field walls. Killebrew's home runs were earned by the sweat of his brow—and by his enormous strength.

The other world-class slugger who was not aided and abetted by the so-called "home field advantage" was Josh Gibson. Josh never even had the glimmer of a home field advantage. In fact, he was usually penalized when he played at home. All his home parks were outlandish pastures, especially to left field and to the left center field power alley, where Gibson hit most of his balls. Griffith Stadium, in Washington, D.C., one of Gibson's home parks with the Homestead Grays, had a distant, 405-foot left field wall in the 1930s and a 421-foot center field wall. The Grays' other home field, Greenlee Field in Pittsburgh, had a 350-foot left field fence and a 400-foot center field fence. Pittsburgh's Forbes Field, where Josh played as a member of the Pittsburgh Crawfords, was 365 feet down the left field foul line and 435 feet to dead center. The happy-go-lucky Gibson played in equally large ballparks in Cuba, Mexico, and Puerto Rico; but it didn't make any difference to him. He hit the long ball in all of them. He won league home run titles in every country he played in. During his nomadic career, he averaged 48 home runs a year in the Negro leagues, 31 home runs a year in

Cuba, 27 home runs a year in Puerto Rico, and 54 home runs a year in Mexico.

The results of this study will be shocking to many people. The majority of people who follow baseball consider Babe Ruth to be the greatest home run hitter of all time. To them, he is "The Sultan of Swat," the ultimate slugger. In truth, Babe Ruth is still the Sultan of Swat in organized baseball. He reigns supreme over the segregated organized leagues that existed during the first half of this century, as well as over the integrated professional leagues that have been in effect since 1946. When the old Negro leagues are taken into consideration, however, the mighty Bambino slips quietly into second place. His spot on the center pedestal is taken by the boyish man who plied his wares up and down the countries of North, Central, and South America during the '30s and '40s.

The number one home run hitter of all time is the slugging catcher of the Homestead Grays, the powerful Josh Gibson—and by a wide margin at that!

Josh Gibson was in a class by himself: a man of great strength, a man of enormous athletic ability, and a man who projected the boyish charm of a teenager. Josh played baseball like it should be played, like a kid's game.

Josh Gibson is the world's greatest home run hitter—the King of Swat.

Gallery of Home Run Kings by League Classification

Minor League Home Run King—Joe Bauman

The undisputed home run king of minor league baseball is Joe Willis Bauman. The big Oklahoman was born in the tiny hamlet of Welch, located in the northeast corner of the state, near the borders of Missouri, Kansas, and Arkansas, on April 17, 1922. His arrival brought the population of Welch up to 651—not counting cows and dogs.

Bauman grew up in Oklahoma City. There, he attended Capital Hill High School, where he first drew the attention of baseball scouts for his prodigious blasts. By the time the lanky first baseman graduated, he had reached his final height of six-feet-five-inches, although his weight was still somewhat less than his professional playing weight of 235 pounds.

After leaving high school, Bauman signed a professional baseball contract with the Little Rock Travellers of the Southern Association. The Travellers immediately farmed him out to Newport in the class D Northeast Arkansas League, where he received his baptism of fire. He quickly discovered that hitting professional pitching was somewhat more difficult than pounding high school kids. His first year totals revealed just 3 home runs and a minuscule .215 batting average in 59 games.

Joe Bauman, shown with Amarillo, hit 48 home runs for the Gold Sox in 1946. Eight years later, he set the all-time professional record, smashing 72 round trippers for the Roswell Rockets of the Longhorn League (credit: Amarillo Globe-News*).*

The following year, on January 10, 1942, Bauman married his high school sweetheart, Dorothy Ramsey. They are still together 55 years later. With the Japanese attack on Pearl Harbor only one month past, Bauman decided to forego another baseball season. Instead, he joined the labor force and waited for his call into military service. In 1943, tired of waiting, he enlisted in the United States Navy and was sent to boot camp at the Great Lakes Naval Training Center.

Bauman spent the war years, 1943 through 1945, at the Norman Navy Base, near the University of Oklahoma campus. He was fortunate to be able to play baseball on the base team with many former minor and major league players. Service ball, which was considered the equivalent of AAA minor league baseball at the time, provided Bauman with an invaluable learning experience. He played against many major league players, including Benny Warren of the Phillies, Al Benton of the Tigers, Rip Radcliffe of the Browns, Charlie Gilbert of the Cubs, and Johnny Rizzo of the Dodgers.

The three years at Norman were, to Bauman, like three years at a baseball academy. The older players on the team took the youngster under their wings and taught him the fundamentals of the game. The manager, who took a liking to the gawky first baseman, kept him in the lineup, through good times and bad. The schedule, which included many of the service installations like Great Lakes was nearly of major league caliber. In the service, Joe Willis Bauman matured, both as a person and as a ballplayer. When the war ended, he was ready to attack baseball with a flourish.

In 1946, fresh out of the Navy, the 24-year-old first baseman joined Amarillo of the West Texas–New Mexico League. He immediately made his mark on professional baseball, hammering a league-leading 48 home runs and driving in 159 teammates, while hitting a respectable .301. Bauman had perfected his batting stroke in Norman—a smooth, uppercut swing that sent baseballs on high arcs to distant territories. His keen eyesight and quick wrists made him a force to be reckoned with on the ballfield. The following year, he brought his batting average up to .350, with 38 round trippers.

The Boston Braves, desperate for some home run punch in Beantown, bought his contract from Little Rock and sent the young slugger to Hartford of the Eastern League. Over the winter, following a lengthy contract dispute, Bauman bolted the Braves with the now famous comment, "I can make more money selling 24-inch shoestrings on a corner."

Joe Bauman sat out the next two seasons, playing semipro ball with Elk City, a town of 7,000 people, located about 100 miles west of Oklahoma City on Route 40. In Elk City, an oil boom town of the early '50s, the town fathers were dedicated to fielding a team capable of winning the national semipro tournament in Wichita. In 1950, Elk City won the state title and traveled to Wichita, where they finished a respectable third. The Fort Wayne-General Electric Voltmen took the championship, their third in a row. In actuality, the Wichita tournament was not a semipro tournament at all. Competing teams routinely recruited the best players available in the country. Many Negro league professionals, such as Satchel Paige, Buck O'Neil, and Chet Brewer, sold their services to the highest bidder year after year.

Elk City rolled through all opposition the next year, taking another state title and returning to Wichita as a favorite. Early in the tournament, they beat defending champion, Fort Wayne-GE, and entered the finals undefeated.

Fort Wayne-GE, determined to capture a fourth title, went out and signed two Negro league pitchers, then proceeded to make their way through the losers bracket without another loss. In the finals, the Voltmen, with their revamped lineup, defeated Elk City twice, by scores of 1–0 in 12 innings, and 5–3.

The next year, the oil wells went dry, the baseball team disbanded, and Bauman returned to professional baseball with the Artesia Drillers of the Longhorn League, who had purchased his contract from Boston. It was the beginning of Joe Bauman's spectacular assault on the home run record book.

Artesia was not exactly a home run haven for lefthanded hitters. Brainard Park had a 345-foot right field fence with a healthy 10–20 mile per hour headwind. These inconveniences didn't bother Bauman, however. The 235-pound strongman poled one long blast after another through the swirling breeze, finishing the year with a league-leading 50 home runs. He also batted .370. The "gentleman first baseman," as he was known, led the league again the next year, walloping 53 homers and stroking the ball at a .371 clip.

In 1954, Joe Bauman moved on to the Roswell Rockets and his meeting with destiny. Hitting with a following wind this time, instead of fighting a blistering headwind, the lefthanded bomber went on a long ball rampage. As the season wound down, his home run total creeped into the 60s—then 65, 66, 67. Finally, with only five games remaining, big Joe drove number 69 over the right field fence at Roswell's Park Field, tying him with Joe Hauser and Bobby Crues for the most single-season home runs in professional baseball history.

A three-game series in Big Spring proved fruitless when the Big Spring pitchers refused to throw anything near the plate. A final twi-night doubleheader in Artesia ended the season, with Bauman at 69 and holding. Artesia manager Jim Adair pitched fireballing, Cuban rookie Jose Gallardo in the opener of the twin bill. The 19-year-old righthander, sporting a 4–1 record, worked the count to 2–2 on Bauman, batting leadoff, then put a fastball in Joe's wheelhouse. The big first baseman promptly sent it on a high arc into the New Mexico dusk. Last seen, it was disappearing over the 352-foot sign in right center field—against the wind—home run number 70, a new professional record. Bauman hit another home run later in the game and then smashed number 72 in the nightcap.

After another big season in 1955, where he piled up 46 more home runs, Bauman called it a day, halfway through the '56 season. During the winter, he had aggravated an old ankle injury from high school football, and it continued to plague him through the summer. Joe Bauman, baseball player, retired; Joe Bauman, businessman, settled down with his two service stations in Roswell. He still lives there after 42 years.

Joe Bauman is the proud possessor of a number of professional baseball slugging records. In addition to hitting the most home runs in a single season, the big Sooner holds the record for the highest single season slugging average in baseball history. He accumulated 456 total bases in 498 at bats in 1954, a slugging average of .916. He also has the second highest single-season RBI total, his 224 runs batted in trailing only Bobby Crues's 254.

His home run average of 54 homers a year, per 550 at bats, has never been equaled in professional baseball.

Major Leagues, Nineteenth Century— Dan Brouthers and Sam Thompson

Big Dan Brouthers and Big Sam Thompson were co-home run kings of nineteenth century major league baseball. It was impossible to differentiate between the two.

Dennis Joseph Brouthers was born in Sylvan Lake, New York, on May 8, 1858. By the time he was 20 years old, he had grown to six-feet-two-inches in height and had tipped the scales at a muscular 200 pounds, a veritable giant for his day. He began his baseball career as a lefthanded pitcher with the Troy Trojans of the National League in 1879, but, after only three games, he was shifted to first base to take advantage of his big bat. He stayed there for the next 19 years.

Brouthers was a competent, defensive first baseman in an era before gloves became fashionable. He had sure hands, while his above-average height gave him a distinct advantage when handling wild throws from erratic infielders. He was also a capable baserunner, averaging over 30 stolen bases a year, with a high of 38 in 1894. But it was at bat where Big Dan was a standout. He cut a handsome figure at the plate: tall, muscular, with a neat handlebar mustache. To the opposing pitcher, however, he presented a terrifying visage: a towering demon who could rain destruction on a team with one mighty swing of his enormous club. Brouthers's smooth, powerful, lefthanded stroke sent baseballs to the farthest reaches of the park with monotonous regularity. His .519 slugging average is the highest of any nineteenth-century player; his extra base hit percentage of 11.3 percent is also first for his time; and his .342 lifetime batting average is not only the highest of any nineteenth-century batter, but also is still ninth on the all time list.

Strangely enough, the gentle giant was not a free swinger of the Mantle- or Reggie Jackson-type. Like most of his compatriots, he was a contact hitter, who rarely watched a third strike go by. Over a 19-year career, Brouthers averaged only 20 strikeouts a year, to go along with 67 bases on balls. In 1894, after the pitching distance was lengthened to sixty feet-six inches from the plate, he struck out only nine times in 525 at bats. Twice in his career, he had more home runs than strikeouts, accomplishments matched by only a few of the world class sluggers, like Ted Williams, Joe DiMaggio, Sadaharu Oh, and Josh Gibson.

Big Dan Brouthers, the premier slugger of the nineteenth century, was also a capable first baseman. He played barehanded during the first half of his career, but by 1889 he had adapted to the glove, as shown in this photo (credit: Transcendental Graphics).

Brouthers's widespread reputation as a slugger gained acceptance in 1882 and 1883 when the Buffalo Bisons' star won two consecutive batting titles, with averages of .368 and .371. In '82, he produced 63 runs batted in, in 84 games; in the following year, he led the league in RBIs with 97, in only 94 games. He also showed the way in hits both years, with 129 and 156, and, in the latter year, led the league in triples with 17. Big Dan led the league in slugging average for six straight years, from 1881 through 1886, with averages of .541, .547, .572, .548, .543, and .581. In 1887 he slugged the ball at a .562 clip, but was beaten out for the title by teammate Sam Thompson's .571.

In 1885, the big first baseman was involved in one of the biggest deals of the nineteenth century. The Buffalo club, financially bankrupt, sold its famed "Big Four" infield to the Detroit Wolverines for a whopping $7,500. Accompanying Brouthers to the Motor City was second baseman Hardie Richardson, shortstop Charlie Rowe, and third baseman Deacon White.

Big Dan's most glorious years came with the Wolverines from 1886 through 1888. On September 10, 1886, he had his most memorable day in baseball, smashing three home runs, a double, and a single, good for 15 total bases, against the Buffalo Bisons.

In 1887, he led the mighty Wolverines, often called one of the greatest teams of all time, to the National League pennant by 3½ games over the Philadelphia Phillies. His league-leading numbers included 153 runs scored and 36 doubles. He also stung the ball at a .338 clip. Detroit went on to scuttle the American Association champion St. Louis Browns 10–5 in the World Series, although Brouthers was sidelined for all but one game with a sprained ankle.

Dan Brouthers was a baseball nomad long before Bobo Newsome made 20 pit stops in 20 years during the '30s and '40s. He toiled for 11 different teams in three different leagues between 1879 and 1904, none for longer than four years. The slugging first baseman had wanderlust. He followed the dollar from town to town, and he let his bat do the talking. He slugged the ball wherever he went, winning a total of five batting titles: two in Buffalo, one in Brooklyn, and two in Boston (for both the Beaneaters and the Red Stockings). His teams won four league championships and one World Championship.

The slugging first baseman took his third batting title in 1889, when he hit .373 for the Beaneaters. After switching teams, to the American Association's Boston Red Stockings, Brouthers led the way in hitting again, smacking the ball at a .350 gait. He followed that performance with another batting championship in 1892, this time with the National League's Brooklyn Bridegrooms. In addition to hitting .335, Big Dan also led the league in runs batted in, with 124.

Brouthers hit the ball with authority wherever he played. The size and shape of the field didn't make any difference to him. He played in horseshoe-shaped stadiums with short foul lines and enormous center field fences, and he played in parks that had no outfield fences at all—only wide-open spaces. He hit the ball with enormous power in all of them, spraying extra base hits to the farthest reaches of the field. In Buffalo, the foul lines at Riverside Grounds were only 210 feet from home plate, but the center field fence was 410 feet from the plate. Recreation Park in Detroit had no fences, so Big Dan had to earn every base he got in the Motor City. Boston's South End Grounds, Brouthers's home field in 1889, was another of the popular, oblong-shaped parks of the period. It had typical, short foul lines (255 feet to right field) and a remote center field fence (440 feet). Baltimore's Oriole Park had a distant, 350-foot right field foul line. Brouthers encountered a lot of variety in his home ballparks, if nothing else.

For all intents and purposes, the slugging first baseman called it quits after the 1896 season, at the age of 38. Playing for the Philadelphia Phillies, Big Dan bowed out by hitting the cover off the ball. His .344 batting average was two points higher than his lifetime average. He did return for two games with the New York Giants, at John McGraw's request, in 1904, but that was for token appearances only. He went 0 for 5.

Following his major league career, Big Dan Brouthers played six years in the minors, leading the Eastern League in hitting in 1897 with an average of .415 and showing the way in the Hudson River League in 1904 at the age of 46, with an average of .373. After he put away his uniform for the last time, he became a scout for John McGraw's New York Giants. Later, he worked for more than 20 years as the press gate attendant at the Polo Grounds.

Looking back on his illustrious major league baseball career, the aged war horse just smiled and said, "We slugged 'em to death." The nineteenth-century home run king died quietly in 1932, at the age of 74. He was inducted into baseball's Hall of Fame in 1945.

Samuel Luther Thompson first saw the light of day on March 5, 1860, in Danville, Indiana. As a youngster growing up in the midwest, he played sandlot ball for recreation, but worked as a carpenter to earn his keep. During the summer of 1883, he was recruited by the Detroit Wolverines following an exhibition game against his town team.

Big Sam's career began quietly enough, in 1884, with a short, five-game stint in nearby Evansville. The next year, after cracking the ball at a .316 clip in 30 games with Indianapolis of the Western League, the powerful, six-foot-two, 207-pound, lefthanded hitter was called up to the Wolverines by manager Charlie Morton. Thompson helped the ragtag Detroit club escape their normal cellar position with a display of power unknown in the Motor City. The 25-year-old rookie led the team in batting with an average of .303. He also unloaded 25 extra base hits in just 63 games, including seven triples and seven home runs.

In 1886, after the "Big Four" joined the club from Buffalo, Detroit improved their league standing from sixth place to second place. The following year, they captured the pennant. Big Sam dominated the league statistics, setting the pace in at bats (545), batting average (.372), triples (23), and runs batted in (166). His teammate, Dan Brouthers led the league in doubles and runs scored.

In the fall classic, the husky slugger sparked his team to a 10–5 World Series victory over the powerful St. Louis Browns. His .362 average included two doubles and two home runs. Both his homers came off Brownie ace Parisian Bob Caruthers in game eight. That win gave the Wolverines a comfortable 6–2 Series lead. By the time Detroit clinched the Series, by winning their eighth game in 11 decisions, Big Sam had already accumulated 19 base hits.

Two years later, Thompson was sold to the Philadelphia Phillies, where he teamed up with Billy Hamilton and Ed Delahanty to form the only .400-hitting outfield in major league history. In 1894, from the longer pitching distance, the outfield trio tattooed opposing pitchers almost at will. Big Sam's .404 average was supplemented by Sliding Billy's .404 and Big Ed's .407. In

Big Sam Thompson, shown in action in 1889, starred for both the Detroit Wolverines and the Philadelphia Phillies over a 15-year career. He batted .400 twice, although he never led the league in that category. In 1894, he was part of baseball's only .400 hitting outfield (credit: Transcendental Graphics).

spite of that potent offense, the Phillies limped home a distant 18 games behind Ned Hanlon's pennant-winning Baltimore Orioles.

In 1893, after the rules committee lengthened the pitching distance by over ten feet, major league hitters feasted on the longer, slower serves, as has been noted. As batting averages jumped up by over 35 points, no one capitalized on the situation more than Thompson. In the eight years prior to 1893, Big Sam hit .318, with 10 home runs a year. In the three years after the change, the slugging lefty walloped the ball at a stratospheric .391 clip and increased his home run output to 14.

In 1895, the handsome giant tattooed the ball at a blazing .392 clip. He led the league in home runs, jerking 18 balls over the short, 272-foot right field wall at the newly opened Baker Bowl. He also showed the way in runs batted in, with 165, and in slugging percentage, with .654.

A back injury hampered Thompson's swing in 1896, causing his batting average to plummet to a disappointing .298, a drop of 96 points from his outstanding 1895 season and only the fourth time in his 12-year major league career that he had failed to surpass the .300. His extra base hit output also suffered, dropping from 84 to 47, although he still managed to knock in 100 runs and to score 103 himself. When back problems continued to plague him throughout the next two years, limiting his playing time to just 17 games, the proud slugger called it a day. He came back briefly with Detroit in 1906, responding to an emergency call from manager Bill Armour, but the 46-year-old outfielder barely survived the strain, batting just .226 in eight games.

Thompson was a big, handsome man, with a finely muscled physique and outstanding coordination. His offensive statistics are impressive—a .331 career batting average and 127 home runs—but they were not his only attributes. The good-natured Hoosier was an all-around player. Even though he was a big man, he could still motor, piling up 235 stolen bases in 15 years. He was also an outstanding defensive outfielder, with good range, a dependable glove, and a strong, accurate throwing arm. He has been credited with popularizing the one-hop throw to the catcher to cut down aggressive baserunners.

Samuel L. Thompson was a true home run king. His 127 home runs are second to Roger Connor for nineteenth-century honors, but his home run average of 12 home runs per year is the highest average of the nineteenth century. His 166 runs batted in 1887 is also a nineteenth-century record. Big Sam remains the most productive run producer in major league history. His career RBI average of .923 runs batted in per game puts him slightly ahead of Lou Gehrig and Hank Greenberg, the two most productive twentieth century sluggers.

The modest Thompson retired in his "home town" of Detroit after his playing days ended. Heart disease took the big slugger away from his fans prematurely, in 1922, at the age of 62. He was subsequently elected to the Baseball Hall of Fame in 1974 in recognition of his outstanding achievements on the playing field.

Major Leagues, Twentieth Century, Dead Ball Era—Gavvy Cravath

Clifford Carleton Cravath, better known as "Gavvy," was the greatest home run hitter of the old dead ball era. The wise-cracking, tobacco-chewing outfielder led the National League in dingers six times in seven years, between 1913 and 1919. His average of 17 home runs a year, adjusted for the lively ball that came into play just after he retired, predicted he would have pounded out 43 home runs a year if he had played after 1920. If that were the case, he would have found himself in elite company—just him, The Babe, and Josh Gibson.

Cravath was a southern Californian, born in San Diego on March 23, 1881. He broke into organized ball with his home town team of the California League at the age of 21. Then, after five impressive seasons with Los Angeles of the Pacific Coast League, the young outfielder was purchased by the lowly Boston Red Sox of the American League.

He played in 94 games for Deacon McGuire's Sox in 1908, demonstrating average defense in the outfield, but showing little of the anticipated offense. His 22 extra base hits included only one home run, and he knocked in only 34 runs in 277 at bats. The following year, after disastrous trials with the Chicago White Sox and the Washington Senators, Cravath was back in the minors, with the American Association's Minneapolis Millers.

His three years in Minneapolis were maturing years for the five-foot-eleven, 186-pound slugger. After hitting a respectable .290 in 1909, the 29-year-old Cravath finally came into his own the next year, capturing the batting title with an average of .326 and establishing himself as a long ball threat with a league-leading 14 home runs. In 1911, the righthanded power hitter ran roughshod through the American Association, leading the league in batting (.363), hits (221), doubles (53), and home runs (29). His four-base output led all of professional baseball. By comparison, Frank Schulte of the Chicago Cubs led the National League in homers with 21, while Frank "Home Run" Baker of the Philadelphia Athletics showed the way in the American League with a scant 9 round trippers.

Cravath's Minneapolis home runs were not the result of the notorious dimensions in Nicollet Park, either. The field may have had some advantage for lefthanded batters, but it was no picnic for righthanded ones. The left field fence was 334 feet from home plate, and the center field fence was a distant 432 feet away.

The Philadelphia Phillies, tired of playing second fiddle to Connie Mack's Athletics in the City of Brotherly Love, picked up Cravath's contract from Minneapolis for $3,500. Gavvy was ready this time, at the advanced baseball age of 31. He proceeded to dominate the major leagues in home run output over the next eight years, leading the National League in home runs six times and both major leagues in home runs four times.

In 1912, the Californian cracked 11 home runs, 3 behind the league leader. The following year, taking dead aim on the short right field fences in Baker Bowl, he upped up his home run production to 19, good enough to lead both leagues. He also led both circuits in runs batted in with 128, while stinging the ball at a career-high .341. He hit another 19 home runs in 1914, good enough for another home run crown.

In 1915, Cravath and the Phillies put it all together. Pat Moran's slugging right fielder topped the league in runs scored (89), home runs (24), runs batted in (115), and bases on balls (89). His four-base total was the highest home run total in the major leagues in 31 years. He practically carried the Phils to the pennant single-handedly, on the wings of his blazing bat. He was ably supported by a 28-year-old, righthanded pitcher by the name of Grover Cleveland Alexander. All Pete did was win 31 games against only 10 losses, with a barely visible earned run average of 1.22.

The Phils fortunes declined after 1915, but Cravath kept plugging along. He won three more home run titles, in 1917, 1918, and 1919. In 1919, he captured the title with 12 home runs, even though he came to bat only 214 times. Many players had in excess of 500 at bats that season. By this time, Gavvy's aging legs were beginning to give out, however, and Father Time was sharpening up his scythe.

The San Diego native was promoted to manager halfway through the 1919 season, but his efforts did not prevent the Philadelphia National League entry from finishing dead last with a record of 47–90. Fate did not deal Cravath any better hand in 1920. His Phillies once again stumbled home, winning only 62 of 153 games and finishing 30½ games behind the pennant-winning Brooklyn Dodgers. Cravath batted only 49 times, finishing with 1 home run, 11 runs batted in, and a .289 average, although he did lead the league in pinch hits with 20.

Gavvy Cravath called it quits after the 1920 season. He returned to California and settled in Escondido, where he became a justice of the peace, living to the ripe old age of 82. The powerful slugger from the west coast was one of the outstanding home run hitters in baseball history. He was just born twenty years too soon.

Japanese Leagues—Sadaharu Oh

Sadaharu Oh is the all-time, Japanese, professional career home run leader with a total of 868 home runs over a 22-year period. He completely dominated Japanese baseball for over two decades, leading the Central League

Gavvy Cravath led the National League in home runs six times in seven years, from 1913 through 1919. He was the Major League's home run king during the era of the dead ball (credit: National Baseball Library, Cooperstown, N.Y.).

in home runs a total of 15 times, 13 of those in succession. He also piled up dozens of other records along the way, winning five batting titles, while showing the way in runs scored 15 times and runs batted in 13 times.

Sadaharu Oh was born in Sumida-ku, the older section of Tokyo, on May 10, 1940, to a Chinese father and a Japanese mother. The husky youngster began his baseball career as a pitcher, in grade school, and continued to pitch at Waseda Commercial High School, the recognized "baseball factory," for the professional teams. In his freshman year at Waseda, his team participated in the National High School Tournament in Koshien, the single biggest baseball event of the year in Japan—far exceeding any of the professional events, even the Japan Series, the professional World Series equivalent.

Almost 2,000 high school teams from across Japan participated in the elimination tournament, with the regional winners moving on to Koshien for the finals. It was, by far, the most celebrated athletic event of the year in Japan, with millions of people attending the various regional tournaments, and well over 500,000 fans cramming into Koshien Stadium to witness the championship games.

As a freshman, the young southpaw pitcher had some early success. He tossed a no-hitter in the regionals and hit a home run to support his cause. Unfortunately, in Koshien, he lost his composure in front of 60,000 screaming fans and took a pounding on the mound. The following year he fared better, pitching his team to the Koshien championship by a 4–2 score. In his final year at Waseda, Oh failed to hold a 5–1 lead in the twelfth inning of the regional final in Tokyo, and Waseda was eliminated from the tournament by their cross-town arch rival, Meiji, 6–5. It was a shattering defeat for the 18-year-old youngster and a humiliating end to his high school career.

In spite of his ignominious departure from high school baseball, the Yomiuri (Tokyo) Giants still recruited the pitcher/slugger for their Central League champions. As Oh discovered, professional baseball in Japan is played in a military-like atmosphere, with daily, punishing practice sessions. The variety of body-building exercises, such as push-ups, sprints, and calisthenics, combined with the incessant fielding and batting drills, lasted from sunup to sundown. As a result, most Japanese players are in tiptop physical condition. They are also outstanding defensive players, good hitters with excellent bat control, and thoroughly schooled in the fundamentals of the game.

In high school, Oh was a sensational pitcher, as well as a long ball threat. In the majors, however, his fast ball was below average, causing his manager Mr. Mizuhara, to move him to first base, while taking advantage of his explosive bat. As an infielder, Oh had to learn the ropes from the ground up. History shows he learned his lessons well. He won nine gold gloves as a defensive first baseman.

It was at the plate, however, where Sadaharu Oh excelled. He was not an overnight sensation, to be sure, hitting only 37 home runs in his first three years, with a total of 149 runs batted in and an anemic .242 batting average. Constant work on his part, and the teaching of Arakawa-san, gradually brought Oh to his optimum playing potential. In 1962, at the age of 22, the five-foot-eleven, 174-pound slugger suddenly blossomed in a bona fide home run hitter. He sent a league-leading 38 home runs out of stadiums all over Japan. He also led the league in RBIs with 84 and hit a respectable .272. From there, the young first baseman's career skyrocketed.

Sadaharu Oh won the next 12 home run crowns, giving him 13 in a row. After a one year absence, he took two more titles. The smooth-swinging lefthander, with the pronounced, high leg kick, set a new Japanese professional season record with 55 round trippers in 1964. He also hit 50 home runs in 1977 and, on ten other occasions, exceeded 40 home runs a year.

Oh teamed with all-star third baseman Shigeo Nagashima to give the Giants a slugging duo unmatched in the annals of Japanese baseball. Nagashima himself won two home run crowns, four RBI titles, and a record six batting crowns. Between them they carried the Yomiuri team to an unprecedented 14 Central League pennants and 11 Japan Series titles.

Sadaharu Oh captured two triple crowns along the way, back to back, in 1973 and 1974. His .355 batting average, 51 home runs, and 114 runs batted in led the way in '73, while his .332 average, 49 dingers, and 107 RBIs were tops in '74.

Sadaharu Oh, with his inimitable leg kick, powered his way to the top of the baseball world by slamming a world record 868 home runs during a glorious 22-year career with the Yomiuri Giants of the Japanese Central League (credit: Transcendental Graphics).

Late in 1975, Oh pounded out his 658th home run, breaking the record of Katsuya Nomura, the powerful catcher of the Nankai Hawks. Two years later, on September 3, 1977, Oh reached the pinnacle. In the third inning of a game against the Yakult Swallows, in Korakuen Stadium, the determined first sacker hit a hanging curve ball off Kojiro Suzuki, sending it in a high arc into the right field stands. It was home run number 756, permitting Oh to pass Hammerin' Hank Aaron to become the all-time professional home run leader. Oh continued to play for another two years, adding another 112 home runs to his distinguished total. He bowed out of the sport in 1980, with a 30-home run season, a champion to the end.

On November 8, 1983, Sadaharu Oh was named manager of the Tokyo Yomiuri Giants.

Major Leagues, Twentieth Century, Lively Ball Era—Babe Ruth

George Herman "Babe" Ruth is America's "Sultan of Swat." He stands astride the baseball scene like the Colossus of Rhodes. During baseball's darkest days, in the wake of the infamous Black Sox scandal, the Babe rallied the country around him, thanks mainly to his superhuman slugging feats and his larger-than-life public escapades. It would not be an exaggeration to say that Babe Ruth saved baseball; or, if he didn't save it, he at least nursed it back to health.

George Herman Ruth was born in Baltimore, Maryland, on February 6, 1895. His father, a saloon keeper, had difficulty controlling the unruly youth, and seven-year-old George eventually ended up in the local reform school, St. Mary's Industrial School. Ruth was in and out of St. Mary's over the next 11 years. He learned some discipline there (a minimum), along with the fundamentals of baseball.

Ruth began his baseball career as a lefthanded catcher at St. Mary's, but by the time he left school at the age of 18, he had become a talented southpaw pitcher. Brother Mathias, his school counselor, recommended The Babe to Jack Dunn of the Baltimore Orioles in 1914, and the young hurler ran up a respectable 22–9 record in the International League. Within a year, the six-foot-two, 215-pound hurler was toiling for the Boston Red Sox of the American League, only 300 miles from St. Mary's as the crow flies, but light years away as far as Ruth was concerned.

The Babe was an overnight pitching sensation. He had a good fast ball and a sharp-breaking curve ball that he kept low to the ground. He was stingy with the hits, allowing only seven per game, and meted out only three bases on balls for every nine innings pitched. In 1915, the slick lefty piled up an 18–8 record. He followed that with a 23–12 season, pacing the American League with a 1.75 earned run average and nine shutouts. In 1917, Ruth won

24 games in his last full season as a pitcher. His herculean feats with the bat brought his mound career to a premature end.

The southpaw didn't go quietly, however. He appeared as a pitcher in two World Series, in 1916 against the Brooklyn Dodgers and in 1918 against the Chicago Cubs. The Babe left the pitching rubber in a blaze of glory. In the two Series, he compiled an enviable 3–0 record, with a 0.87 earned run average. Along the way, he established a World Series record of 29 consecutive scoreless innings. Whitey Ford broke the record in 1962, completing a string of 33 scoreless innings that began in 1960 and continued through 1961 and into 1962.

The Bambino's first year as a full-time outfielder was 1919, and he immediately broke the all-time major league home run record by banging out 29 circuit clouts. He still managed to win nine games on the mound that year, but that was his swan song as a pitcher. He saw action on the mound only five more times in 17 years.

Babe Ruth completed his short, six-year pitching career with 94 wins against only 46 losses. He finished with 17 shutouts and a microscopic 2.24 earned run average. The all-time ERA leader is Ed Walsh with 1.82. Ruth's total would place him eighth on the list, just behind Walter Johnson, if he had enough innings to qualify. As noted earlier, the crafty southpaw bested "The Big Train" eight times in ten head-to-head duels. As a pitcher, Ruth had few equals. He was the top lefthanded pitcher in the American League during his brief tenure on the mound. If he had concentrated on a pitching career instead of opting for the outfield, he might well have duplicated Johnson's record of 400+ victories and 100+ shutouts. He was that good.

After his spectacular 1919 season, Babe Ruth became an immediate celebrity, a larger-than-life hero to millions of people, young and old alike. His extraordinary prowess with the bat made eyes pop wherever he went. In 1920, he almost doubled his previous year's home run output, racking up 54 dingers in 142 games. His home run total represented 15 percent of all the home runs hit in the American League that year. He outhomered every other league team, single-handedly. All of them!

From there, the legend of the Bambino grew by leaps and bounds. In 1922, he extended his single-season home run record to 59 and, in 1927, he established a new standard with 60 home runs, once again outhomering every other team in the league. This time, his total accounted for 14 percent of the entire league's home run production—one out of every seven home runs hit in the American League.

Over the course of 22 years, as a pitcher and an outfielder, Babe Ruth led the American League in homers 12 times. He hit over 50 home runs four times and over 40 home runs 11 times. His home run frequency of 11.8 at bats per home run is unchallenged in major league history. By comparison, Hank Aaron's frequency was 16.4. Roger Maris's was 18.5.

A svelte, 190-pound Babe Ruth, 1919, broke the Major League record for home runs by hitting 29 for Boston that year. Twenty of the round trippers were hit on the road, as Boston's spacious right field stands were almost unreachable during the dead ball era (credit: National Baseball Library, Cooperstown, N.Y.).

The Sultan of Swat was at his peak during the decade of the '20s, the so-called "Golden Age" of sports. Great athletes with extraordinary talent seemed to rule all major sports during this period, heroic figures that were larger than life to the American sporting public. Babe Ruth towered over the baseball world. Jack Dempsey, the 182-pound fighting Irishman out of Manassa, Colorado, destroyed heavyweight champion, Jess Willard, the supposedly unbeatable six-foot-six, 250-pound Pottawatomie Giant, in 1919, then dominated the heavyweight boxing scene for eight long years. Robert T. "Bobby" Jones, a lifetime amateur golfer, had no equal on the links during his career. In eight years, the young Georgian captured four United States Open titles and four times finished second, twice in playoffs. He made the other golfers happy when he retired in 1930. Big Bill Tilden, the king of tennis during the '20s, is still considered by many experts to be the greatest tennis player of all time. The tall, skinny racquet artist won the National Tennis Championship seven times in ten years. Six of those titles came in succession, from 1920 through 1925. Harold "Red" Grange, the legendary "Galloping Ghost" of Illinois football, was one of the greatest running backs in college football history, piling up over 3,600 rushing yards during his three years with the Fighting Illini. In 1924, against Michigan, the Ghost scored five touchdowns, including a 95-yard gallop with the game's opening kickoff. He scored three more first quarter touchdowns, on runs of 65, 55, and 45 yards, respectively. On the distaff side, Helen Wills Moody, a young American housewife, won the United States National Tennis Championship seven times. Gertrude Ederle, a plucky, 19-year-old New Yorker, became the first woman to swim the English Channel, crossing from France to England in 14 hours, 31 minutes. And Mildred "Babe" Didrickson, a fiery redhead, left Texas in 1928 at the age of 13 to become a true superstar. After winning several track and field events in the 1932 Olympics, the talented Didrickson went on to star on both the golf links and the baseball diamond. She was also an outstanding basketball player, high diver, and archer. The 1920s truly bred a contingent of world-class athletes unmatched in the history of American sports. There were mythical heroes in every field of athletic endeavor; and the mighty Bambino towered over all of them.

Ruth and the New York Yankees dominated major league baseball during his tenure in the big city. The Bronx Bombers won seven American League flags in 15 years and walked off with four world titles. Ruth won three other World Championships with the Boston Red Sox during his pitching days. In 41 World Series games, in addition to his pitching records, the Bambino hit 15 home runs, knocked in 33 runs, and batted .326.

Babe Ruth was more than the world's greatest home run hitter. He also hit for average, his .342 career batting average places him ninth on the all-time batting list. He put together season marks of .376, .378, .393, .378, .372, and .373. He won the batting title in 1924 and set the pace in runs scored 7 times, runs batted in 6 times, slugging percentage 12 times, and bases on balls 11 times. He scored 2,174 runs during his career, second only to Ty Cobb.

Often overlooked in the light of his prodigious home run feats are his many other talents. He was an intelligent baserunner, with above-average speed, and was a good slider. He stole 123 bases during his career, even though the Yankees were not a running ball club at the time. He stole 17 bases in 1921 and again in 1923.

The Babe was also an excellent defensive outfielder, with good range and an accurate throwing arm. He averaged about 15 assists a year from his right field position in Yankee Stadium during his prime, with a high of 21 in 1920. The New York sports writers claimed that Ruth never made a bad play in the outfield during his Yankee career. If that isn't quite true, it is correct to say that he more than held his own in the field.

Babe Ruth left the New York Yankees in 1935 to play for the Boston Braves, hoping his presence in Boston would lead to a managerial position. It didn't. He did, however, have one more glorious day at bat to give to his fans. On a warm May afternoon in Pittsburgh, the 40-year-old Sultan of Swat smashed three balls out of Forbes field, the last one a mighty wallop of more than 400 feet.

Babe spent the 1938 season as a coach for the Brooklyn Dodgers, still hoping for an opportunity to manage a major league club. He was already a Hall-of-Famer, having been presented with that honor in 1936. When Larry McPhail brought Leo Durocher in to manage the Brooks, Ruth took off his uniform for the last time and went home. He spent the remaining years of his life as a goodwill ambassador for the sport, particularly with the youth of America, whose hero he remained to the end.

George Herman Ruth died in 1948, at the young age of 53, after a long, courageous battle with throat cancer. The Babe was one of a kind. He was the ugly duckling who became a prince—the juvenile delinquent who grew up to socialize with kings and presidents. He was their hero also.

The King of Swat—Josh Gibson

Josh Gibson, in his prime, stood six-feet-two-inches tall and weighed in at a solid 217 pounds. He was the strongest man in baseball, capable of hitting the ball out of any stadium in the world. Physically, he resembled a weightlifter, with mighty forearms and a barrel-like chest; but inside that muscular body beat the heart of a child. Josh Gibson was a big, good-natured youngster who loved to play baseball and who could play it better than any man alive.

Gibson was born in Buena Vista, Georgia, about 20 miles east of Columbus on Route 26, on December 21, 1911, to Mark and Nancy Gibson. In 1924, Mark Gibson, a dirt-poor sharecropper, moved his family to Pittsburgh, Pennsylvania, to escape the stifling bigotry and segregation of the south and to make a better life for his family. They settled in the Pleasant Valley section of city, in the black ghetto across the Allegheny, known as "The Hill."

Twelve-year-old Josh quickly adapted to his new environment and began to develop a new interest—baseball. He spent all his free time shagging flies and swinging a bat in the summer sandlot games along Bedford Avenue. Being a natural athlete, young Josh soon developed into the hottest young baseball player on "The Hill." Off the field, his imagination was stimulated by the exploits of the local Homestead Grays, one of the leading professional teams in Negro baseball. The feats of his heroes, such as fireballing Smokey Joe Williams, slugging John Beckwith, and superstar Martin Dihigo, convinced the teenage slugger to pursue a career in professional baseball.

Young Gibson was not only an outstanding baseball player in his teens. He was also a top amateur swimmer, football player, and basketball player, but baseball was his first love. Four years after his arrival in the Steel City, the 16-year-old catcher buttoned on his first real uniform shirt, as a member of Gimbel's Athletic Club, a local amateur team.

The Gibson myth was born in western Pennsylvania in the late '20s, as the gifted young catcher sent titanic home runs out of ballparks up and down the Monongahela. In addition to his extraordinary baseball talent, he had a natural charisma that mesmerized the fans. His friendly disposition, youthful good looks, Grecian body, and great strength brought out large crowds wherever he played.

The precocious slugger didn't remain an amateur for long. He was quickly recruited by the Crawford Colored Giants, a local semipro team, where his powerful drives added to his already burgeoning reputation in the Pittsburgh area. His notoriety brought him to the attention of the Homestead Grays' manager, Judy Johnson, who followed his progress with increasing interest. One night in 1930, as Josh sat in the stands at Grays Field, watching Johnson's cohorts do battle with the Kansas City Monarchs, the Grays' catcher went down with a split finger. Gibson was quickly recruited to fill the void. He was a professional from that day on.

Within a year, the 19-year-old phenom was the talk of Negro league baseball. He slugged the ball at a sizzling .368 clip in '31, and led the Eastern Colored League in home runs with six in just 32 games. He repeated as home run champion the following year, smashing seven round trippers in 46 games.

Over the course of a 17-year career with the Grays and the Pittsburgh Crawfords, Josh Gibson led the league in home runs a total of nine times. He showed the way with 12 homers in 50 games in 1934, 13 homers in 49 games in 1935, 11 homers in 23 games in 1936, 16 home runs in only 27 games in 1939, 11 home runs in 40 games in 1942, 14 homers in 49 games in 1943, and 18 homers in 31 games in 1946.

Showing he was not a one dimensional baseball player, the speedy catcher led the league in triples three times and in stolen bases once. He also led the league in hitting in 1943. His .521 batting average in 1943 is the second highest in Negro league annals, trailing only John Henry Lloyd, who pounded the ball at a .564 clip in 1929.

Josh Gibson was one of the most feared hitters in baseball history. He starred in the Negro leagues, as well as in Cuba, Mexico, the Dominican Republic, and Puerto Rico. His home run prowess matched that of any slugger who ever played the game (credit: Noir Tech Sports, Inc.).

When Josh played with the Crawfords from 1934 through 1936, he teamed with Satchel Paige to form what many baseball experts consider to be the greatest battery in baseball history. When the two players barnstormed together after the season ended, the advertising posters would read, "Satchel Paige, guaranteed to strike out the first nine men, and Josh Gibson, guaranteed to hit two home runs." Not many fans went home disappointed.

As a member of the Homestead Grays, Gibson teamed with first baseman Buck Leonard to lead the Grays to an unprecedented nine consecutive Negro National League pennants, beginning in 1937. The dynamic duo, known as the "Thunder Twins" were the Negro league counterparts of Ruth and Gehrig.

Like many of the Negro players of his day, Josh played baseball year-round. In addition to the regular Negro league season and the barnstorming junkets around the United States in the fall, Josh usually played baseball south of the border during the winter. Over the years, his baseball travels took him to Mexico, Cuba, Puerto Rico, and the Dominican Republic. He made eyes pop wherever he played. His 11 home runs in 186 at bats led the Cuban League in 1938. Three years later, he led two different leagues in two different countries in home runs. Playing 94 games for Vera Cruz in the Mexican League, the young slugger banged out 33 homers in 358 at bats. Moving on to Puerto Rico that winter, Gibson hit another 13 home runs for Santurce in 32 games, giving him a total of 46 homers in 126 games and two home run titles.

Josh Gibson's career Negro league batting average was .362, which he complemented with a total of 48 home runs a year. The big catcher averaged 27 home runs a year during three winters in Puerto Rico, while hitting a solid .355. His winter Cuban League averages over three years were 31 home runs and a .352 batting average. In two years in Mexico, the young slugger averaged 54 homers, to go along with a .393 batting average.

Josh also had outstanding success against major league pitching. The records show that he faced big league pitchers 61 times over a 16-year period. Batting against the likes of Dizzy Dean, Paul Dean, Larry French, Fred Frankhouse, and Johnny VanderMeer, the big catcher ripped the ball at a .426 gait, with five home runs.

Josh Gibson was the Peter Pan of Negro league baseball, refusing to grow up and playing the game for the sheer enjoyment of it. He remained a cheerful and enthusiastic ambassador of the sport until the day he died, much like another Negro league catcher, Roy Campanella. He loved the daily contests, and he cherished the companionship of his teammates and the familiarity of the fans. His great affection for the sport was reflected in his Bunyan-like performances. Baseball was a year-round recreation for the gentle giant. He would have played it for nothing.

Over the last three years of his life, the genial catcher was weakened by a life threatening brain tumor. The deadly growth gnawed away at his uncompromising zest for life, causing erratic behavior patterns to emerge. The pain, the painkillers, and various chemical dependencies all contributed to a gradual decline in the big slugger's health. In 1946, Josh Gibson, crippled by arthritis, struggling with the tumor, and depressed that he was not recruited by the major leagues, still managed to put together one of his greatest seasons, rapping the ball to the tune of .361 and smashing 18 homers, in only 119 at bats.

That last sensational season was Josh Gibson's swan song. Shortly after the Christmas holidays, on January 20, 1947, tragedy struck the baseball superstar. He suffered a paralyzing stroke at his mother's home, at 2410 Strauss. He died within hours, just blocks away from his old sandlot haunts. He had just turned 35.

Josh Gibson could do it all. He hit for average, hit with fearsome power, had above-average speed, and was an outstanding catcher with a rifle arm. His lifetime Negro league batting average of .362, even adjusted to major league levels, would have made him one of the top hitting catchers in major league history. His adjusted home run average of 61 home runs for every 550 at bats is unmatched in baseball annals. It is mind boggling to imagine what his numbers might have been if he had played his home games in Atlanta's Fulton County Stadium—or perhaps at Coors Field!

The King of Swat was finally elected to the Baseball Hall of Fame in Cooperstown, New York, in 1972—a fitting tribute long overdue.

APPENDIX:
STATISTICAL TABLES

Comparison of Professional Leagues

Leagues	AB	H	D	T	HR	BA
Major Leagues	550	143	25	6	19	.260
Minor Leagues (Total)	550	163	26	6	26	.296
Class AAA	550	157	—	—	20	.287
Class AA	550	168	—	—	31	.306*
WT-NM, Longhorn Leagues	550	177	—	—	32	.321*
Negro Leagues	550	173	24	8	15	.311
Japanese Leagues	550	152	21	1	42	.278

Notes: Japanese parks were 297 feet down the foul lines, and 387 feet to center field.

Comparison of leagues, data points—
Japanese leagues (90,332 AB) to major leagues (170,380 AB)
Japanese leagues (11,475 AB) to lower minor leagues (41,932 AB)
Negro leagues (13,469 AB) to high minor leagues (45,551 AB)
Negro leagues (13,469 AB) to major leagues (65,240 AB)
* *Small data base.*

Comparison of Negro Leagues to Major Leagues

Name	Negro League Avgs.				Major League Avgs.			
	AB	H	HR	BA	AB	H	HR	BA
Artie Wilson	1,046	393	6	.376	22	4	0	.182
Luke Easter	434	146	23	.336	1,725	472	93	.274
Sam Jethroe	1,331	453	20	.340	1,763	460	49	.261
Roy Campanella	618	197	15	.319	4,205	1,161	242	.276
Ernie Banks	196	50	1	.255	9,421	2,583	512	.274
Willie Mays	460	141	5	.307	10,881	3,283	660	.302
Willard Brown	1,773	624	65	.352	67	12	1	.179
Monte Irvin	850	293	33	.345	2,499	731	99	.293
Jackie Robinson	163	63	5	.387	4,877	1,518	137	.311
Junior Gilliam	432	114	2	.264	7,119	1,889	65	.265
Hank Thompson	641	220	21	.343	3,003	801	129	.267
Larry Doby	513	194	25	.378	5,348	1,515	253	.283
Minnie Minoso	287	84	4	.293	6,579	1,963	186	.298
Elston Howard	495	143	3	.289	5,363	1,471	167	.274
Bob Boyd	1,129	409	11	.362	1,936	567	19	.293
Sandy Amoros	136	46	4	.338	1,311	334	43	.255
Bus Clarkson	517	165	11	.319	25	5	0	.200
Hector Rodriguez	130	31	0	.238	407	108	1	.265
Al Smith	431	126	8	.292	5,357	1,457	164	.272
Total	7,592	2,519	174	.332	51,492	14,447	1,647	.281
Average	550	182	13	.332	550	155	18	.281

Major league averages from *Total Baseball*, edited by John Thorn and Pete Palmer.

Negro league averages for Wilson, Clarkson, and Rodriguez from SABR.

Negro league averages for Easter, Campanella, Banks, Mays, Brown, Irvin, Robinson, Gilliam, Thompson, Minoso, Doby, Howard, and Boyd: © 1995 John B. Holway and Dick Clark, used with permission.

Note: Wilson, Brown, and Clarkson were not included in averages because of their limited major league at bats. Banks and Mays were not included in averages because they were very young when they played in the Negro leagues (Banks, 21–22 years old; Mays 17–19, years old). They had not developed physically and their major league home run totals would have skewed the averages. The major league average would be 22 home runs a year, instead of 18, if Banks and Mays were included.

Comparison of Negro Leagues to High Minor Leagues

Name	Negro League Avgs.				Minor League Avgs.			
	AB	H	HR	BA	AB	H	HR	BA
Artie Wilson	1,046	393	6	.376	5,152	1,609	8	.312
Bill Wright	908	305	21	.336	3,438	1,146	78	.333
Luke Easter	434	146	23	.336	4,150	1,227	269	.296
Ray Dandridge	878	263	5	.322	2,699	852	27	.316
Sam Jethroe	1,331	453	20	.340	3,750	1,108	119	.295
Roy Campanella	618	197	15	.319	959	275	39	.287
Willie Mays	460	141	5	.307	455	179	12	.393
Willard Brown	1,773	624	65	.352	2,213	684	95	.309
Monte Irvin	850	293	33	.345	581	207	33	.356
Jackie Robinson	163	63	5	.387	444	155	3	.349
Junior Gilliam	432	114	2	.264	1,126	331	16	.294
Hank Thompson	641	220	21	.343	505	140	23	.277
Larry Doby	513	194	25	.378	27	6	0	.222
Minnie Minoso	287	84	4	.293	1,309	408	46	.312
Elston Howard	495	143	3	.289	994	306	32	.308
Bob Boyd	1,129	409	11	.362	2,113	672	20	.318
Sandy Amoros	136	46	4	.338	2,229	710	98	.319
Total	11,581	3894	243	.336	32,117	10,009	918	.312
Average	550	185	12	.336	550	171	16	.312

Note: Negro league averages for Wright, Easter, Dandridge, Jethroe, Campanella, Mays, Brown, Irvin, Robinson, Gilliam, Thompson, Doby, Minoso, Howard, Boyd, and Amoros; © 1995 John B. Holway and Dick Clark, used with permission.

Doby was not included in the averages because of his limited minor league at bats.

Minor league averages of Wilson, Wright, Easter, Dandridge, Jethroe, Campanella, Mays, Brown, Irvin, Robinson, Gilliam, Thompson, Doby, Minoso, Howard, Boyd, and Amoros, as well as Amoros's Negro league averages, compliments of SABR, from the book, *The Negro Leagues Book*, edited by Dick Clark and Larry Lester.

Comparison of Japanese Leagues to Major Leagues

Name	Japanese League Avgs.				Major League Avgs.			
	AB	H	HR	BA	AB	H	HR	BA
Matty Alou	913	258	15	.283	5,789	1,777	31	.307
George Altman	3,183	985	205	.309	3,091	832	101	.269
Mike Andrews	389	90	12	.231	3,116	803	66	.258
Ken Aspromonte	943	257	31	.273	1,483	369	19	.249
Don Blasingame	1,356	371	15	.274	5,296	1,366	21	.258
Clete Boyer	1,486	382	71	.257	5,780	1,396	162	.242
Don Buford	1,779	480	65	.270	4,553	1,203	93	.264
Warren Cromartie	2,961	951	171	.321	3,796	1,063	60	.280
Willie Davis	797	237	43	.297	9,174	2,561	182	.279
Wayne Garrett	606	146	28	.241	3,285	786	61	.239
Dave Johnson	660	159	39	.241	4,797	1,252	136	.261
Cecil Fielder	384	116	38	.302	2,870	743	191	.259
Willie Kirkland	2,323	559	126	.246	3,494	837	148	.240
LeRon Lee	4,934	1,579	283	.320	1,617	404	31	.250
Jim Lefebvre	1,098	289	60	.263	3,014	756	74	.251
Norm Larker	727	194	14	.267	1,953	538	32	.275
Jim Lyttle	3,319	945	166	.285	710	176	9	.248
Jim Marshall	1,501	402	78	.268	852	206	29	.242
Felix Millan	1,139	348	12	.306	5,791	1,617	22	.279
Bobby Mitchell	1,718	429	113	.250	617	150	3	.243
Steve Ontiveros	2,458	768	82	.312	2,193	600	24	.274
Roger Repoz	1,787	469	122	.262	2,145	480	82	.224
Dave Roberts	2,774	764	183	.275	194	38	2	.196
Reggie Smith	494	134	45	.271	7,033	2,020	314	.287
Daryl Spencer	2,233	615	152	.275	3,689	901	105	.244
Dick Stuart	685	176	49	.257	3,997	1,055	228	.264
Terry Whitfield	1,407	406	85	.289	1,913	537	33	.281
Walt Williams	952	264	44	.277	2,373	640	33	.270
Bump Wills	633	164	16	.259	3,030	807	36	.266
Roy White	1,229	348	54	.283	6,650	1,803	160	.271
Randy Bass	2,208	743	202	.337	325	69	9	.212
Boomer Wells	3,482	1,137	231	.327	127	29	0	.228
Ralph Bryant	1,173	323	112	.275	1,997	515	30	.258
Mike Diaz	943	288	72	.305	683	169	31	.247
Kent Hadley	2,825	727	131	.257	363	88	14	.242
Ken Macha	1,699	516	82	.303	380	98	1	.258
Carlos May	1,397	431	70	.308	4,120	1,127	90	.274

	Japanese League Avgs.				Major League Avgs.			
Name	AB	H	HR	BA	AB	H	HR	BA
Larry Parrish	874	227	70	.260	6,792	1,789	256	.263
Tony Solaita	1,786	479	155	.268	1,316	336	50	.255
Gordy Windhorn	1,966	501	86	.255	108	19	2	.176
Dick Davis	1,703	564	117	.331	1,217	323	27	.265
Mike Easler	517	156	26	.302	3,677	1,078	118	.293
Vic Harris	968	245	35	.253	1,610	349	13	.217
Willie Upshaw	653	160	39	.245	4,203	1,103	123	.262
George Vukovich	754	193	32	.256	1,602	430	27	.268
Chuck Essegian	300	79	15	.263	1,018	260	47	.255
Ben Oglivie	805	246	46	.306	5,913	1,615	235	.273
Bob Nieman	355	107	13	.301	3,452	1,018	125	.295
Bombo Rivera	541	130	37	.240	831	220	10	.265
Gary Thomasson	477	119	20	.249	2,373	591	61	.249
Bobby Tolan	360	96	6	.267	4,230	1,121	86	.265
Lee Walls	343	82	14	.239	2,550	670	66	.262
Jim Trabor	495	150	24	.303	819	186	27	.227
Brian Dayett	481	126	21	.262	426	110	14	.258
Orestes Destrade	1,655	436	154	.263	635	157	21	.247
Adrian Garrett	1,302	338	102	.260	276	51	11	.185
Woody Jones	3,182	762	246	.239	137	34	2	.248
Stan Palys	1,525	419	66	.275	333	79	10	.237
Jack Pierce	291	66	13	.227	199	42	8	.211
Jose Vidal	122	27	2	.221	146	24	3	.164
George Wilson	624	161	27	.258	209	40	3	.191
Kevin Reimer	470	140	26	.298	1,455	376	52	.258
Glenn Braggs	712	232	54	.326	2,336	601	70	.257
Tom O'Malley	1,721	548	74	.318	1,213	310	13	.256
Mel Hall	939	269	52	.286	4,212	1,168	134	.277
Jack Howell	1,146	336	86	.293	2,268	535	84	.236
Total	90,332	25,539	5,096	.283	170,380	45,200	4,412	.265
Average	550	156	31	.283	550	146	14	.265

Japanese league averages compliments of the Office of the Baseball Commissioner, Japan.

Major league averages from *Total Baseball*, edited by John Thorn and Pete Palmer.

Comparison of Japanese Leagues to Lower Minor Leagues (AA–A)

Name	Japanese League Avgs.				Lower Minor League Avgs.			
	AB	H	HR	BA	AB	H	HR	BA
Orestes Destrade	1,655	436	154	.263	3,051	779	137	.255
Adrian Garrett	1,302	338	102	.260	5,182	1,344	280	.259
Woody Jones	3,182	762	246	.239	3,830	1,068	211	.279
Stan Palys	1,525	419	66	.275	4,919	1,586	189	.322
Jack Pierce	291	66	13	.227	6,926	2,039	395	.294
Dave Roberts	2,774	764	183	.275	6,582	1,858	244	.282
Jose Vidal	122	27	2	.221	5,337	1,486	251	.278
George Wilson	624	161	27	.258	6,105	1,901	275	.311
Total	11,475	2,973	793	.259	41,932	12,061	1,982	.288
Average	550	143	38	.259	550	158	26	.288

Note: Minor league averages from SABR, *Minor League Baseball Stars*.

Japanese averages compliments of the Office of the Baseball Commissioner, Japan.

Home Run Frequency by American Players in Japan

Orestes Destrade's Japanese league home run frequency was 51 homers a year (per 550 at bats). Destrade had a total of 1,655 at bats in Japan through 1994.

Adrian Garrett averaged 43 home runs a year, on 1302 at bats.

Woody Jones averaged 43 home runs a year, on 3,182 at bats.

Randy Bass averaged 50 home runs a year, on 2,208 at bats.

Ralph Bryant averaged 49 home runs a year, on 2,794 at bats.

Tony Solaita averaged 48 home runs a year, on 1,786 at bats.

Larry Parrish averaged 44 home runs a year, on 874 at bats.

Mike Diaz averaged 41 home runs a year, on 1,256 at bats.

Cecil Fielder averaged 54 home runs a year, on 384 at bats.

Charley Manuel averaged 50 home runs a year, on 2,127 at bats.

Note: Sadarahu Oh's home run frequency was 52 home runs a year, on 9,250 at bats. The next highest home run frequency by a Japanese player was the 40 home runs a year hit by outfielder Hiromitsu Ochiai. Ochiai was still active at the end of the 1995 season.

Negro League Averages

Batting Statistics Per 550 At Bats

Name	AB	H	D	T	HR	BA
Josh Gibson	550	199	29	11	48	.362
Roy Campanella	550	175	31	3	13	.319
Buck Leonard	550	178	30	12	24	.328
Mule Suttles	550	181	31	12	34	.329
Ed Wesley	550	178	28	7	28	.324
Willie Wells	550	180	33	8	20	.328
Dobie Moore	550	201	35	15	12	.365
Judd Wilson	550	191	30	6	14	.34
Oscar Charleston	550	192	32	12	26	.350
Turkey Stearnes	550	194	33	18	30	.352
Martin Dihigo	550	174	21	8	25	.319
Chino Smith	550	235	50	8	33	.428
John Beckwith	550	194	33	8	30	.356
Frog Redus	550	176	27	9	21	.319
Heavy Johnson	550	200	—	—	20	.363
Monte Irvin	550	189	28	5	21	.345
Larry Doby	550	208	27	15	27	.378
Luke Easter	550	185	42	10	29	.336
Willard Brown	550	194	26	7	20	.352

Averages Adjusted To Major Leagues

Name	AB	H	D	T	HR	BA
Josh Gibson	550	170	30	8	61	.312
Roy Campanella (Proj.)	550	145	33	3	16	.269
(Actual)	550	152	23	2	32	.276
Buck Leonard	550	150	26	8	30	.278
Mule Suttles	550	152	32	8	43	.279
Ed Wesley	550	149	29	5	36	.274
Dobie Moore	550	169	32	10	15	.315
Oscar Charleston	550	163	33	9	33	.300
Turkey Stearnes	550	164	34	13	38	.302
Martin Dihigo	550	146	22	6	32	.269
Chino Smith	550	204	52	6	42	.378
John Beckwith	550	167	34	6	38	.306

Note: Negro league averages, © 1995 John B. Holway and Dick Clark, used with permission.

Professional Baseball's 50+ Home Run Hitters

Name	Team	League	Year	HR
Babe Ruth	New York Yankees	American	1920	54
			1921	59
			1927	60
			1928	54
Jimmie Foxx	Philadelphia A's	American	1932	58
	Boston Red Sox	American	1938	50
Hank Greenberg	Detroit Tigers	American	1938	58
Mickey Mantle	New York Yankees	American	1956	52
			1961	54
Roger Maris	New York Yankees	American	1961	61
Hack Wilson	Chicago Cubs	National	1930	56
Ralph Kiner	Pittsburgh Pirates	National	1947	51
			1949	54
Willie Mays	New York Giants	National	1955	51
	San Francisco Giants	National	1965	52
George Foster	Cincinnati Reds	National	1977	52
Johnny Mize	New York Giants	National	1947	51
Cecil Fielder	Detroit Tigers	American	1990	51
Albert Belle	Cleveland Indians	American	1995	50
Mark McGwire	Oakland Athletics	American	1996	52
Brady Anderson	Baltimore Orioles	American	1996	50
Sadaharu Oh	Yomiuri Giants	Japanese	1964	55
			1973	51
			1977	50
Makoto Otsuru	Shochiku	Japanese	1950	51
Katsuya Nomura	Nankai Hawks	Japanese	1963	52
Randy Bass	Hanshin Tigers	Japanese	1985	54
Hiromitsu Ochiai	Lotte Marines	Japanese	1985	50
			1986	52
Buzz Arlett	Baltimore	IL	1932	54
Joe Bauman	Artesia	Longhorn	1952	50
			1953	53
	Roswell	Longhorn	1954	72
Steve Bilko	Los Angeles	PCL	1956	55
			1957	56
Ike Boone	Mission	PCL	1929	55
Moose Clabaugh	Tyler	E. Texas	1926	62
Bobby Crues	Amarillo	WT-NM	1947	52
			1948	69

Name	Team	League	Year	HR
Nick Cullop	Minneapolis	AA	1930	54
John Gravino	Fargo-Moorehead	Northern	1953	52
			1954	56
Ken Guettler	Shreveport	Texas	1956	62
Joe Hauser	Baltimore	IL	1930	63
	Minneapolis	AA	1933	69
Frosty Kennedy	Plainview	Southwest	1956	60
Tony Lazzeri	Salt Lake City	PCL	1925	60
Big Boy Kraft	Fort Worth	Texas	1924	55
Bob Lennon	Nashville	Southern	1954	64
Gene Lillard	Los Angeles	PCL	1935	56
Pud Miller	Wichita Falls	Big State	1947	57
	Lamesa	WT-NM	1949	52
Howie Moss	Baltimore	IL	1947	53
James Poole	Nashville	Southern	1930	50
George Puccinelli	Baltimore	IL	1935	53
Tony Robello	Pocatello	Pioneer	1939	58
Leo Shoals	Reidsville	Carolina	1949	55
Dick Stuart	Lincoln	Western	1956	66
Jerry Witte	Dallas	Texas	1949	50
Chuck Workman	Nashville	Southern	1948	52
Bill McNulty	Sacramento	PCL	1974	55
Gorman Thomas	Sacramento	PCL	1974	51
Ron Kittle	Edmonton	PCL	1982	50
Bill Serena	Lubbock	WT-NM	1947	57
James Mathews	Amarillo	WT-NM	1953	50
Ramiro Caballero	Guanajuato	Mex. Cntr.	1962	59
Bud Davis	Okmulgee	West Ass.	1924	51
Buck Frierson	Sherman-Dennison	Big State	1947	58
Jack Pierce	Leon	Mexican	1986	54
Bud Heslet	Visalia	California	1956	51
Leonard Tucker	Pampa	Southwest	1956	51
Tom Winsett	Columbus	AA	1936	50
Pat Wright	Fort Wayne	Central	1930	52
Orrin Snyder	Borger	WT-NM	1947	54
Calvin Felix	Las Vegas	Sunset	1947	52
Jesse McLain	Harlingen	Rio G'de Vl.	1950	53
Leon Wagner	Danville	Carolina	1956	51
Heriberto Vargas	Guanajuato	Mex. Ctr.	1966	55

Legend:

IL	International League
PCL	Pacific Coast League
WT-NM	West Texas-New Mexico League
AA	American Association
Mex. Cntr	Mexican Central League
West Ass.	Western Association
Rio G'devl	Rio Grande Valley League

Professional Baseball's 50+ Home Run Hitters,
By League Classification

League Classification	No. Players 50+	No. Players 60+
Major Leagues	21 (AL 14, NL 7)	2 (Ruth, Maris)
High Minor Leagues (AAA)	14 (IL 4, AA 3, PCL 7)	3 (Hauser x2, Lazzeri)
Lower Minors		
AA, A	7	3 (Guettler, Lennon, Stuart)
B, C, D	26	4 (Bauman, Clabaugh, Crues, Kennedy)
Japanese Leagues	8	0

Note: Only one player has hit more than 69 home runs in one season. Joe Bauman of Roswell in the Class C Longhorn League, smashed 72 home runs in 1954.

Legend: AL ....American League
NL ....National League
AAA, AA, A, B, C, D ....Minor League Classifications
AA ....American Association
IL ....International League
PCL ....Pacific Coast League

Professional Baseball's 50+
Home Run Hitters, By Decade

1920–1929	Major League	4	(Babe Ruth, x4)
	Class AAA	3	(Lazzeri, Boone, Kraft)
	Class B	1	(Davis)
	Class C	1	(Clabaugh)
1930–1939	Major League	4	(Foxx x2, Greenberg, Wilson)
	Class AAA	7	(Hauser x2, Arlett, Cullop, Lillard, Puccinelli, Winsett)
	Class AA	1	(Poole)
	Class A	1	(Wright)
	Class B	1	(Robello)
1940–1949	Major League	3	(Kiner x2, Mize)
	Class AAA	1	(Moss)
	Class AA	2	(Witte, Workman)
	Class B	3	(Miller, Shoals, Frierson)
	Class C	6	(Crues x2, Miller, Serena, Snyder, Felix)
1950–1959	Major League	2	(Mantle, Mays)
	Japan	1	(Otsuru)
	Class AAA	2	(Bilko x2)
	Class AA	2	(Guettler, Lennon)
	Class A	1	(Stuart)
	Class B	2	(Tucker, Wagner)
	Class C	9	(Bauman x3, Gravino x2, Kennedy, Mathews, Heslitt, McClain)
1960–1969	Major League	3	(Mantle, Maris, Mays)
	Japan	2	(Oh, Nomura)
	Class A	1	(Vargas)
	Class C	1	(Caballero)
1970–1979	Major League	1	(Foster)
	Japan	2	(Oh)
	Class AAA	2	(McNulty, Thomas)
1980–1989	Japan	3	(Bass, Ochiai x2)
	Class AAA	2	(Kittle, Pierce)
1990–1996	Major League	4	(Fielder, Belle, McGwire, Anderson)

Note: The classifications of all leagues, prior to 1946, have been upgraded by one classification to maintain consistency. Prior to 1946, the highest league classification was AA. Since 1946, the highest classification has been AAA.

Average Number of Home Runs
Hit by League Leader Per Decade

				League			
Decade	NL	AL	IL	AA	PCL	LH	WT-NM
1900–1910	10	11	—	—	—	—	—
1911–1920	16	16	—	—	—	—	—
1921–1930	35	47	—	—	—	—	—
1931–1940	34	47	40	44	40	—	36
1941–1950	37	35	34	29	33	37	45
1951–1960	45	40	34	34	39	51	42
1961–1970	45	44	32	29	32	—	—
1971–1980	43	37	28	33	34	—	—
1981–1990	38	39	28	31	32	—	—
Average	39	41	36	36	37	44	41

Notes: The averages represent the average number of home runs yearly, between the years 1931 and 1960.

The average number of home runs for the home run leader in the LH, excluding Joe Bauman, was 37.

The PCL played as many as 200 games in a season. Their average, adjusted to the major league totals, is 33.

Legend: NL .... National League—Major League
AL .... American League—Major League
IL .... International League—Class AAA Minor League
AA .... American Association—Class AAA Minor League
PCL .... Pacific Coast League—Class AAA Minor League
LH .... Longhorn League—Class C Minor League
WT-NM .... West Texas-New Mexico League—Class C Minor League

Home Run Leaders,
By League

League	Name	Year	HR	League in Existence, Years	No. Players 50+ HRs
NL	Ralph Kiner	1949	54	117	7 (Kiner 51, 54; Mays 51, 52)
AL	Roger Maris	1961	61	92	14 (Ruth 54, 54, 59,60; Mantle 54,52; Foxx 50, 58)
IL	Joe Hauser	1930	63	82	4
AA	Joe Hauser	1933	69	84	2
PCL	Tony Lazzeri	1925	60	89	6
LH	Joe Bauman	1954	72	9	3 (Bauman 50, 53, 72)
WT-NM	Bobby Crues	1948	69	16	4 (Crues 52, 69)
Texas	Ken Guettler	1956	62	87	3
Japan					
CL	Sadaharu Oh	1964	55	46	5 (Oh 55, 51, 50)
PL	Katsuya Nomura	1963	52	46	3
	H. Ochiai	1986	52	46	3 (Ochiai 52, 50)

Legend:

NL . . . . National League—Major League
AL . . . . American League—Major League
IL . . . . International League—Class AAA Minor League
AA . . . . American Association—Class AAA Minor League
PCL . . . . Pacific Coast League—Class AAA Minor League
LH . . . . Longhorn League—Class C Minor League
WT-NM . . . . West Texas–New Mexico League—Class C Minor League
Texas . . . . Texas League—Class AA Minor League
CL . . . . Japan, Central League
PL . . . . Japan, Pacific League

Home Run Leaders,
Batting Statistics

Name	Slugging %	Extra Base Hit %	Home Run Frequency, %
Babe Ruth	.690	16.1	8.5
Harmon Killebrew	.509	10.9	7.0
Ralph Kiner	.548	12.0	7.1
Dan Brouthers	.519	11.3	1.5
Sam Thompson	.505	10.0	2.1
Gavvy Cravath	.478	11.0	3.0
Tilly Walker	.427	10.5	2.3
Josh Gibson	.804	16.1	8.7
Mule Suttles	.612	13.8	6.2
Turkey Stearnes	.638	14.6	5.4
Sadaharu Oh	.634	14.2	9.4
Joe Bauman	.702	16.6	9.7
Joe Hauser (Minor Leagues)	.575	13.3	6.2
(Major Leagues)	.478	10.3	3.9
Dick Stuart (Minor Leagues)	.595	13.5	8.4
(Major Leagues)	.514	10.1	5.6

Major League Ballpark Dimensions,
1900–1910

City & Park	Distance, Feet		
	LF	CF	RF
National League			
New York—Polo Grounds IV	335	500	335
Chicago—West Side Grounds	340	560	316
Pittsburgh—Exposition Park III	400	450	400
Philadelphia—Baker Bowl	335	408	272
St. Louis—Robison Field	470	500	290
Cincinnati—Palace of the Fans	—	—	450
Brooklyn—Washington Park	335	445	295
Boston—South End Grounds	250	450	255
Average	352	473	327
American League			
Philadelphia—Shibe Park	360	502	340
Detroit—Bennett Park	345	467	370
Chicago—South Side Park III	400+	400+	400+
Cleveland—League Park I	—	—	290
Boston—Huntington Avenue BB Grounds	350	530	280
New York—Hilltop Park	365	542	400
Washington—American League Park II	—	—	—
St. Louis—Sportsmans Park II	—	—	—
Average	355	510	336

Major League Ballpark Dimensions,
1910–1920

City & Park	Distance, Feet		
	LF	CF	RF
National League			
New York—Polo Grounds V	277	433	256
Chicago—Wrigley Field	345	440	356
Pittsburgh—Forbes Field	360	422	376
Philadelphia—Baker Bowl	335	408	272 (40' Fence)
St. Louis—Robison Field	380	435	290
Cincinnati—Crosley Field	360	420	360
Brooklyn—Ebbets Field	410	450	300
Boston—Braves Field	402	440	402/365
Average	359	431	331
American League			
Philadelphia—Shibe Park	360	502	340
Detroit—Navin Field	345	467	370
Chicago—Comiskey Park	362	420	362
Cleveland—League Park II	385	420	290 (45' Fence)
Boston—Fenway Park	324	488	314
New York—Polo Grounds V	277	433	256 (11' Fence)
Washington—Griffith Stadium	407	421	328
St. Louis—Sportsmans Park III	350	430	325
Average	351	448	323

Major League Ballpark
Dimensions, 1994

City & Park	Distance, Feet		
	LF	CF	RF
Anaheim Stadium, California	333	406	333
Arlington Stadium, Texas	330	400	330
Fulton County Stadium, Atlanta	330	402	330
Oriole Stadium, Baltimore	333	410	318
Fenway Park, Boston	315	390	302
Wrigley Field, Chicago	355	400	353
Comiskey Park II, Chicago	347	400	347
Tiger Stadium, Detroit	340	440	325
Astrodome, Houston	330	400	330
Royals Stadium, Kansas City	330	410	330
Dodger Stadium, Los Angeles	330	400	330
County Stadium, Milwaukee	315	402	315
H. H. Humphrey Metrodome, Minnesota	343	408	327
Olympic Stadium, Montreal	325	404	325
Yankee Stadium, New York	318	408	314
Shea Stadium, New York	338	410	338
Oakland Coliseum, California	330	400	330
Veterans Stadium, Philadelphia	330	408	330
Three Rivers Stadium, Pittsburgh	335	400	335
Busch Stadium, St. Louis	330	402	330
Jack Murphy Stadium, San Diego	329	405	329
Candlestick Park, San Francisco	335	400	335
Kingdome, Seattle	331	405	314
Skydome, Toronto	328	400	328
Average	332	405	329

Famous Ballparks—Dimensions

		Distance, Feet		
Player	Home Park	LF	CF	RF
Babe Ruth	Yankee Stadium	281	490	295
Harmon Killebrew	Griffith Stadium	350	421	320
	Metropolitan Stadium	344	430	330
Ralph Kiner	Forbes Field	335	435	300
Dan Brouthers	Riverside Grounds	210	410	210
	Recreation Park	—	430+	—
Sam Thompson	Phil. Baseball Grnds.	500	—	310
	Baker Bowl	335	408	300
Gavvy Cravath	Baker Bowl	335	408	300
Tilly Walker	Shibe Park	380	502	340
Josh Gibson	Griffith Stadium	405	421	320
	Forbes Field	365	435	300
	Greenlee Field	350	400	—
Turkey Stearnes	Tiger Stadium	340	467	370
Mule Suttles	Rickwood Field	405	470	334
	Stars Park	250	425+	—
Joe Bauman	Park Field	329	380	329
	Brainard Park	349	355	349
Joe Hauser	Terrapin Park	300	450	335
	Nicollet Park	334	432	279
Sadaharu Oh	Korakuen Stadium	297	387	297
Dick Stuart	Sherman Field	330	380	330
Bobby Crues	Gold Coast Stadium	324	360	324

Home Run Factors

Park	Distance, Feet (LF-CF-RF)	Published HRF	Actual HRF by Player LF	RF	Avg.
Fenway Park	315-420-302	112	134(JF)	90(TW)	112
Yankee Stadium	301-461-295	102	71(JD)	113(LG)	98
				106(BR)	—
				103(MM)	—
Griffith St. (B)	350-421-320	99	95(HK)		95
Griffith St. (A)	402-421-320	39	−(JG)		—
Forbes Field (A)	360-435-300	69	−(JG)		—
Forbes Field (B)	335-435-300	121	−(RK)		—
Metropolitan St.	329-412-329	110	114(HK)		114
Fulton Co. St.	325-402-325	143	138(HA)		138
County Stadium (Milw)	320-402-315	82	94(HA)		94
Polo Grounds	280-480-258	169	106(WM)	186(MO)	146
Shibe Park	334-410-330	126	126(JF)		126
Candlestick Pk.	330-410-330	97	116(WM)		—

Note: Mickey Mantle was a switch hitter, but most of his at bats were lefthanded. I have taken the liberty of listing him here as a lefthanded hitter.

Legend: HRF .... Home Run Factor, published in *Total Baseball*, edited by John Thorn and Pete Palmer
Griffith St. (B) .... Dimensions, 1956–1961
Griffith St. (A) .... Dimensions, 1911–1955
Forbes Field (A) .... Dimensions 1909–1970, except 1947–1953
Forbes Field (B) .... Dimensions, 1947–1953, "Kiner's Korner"
JF .... Jimmie Foxx
TW .... Ted Williams
JD .... Joe DiMaggio
LG .... Lou Gehrig
BR .... Babe Ruth
MM .... Mickey Mantle
HK .... Harmon Killebrew
JG .... Josh Gibson
RK .... Ralph Kiner
HA .... Hank Aaron
WM .... Willie Mays
MO .... Mel Ott

Home Run Kings,
Lifetime Batting Statistics

Name	League	G	AB	H	D	T	HR	BA
Joe Bauman	Minor	1,019	3,463	1,166	221	17	337	.337
Bobby Crues	Minor	843	3,216	1,083	214	35	232	.337
Joe Hauser	Minor	1,854	6,426	1,923	340	116	399	.299
	Major	629	2,044	580	103	29	79	.284
Dick Stuart	Minor	680	2,487	712	113	13	210	.286
	Major	1,112	3997	1,055	157	30	228	.264
	Japan	208	685	176	—	—	49	.257
Hank Aaron	Major	3,298	12,364	3,771	624	98	755	.305
Dan Brouthers	Major	1,673	6,711	2,296	460	205	106	.342
Gavvy Cravath	Major	1,220	3,951	1,134	232	83	119	.287
Jimmie Foxx	Major	2,317	8,134	2,646	458	125	534	.325
Harmon Killebrew	Major	2,435	8,147	2,086	290	24	573	.256
Ralph Kiner	Major	1,472	5,205	1,451	216	39	369	.279
Dave Kingman	Major	1,941	6,677	1,575	240	25	442	.236
Mickey Mantle	Major	2,401	8,102	2,415	344	72	536	.298
Roger Maris	Major	1,463	5,101	1,325	195	42	275	.260
Babe Ruth	Major	2,503	8,399	2,873	506	136	714	.342
Mike Schmidt	Major	2,404	8,352	2,234	408	59	548	.267
Sam Thompson	Major	1,407	5,984	1,979	340	160	127	.331
Tilly Walker	Major	1,418	5,067	1,423	244	71	118	.281
Ted Williams	Major	2,292	7,706	2,654	525	71	521	.344
John Beckwith	Negro	453	1,638	583	98	25	91	.356
Josh Gibson	Negro	501	1,679	607	89	35	146	.362
Chino Smith	Negro	163	610	261	56	9	37	.428
Turkey Stearnes	Negro	903	3,358	1,183	201	107	181	.352
Mule Suttles	Negro	870	3,077	1,011	171	65	190	.329
Ed Wesley	Negro	—	1,629	528	84	22	84	.324
Sadaharu Oh	Japan	2,831	9,250	2,786	422	25	868	.301

Note: Minor league averages from SABR, *Minor League Baseball Stars.* Major league averages from *Total Baseball*, edited by John Thorn and Pete Palmer. Negro league averages, © 1995 John B. Holway and Dick Clark, used with permission.
Japanese averages compliments of the Office of the Baseball Commissioner, Japan.

Home Run Kings,
Average Season Performance Based on 550 at Bats

Name	League	AB	H	D	T	HR	BA
Joe Bauman	Minor	550	185	35	3	54	.337
Bobby Crues	Minor	550	185	37	6	40	.337
Joe Hauser	Minor	550	165	29	10	34	.299
	Major	550	156	28	8	21	.284
Dick Stuart	Minor	550	158	25	3	46	.286
	Major	550	145	22	4	31	.264
	Japan	550	141	—	—	39	.257
Hank Aaron	Major	550	168	28	4	34	.305
Dan Brouthers	Major	550	188	38	17	9	.342
Gavvy Cravath	Major	550	158	32	12	17	.287
Jimmie Foxx	Major	550	179	31	8	36	.325
Harmon Killebrew	Major	550	141	20	2	39	.256
Ralph Kiner	Major	550	153	23	4	39	.279
Dave Kingman	Major	550	130	20	2	36	.236
Mickey Mantle	Major	550	164	23	5	36	.298
Roger Maris	Major	550	143	21	5	30	.260
Babe Ruth	Major	550	188	33	9	47	.342
Mike Schmidt	Major	550	147	27	4	36	.267
Sam Thompson	Major	550	182	31	15	12	.331
Tilly Walker	Major	550	155	26	8	13	.281
Ted Williams	Major	550	189	37	5	37	.344
John Beckwith	Negro	550	196	33	8	31	.356
Josh Gibson	Negro	550	199	29	11	48	.362
Chino Smith	Negro	550	235	50	8	33	.428
Turkey Stearnes	Negro	550	194	33	18	30	.352
Mule Suttles	Negro	550	181	31	12	34	.329
Ed Wesley	Negro	550	178	28	7	28	.324
Sadaharu Oh	Japan	550	166	25	1	52	.301

Home Run Kings,
Average Season Performance Based on 550 at Bats, Adjusted to Major League Basepoint

Name	League	AB	H	D	T	HR	BA
Joe Bauman	Minor	550	152	—	—	32	.276
Bobby Crues	Minor	550	152	—	—	24	.276
Joe Hauser	Minor	550	145	28	10	25	.263
	Major	550	156	28	8	21	.284
Dick Stuart	Minor	550	138	24	3	34	.250
	Major	550	145	22	4	31	.264
	Japan	550	132	—	—	18	.240
Hank Aaron	Major	550	168	28	4	34	.305
Dan Brouthers	Major	550	188	—	—	30+	.342
Gavvy Cravath	Major	550	158	32	12	43	.287
Jimmie Foxx	Major	550	179	31	8	36	.325
Harmon Killebrew	Major	550	141	20	2	39	.256
Ralph Kiner	Major	550	153	23	4	39	.279
Dave Kingman	Major	550	130	20	2	36	.236
Roger Maris	Major	550	143	21	5	30	.260
Mickey Mantle	Major	550	164	23	5	36	.298
Babe Ruth	Major	550	188	33	9	50	.342
Mike Schmidt	Major	550	147	27	4	36	.267
Sam Thompson	Major	550	182	—	—	35	.331
Tilly Walker	Major	550	155	26	8	33	.281
Ted Williams	Major	550	189	37	5	37	.344
John Beckwith	Negro	550	163	34	6	38	.306
Josh Gibson	Negro	550	166	30	9	61	.312
Chino Smith	Negro	550	202	52	6	42	.378
Turkey Stearnes	Negro	550	161	34	14	38	.302
Mule Suttles	Negro	550	148	32	9	43	.279
Ed Wesley	Negro	550	145	29	5	36	.274
Sadaharu Oh	Japan	550	156	30	6	23	.284

BIBLIOGRAPHY

Bak, Richard. *Turkey Stearnes and the Detroit Stars.* Wayne State University Press, Detroit, Mich, 1994.

The Ballplayers. Mike Shatzkin, editor. William Morrow and Co., New York, 1990.

Bankes, James. *The Pittsburgh Crawfords.* Wm. C. Brown Publishers, Dubuque, Iowa, 1991.

The Baseball Encyclopedia. Joseph L. Reichler, editor. Macmillan Publishing Co., New York, 1979.

The Baseball Research Journal, no. 24. Mark Alvarez, editor. The Society for American Baseball Research, Cleveland, Ohio, 1995.

The Baseball Research Journal, no. 23, Mark Alvarez, editor. The Society for American Baseball Research, Cleveland, Ohio 1994.

The Baseball Research Journal, no. 22. Mark Alvarez, editor. The Society for American Baseball Research, Cleveland, Ohio, 1993.

The Baseball Research Journal, no. 21. Mark Alvarez, editor. The Society for American Baseball Research, Cleveland, Ohio, 1992.

Baseball's Hall of Fame, Cooperstown. *Where the Legends Live and Die.* Joe Hoppel, editor. Arlington House, New York, 1988.

Benson, Michael. *Ballparks of North America.* McFarland & Co., Publishers, Jefferson, N.C., 1989.

Bruce, Janet. *The Kansas City Monarchs.* University Press of Kansas, Wichita, Kans., 1985.

Couzens, Gerald Secor. *A Baseball Album.* Lippencourt & Crowell, Publishers, New York, 1980.

Cult Baseball Players, Danny Peary, editor. Simon & Schuster, New York, 1990.

Daguerreotypes, 8th edition. Craig Carter, editor. The Sporting News, St. Louis, Mo., 1990.

"Dodger Yearbooks." Brooklyn and Los Angeles, 1950 to 1993.

Durant, John. *The Story of Baseball in Words and Pictures.* Hastings House Publishers, New York, 1973.

The Encyclopedia of Minor League Baseball. Lloyd Johnson and Miles Wolff, editors. Baseball America, Durham, N.C., 1993.

Grayson, Harry. *They Played the Game.* A. S. Barnes and Co., New York, 1945.

Holway, John. *Voices from the Great Black Baseball Leagues.* Da Capo Press, New York, 1992.

Holway, John B. *Black Diamonds.* Stadium Books, New York, 1991.

Holway, John B. *Josh and Satch.* Carroll and Graf Publishers, New York, 1991.

Holway, John B. *Blackball Stars.* Meckler Books, Westport, Conn. 1988.

Japan Pro Baseball Fan Handbook and Media Guide. Compiled by Wayne Graczyk. Japan Pro Baseball Fan Handbook and Media Guide, Tokyo, Japan, 1991.

Japan Pro Baseball Fan Handbook and Media Guide. Compiled by Wayne Graczyk. Japan Pro Baseball Fan Handbook and Media Guide, Tokyo, Japan, 1995.

Lowry, Philip J. *Green Cathedrals.* Addison-Wesley Publishing Co., Reading, Mass. 1992.

Maitland, Brian. *Japanese Baseball; A Fan's Guide.* Charles E. Tuttle Co., Rutland, Vt., 1991.

McNary, Kyle P. *Ted "Double Duty" Radcliffe.* McNary Publishing, Minneapolis, Minn. 1994.

Minor League Baseball Stars, vol. 1. The Society for American Baseball Research, Cleveland, Oh. 1984.

Minor League Baseball Stars, vol. 2. The Society for American Baseball Research, Cleveland, Ohio 1985.

Minor League Baseball Stars, vol. 3. The Society for American Baseball Research, Cleveland, Ohio, 1992.

Minor League History Journal, vol. 1, no. 1. The Society for American Baseball Research, Cleveland, Ohio, 1992.

Minor League History Journal, vol. 2, no. 1. The Society for American Baseball Research, Cleveland, Ohio, 1993.

Minor League History Journal, vol. 3. The Society for American Baseball Research, Cleveland, Ohio, 1994.

Mooreland, George L. *Balldom.* Balldom Publishing Co., New York 1914.

The National Pastime. John Thorn, editor. Bell Publishing Co., New York, 1987.

The National Pastime, no. 10. The Society for American Baseball Research, Cleveland, Ohio, 1990.

The National Pastime, no. 11. The Society for American Baseball Research, Cleveland, Ohio, 1992.

The National Pastime, no. 12. The Society for American Baseball Research, Cleveland, Ohio, 1992.

The National Pastime, no. 13. The Society for American Baseball Research, Cleveland, Ohio, 1993.

The National Pastime, no. 14. The Society for American Baseball Research, Cleveland, Ohio, 1994.

The National Pastime, no. 15. The Society for American Baseball Research, Cleveland, Ohio, 1995.

The Negro Leagues Book, Dick Clark and Larry Lester, editors. The Society for American Baseball Research, Cleveland, Ohio, 1994.

Oh, Sadaharu, and David Falkner, *Sadaharu Oh.* Random House, New York, 1984.

Peterson, Robert. *Only the Ball Was White.* McGraw-Hill Book Co., New York, 1970.

Riley, James A. *The Biographical Encyclopedia of the Negro Baseball Leagues.* Carroll & Graf Publishers, New York, 1994.

Ritter, Lawrence S. *The Glory of Their Times.* William Morrow and Co., New York, 1984.

Seymour, Harold. *Baseball: The Early Years.* Oxford University Press, New York, 1960.

Rogosin, Donn. *Invisible Men.* Macmillan Publishing Co., New York, 1987.

Spalding, Albert G. *America's National Game.* Halo Books, San Francisco, Calif. 1991.

Total Baseball. John Thorn and Pete Palmer, editors. Warner Books, New York, 1989.

Whiting, Robert. *You Gotta Have Wa.* Vintage Books, New York, 1990.

Who's Who in Baseball, Who's Who in Baseball Magazine Co., New York, *1916-1994.*

INDEX